SUBWAY LIVES

SUBWAY LIVES

24 HOURS IN THE LIFE OF THE NEW YORK CITY SUBWAY

JIM DWYER

CROWN PUBLISHERS, INC.   NEW YORK

Grateful acknowledgment is made to Warner/Chappell Music, Inc., for permission to reprint excerpts of lyrics from: "Blue Suede Shoes" (Carl Lee Perkins) © 1956 Carl Perkins Music Inc. (Renewed). All rights administered by Unichappell Music Inc. All rights reserved. "Love Me Tender" (Elvis Presley, Vera Matson) © 1956 Elvis Presley Music (Renewed). All rights administered by Unichappell Music Inc. All rights reserved. "Hound Dog" (Jerry Leiber, Mike Stoller) © 1956 Gladys Music & MCA Music Publishing (Renewed). All rights on behalf of Gladys Music for the U.S.A. administered by Chappell & Co. All rights reserved. Grateful acknowledgment is made to Leiber and Stoller for permission to reprint excerpts of lyrics from "Jailhouse Rock" by Jerry Leiber and Mike Stoller. © 1957 Jerry Leiber Music & Mike Stoller Music (Renewed). All rights reserved. Canadian rights administered by Warner/Chappell Music, Inc. © 1957 Gladys Music. Grateful acknowledgment is made to Sony Music Publishing for permission to reprint excerpts from "Heartbreak Hotel" by Mae Boren Axton, Tommy Durden, Elvis Presley. © 1956 Tree Publishing Co., Inc. Copyright Renewed. All rights reserved. Reprinted by permission.

Published by Crown Publishers, Inc., 201 East 50th Street, New York, New York 10022. Member of the Crown Publishing Group.

CROWN is a trademark of Crown Publishers, Inc.

Book design by June Bennett-Tantillo

Manufactured in the United States of America

Library of Congress Cataloging-in-Publication Data
Dwyer, Jim
    Subway lives : 24 hours in the life of the New York City subway / by Jim Dwyer. — 1st ed.
       p.   cm.
    1. Subways—New York (N.Y.) 2. New York (N.Y.)—Social life and customs. I. Title.
  TF847.N5D88 1991
  388.4′28′097471—dc20   91-3097
                                       CIP

ISBN 0-517-58445-X

10 9 8 7 6 5 4 3 2 1

First Edition

for Cathy

Acknowledgments

My thanks to the people who generously permitted lengthy interviews about their subway lives: Ramiro Casiano and Kathy Quiles, Joe Caracciolo, Jim Christie, David Gunn, Tom McGurl, Thomas Thomasevich, Roger Smith, David Smith, John Avildsen, REAS, the families of Danny Gomez and Rubin Fernandez, and Joyce Bresa.

Among the many men and women of the transit system who freely shared their expertise are Joe Davis, Bob Slovak, Termaine Garden, Donna Evans, Caren Gardner, Peter Barrett, Bob Previdi, Jared Lebow, Howard Benn, Charles Monheim, John Cunningham, Tito Davila, Al O'Leary, Bob Valentino, Richard Hellinger, Robert Jermolowitz, Robert Giglio, Robert Kiley, George Miller, Steve Polan, Robert Olmstead, Peter Derrick, Daniel T. Scannell, Sonny Hall, Tom Casano, Mel Levy, Barry Feinstein, John Pritchard, Jim Miley, Alan F. Putre, George Ziegler, Beverly Dolinsky, Jim Eastland, John Gaito, Terrie Rouse, Gail Dawson, and Al Garner.

Thanks to them, and of course, to the unmentioned and unmentionable others. Great citizens work in the subways.

Other transit experts who have been most helpful include Clifton Hood, Brian Cudahy, Sally Charnow, Cathy Nolan, Ira Greenberg, Gene Russianoff, Joe Rappaport, Daniel McCarthy, and John Tauranac.

I appreciate the assistance of Lorraine Tozzo, Jesus Torres, Junior Crespo, Les Bridges, Ellen Weyman, James Suarez, and Stan Skalski.

At *New York Newsday,* I owe much to many, but the most to the brains and diligence of Kirsten Hamilton and Michele Parente. Christine Baird, Karen von Rossen, Mary Ann Skinner, and Caroline Brooks are marvelous people and librarians.

My boss, Don Forst, gave me a yard of newspaper space every other day, unlimited tokens, and four years in the subways. In all, a ticket to ride.

It was in Dennis Duggan's "In the Subways" columns that New Yorkers first saw a newspaper capture the molten soul of the city. I had the benefit as consumer and colleague of Molly Gordy's extraordinary beat reporting. My appreciation to Katherine Foran and Ellis Henican for their help, and to Joel Siegel of the *Daily News,* Margie Feinberg and Joanna Molloy of the *New York Post,* and Kevin P. Hayes of the *Bergen Record.* Among a score of friends at *New York Newsday* who helped: Renee Lolya, Joe Hurley, Robert Friedman, Sylvia Moreno, Jim Sleeper, Richard Esposito, Nathan Jackson, Gail Scott, Sandy Widener, Julie Shpiesel, Yolanda Edwards, and Steve Isenberg. Syd Schanberg's files were invaluable; so is his company. For various kindnesses, I thank Tony Marro, Bob Johnson, Stan Asimov, and Jim Toedtman. Other friends and coworkers ought to be credited here but aren't, because I get better than I give. But thank you.

Stanley Gruss, neighbor, and Bob and Cathy Muir, in-laws, provided shelters for this work. Peter Cohn spoiled me for accommodations. Mary Lamont transcribed miles of tape. Flip Brophy is an excellent agent and advisor. Lisa Wagner and Walt Bode jump started this book. David Groff made sure the job was finished. María Bottino shepherded it into print.

I have many reasons to thank my good friend and colleague Tom Curran; most recently, he, Steve Dobrow, and Mike Mauro, read the manuscript on short notice. These three formidable minds did it nothing but good.

Sheila Carmody and Julia Sullivan are two dauntless and inspiring voyagers. Kevin Doyle is the best reader a friend could ask for. Dick Goldensohn innoculated everyone he met against complacency. I get booster shots from Pat Dwyer, Phillip Dwyer, John Dwyer, and Cathy Sullivan Cipressi and Mike Cipressi.

At the end of a day, my wife, Cathy, would send Maura down the hall to bring me home, and what better place to be than with those two? And Maura, it seemed, shows up at the right moments. Phil and Mary Dwyer always have.

Midnight, Brooklyn: Scene

So deep in the dark, the three men cannot qualify as shadows. They stoop through a hole in the fence border of Prospect Park, grunt past brambles and brush, and half slide down an embankment to the side of the tracks. Even on a moonless night the lights of the city pump a mild glow across the clouds. But no light spills from Prospect Park, 526 acres of meadows and quiet groves. A few yards to the west is the mouth of a subway tunnel. The train tracks rise from the tunnel like a swimmer breaching the water, and as they run next to the silent park, mark the darkest corner in all of New York City.

Which is just as well, because the men see the train long before they hear it: headlights gashing the black pitch of the tunnel, beams rising and bouncing along the walls as the train drives from the tail end of Brooklyn toward the ever-lighted island of Manhattan. The men flatten their backs against the concrete wall and suck in their fronts.

Now the rays sting across their faces, nailing bright white spots to their eyes, and they can feel the train looming.

To the men standing on the tracks, two-thirds of the subway car is over their heads; most of what they see is motors and wheels moving, at such close quarters, beyond the shutter speed of the human eye. Everything about the cars is colossal: each is 75 feet long, and is linked in strings of eight by powerful metal couplers and thick electrical cables, in all, 800,000 pounds of metal and plastic and another quarter million of flesh and blood, the greatest moving mass of human tissue in the universe, apart from the planet earth, shooting a mighty roar of wind at 40 miles an hour past their ears.

Above the men the train is a silver blur of cars, their aluminum skins free of blemish. In eleven seconds, a long time to hold a breath, the train is by them.

Nothing moves except the canvas sack that the first man has been holding at his side.

"A new train," he says. "From France. They're very quiet. They sneak up on you before you know they're coming." He knows this because during the day he is a mechanic who fixes them.

But tonight, he is the Obeahman, the man of magic, and when he steps out from the wall and walks between the rails, the other two men fall in behind him. Their footfall is measured by a constant crunching of gravel. About 100 yards away is a station, and a junction for another subway line known as the Franklin Avenue shuttle.

Quickly, the men find a clear space near the track. The canvas sack is laid squirming on the ground.

"Loa," says the Obeahman.

"Santo," says another.

Chanting begins in an island dialect. They are praying in anticipation of the sacrifice of the contents of the canvas sack, a white hen. In this part of Brooklyn, hundreds of thousands of people from the poor islands of the Caribbean and Central America have landed, bringing lilting song to the streets and sacrifice to the subways.

Their religion is a brew of Catholicism, witness to Christ, and voodoo, the magic of the crossroads. To send energy to the saints, sacrificial offerings are made at crossroads, the meeting place between the physical world and the spiritual.

This spot in the subway has the makings of a crossroad; here, two of New York City's twenty-three train lines meet, the Franklin Avenue shuttle and the Brighton line.

From the Obeahman's coat pocket comes a slim butchering knife, its blade sheathed in leather. The plump hen, pure white, except for a pale red comb, is pulled from the bag.

This time, they hear the train before they see it. There is a sound like a bowling ball being dropped, a crash upon crash, which comes from spots on three of the train wheels that are not perfectly round; in fact, there are flat spots in the metal, four or five inches long, and each bangs the rails with hammer blows.

The men press against a wall, not needing clearance from the train, really, but to escape the fierce reports. Half a minute later, the train catches up with its own noise. After twenty-seven years of rolling under and over New York, its grime has hardened into a shell that is a kind of canvas for graffiti, the desolate black marker scrawls on maps and benches, walls and windows, and the soaring four-colored murals splashed 500 feet along the outside of the cars.

And here at midnight, May 12, 1989, three decades and a million miles down the road, the cars are making their last trip along the rails of New York. This is the last train in New York covered with graffiti; its lead car is 8205 and designated S, because the train is heading in the subway's version of south. The train is being scrapped.

When it has passed, the Obeahman flashes the knife.

"Where is the bird?" he asks.

The men look at each other. In the retreat from the noisy train, the hen had wriggled out of someone's arms. Now it is trotting down the tracks behind the noisy train. They start to chase it. The hen spurts ahead.

"Let it go," says the Obeahman, disgustedly. "You cannot catch a hen on the run unless it is cornered."

Somewhere down the railroad, the battered 8205-S passes the gleaming new French train.

Midnight, Command Center, Brooklyn

Ride the New York subways one day. You could fall in love or get snake bitten or see a baby born. Hear a conductor do Elvis routines between stops. Buy a cabbage or a condom. Watch an actress rehearse García Lorca. Study Islam. Salvage a soul. Shinny up a banister in a station where the stairs have been stolen.

Maybe nothing like that will happen—maybe it'll just be a routine ride on America's greatest public work. Also its goofiest. And its most sinister.

New York opened for business in 1624 and managed for most of its first three centuries to mash everyone, more or less, into the bottom—southern—half of Manhattan Island. In 1904, the first subways were opened, supposedly to take the people away from this teeming squalor. And bring them back again, of course, the next morning.

Naturally, the real estate speculators, with no money to be made by turning the Bronx and Harlem and upper Manhattan into suburbs with single-family houses and big lawns, threw up jam-packed tenements around the new subway stations—just like the ones on the Lower East Side that, in theory, the trains were taking people away from. In a bare instant, the subways created fantastic fortunes, carving Manhattan Island into the most valuable real estate in the hemisphere. (The transit system itself has been broke for most of its existence.)

Nine decades later, the subways have become the great public commons of the city, where acts of the heart and warped adventures are played out every day. Every rank of New Yorker is indentured to the subway. Nobody rides first class. Only in the dim warrens of the subway, cursed accomplice of daily existence, can the full spectrum of city life—with all the bewildering diversity of its pathologies and its glories—be glimpsed, felt, and at times even understood.

Children are lost every day on the subway. More are found than were reported missing. Property, too, is mislaid and recovered, then moved to a storeroom where wallets—yes, more than one, dozens at a time, in fact—with thousands of dollars in cash are kept, awaiting their owners. Also false teeth by the drawerful, artificial legs, a Hammond organ, bushels of umbrellas, boxes of gloves, bags of rings and shelves of baby strollers—empty, thank God, whose name, by the way, is invoked on locals and expresses, in a half dozen languages, by supplicants ranging from a murderous cult that wears nuns' habits and pious smiles, to devout Indian monks in clown costumes and painted grins.

The subways cannot be hurt. It has been tried. One fall day in 1989, a water main broke in Harlem and washed a park—*a park*—into the 125th Street station at Eighth Avenue, home of the A train (and the B, C, and D). Before the faucet was turned off, 18 million gallons of water had flowed into the tunnels; the only way to reach the roofs of the trains was to swim straight down ten feet. Forty pumps ran around the clock for four days. Then there was the park—which, when a transit worker named Mike Hardiman was through with it, was in forty thousand bags, fifty muddy pounds apiece. The city collapses, now and then, but the trains keep running.

The subways are infinitely absorbent.

On a typical Friday in early September, there are 3,200,000 riders. It is the last weekend of summer vacation for schools, so by Monday, with the return of the students and teachers, there are a half million more riders, 3,700,000. With the exception of a rambunctious air to the cars at dismissal time, the subway feels no different.

It is as if most of Boston or San Francisco were flown to New York, were handed subway tokens, and then vanished. The subways can swallow major cities without even burping.

Then again: A wire burns out on a train in a tunnel under the East River. Now 150,000 people, backed up over 11 miles and two islands, will not get home for dinner. One tiny problem in one car on one train has brewed an unenchanted evening for, say, the population of Chattanooga, Tennessee.

Where can you see this sprawling register of a city's temperature?

Logically, the grand tour of the New York subways should begin in a grim fourteen-story building on Jay Street in Brooklyn, the headquarters of the New York City Transit Authority. On the third floor is a room called the Command Center, which looks just like those big brain-center places at NASA headquarters or in war movies.

New York is wrapped in 731 miles of track that winds under, over, and on the streets. Here in the command center—oops, the Command Center—every mile can be viewed on a model board that stretches for 70 feet across the front of the room. A dozen men and women are staring at radio consoles, muttering into microphones, sometimes into one of four phones on each desk.

It is very impressive. This, you imagine, is where it all happens: the exacting coordination of the greatest mass transit system anywhere. You envision a full day in the Command Center, as the dispatchers monitor 6,800 train trips, blinking from light to light on the model board. You conjure the staccato reports from train crews and police and station personnel that pour in over the course of a day. You muse on the hundreds of split-second adjustments made when a train breaks down, the rerouting, the announcements, the switches thrown, all to keep the railroad and its cargo of millions on the move, steadily, across the blinking board.

You might see all this, but you'd be dreaming.

The board never has been plugged in to the track circuits.

"We don't know where most of the trains are at a given moment, because the model board was built before the city's fiscal crisis and then never finished," explains John Gaul, the director of planning for the subways. "No one can see the entire system."

There is no omniscient brain center, after all. Maybe, officials say, there'll be one by the turn of the century.

Meanwhile, the board lights twinkle, but no one pays much attention; to find the trains, dispatchers use a Pony Express–type system. Local towers on each route have model boards that actually work—but they display only a few miles of track nearby, and the trains moving on them. To send a message to the other end of the line about, say, an F train departing from Coney Island, word is passed from one tower to the next along its route. In all, fourteen towers hand that F train off to each other over a distance of 27 miles, through Brooklyn, into Manhattan, then east to the terminal in Queens.

Yes, the Command Center is the logical place to start this voyage, for it provides a swift lesson in the limits of a global view of the masses and our transit.

The best glimpse of the subway, it turns out, can be had as trains pass the switch towers, which sit at junctions. If the tower operator knows of a problem, he or she can throw a switch and send the train onto a different track. That's what the switch tower's there for—to steer the trains onto the best routes.

So perhaps the best portal to this mass of machinery and people is at a junction—not of mere train lines, but of New York lives and New York subways; not in any single place, but on a meandering trip with these people, in and out of the underground, as their lives are shaped at their crossings with the subway.

Tom Thomasevich is a conductor—a Brooklyn boy who works on the East Side of Manhattan, the city's gold coast. His line runs from City Hall to the Bronx—with stops along the way near Bloomingdale's and the Metropolitan Museum of Art. Things haven't always fallen Tom's way—he might have made the Mets, but he should have worked out more; he might have been a singer, but he should have practiced more. Still, he rides with a song in his heart. And in his mouth.

Kathy Quiles is at the bursting point. For two years, she has been living in one room of a welfare hotel—along with six kids and a husband who quit a good job in the post office because he didn't like getting up in the morning. Their hotel is on a peninsula at the southeastern edge of the city, facing the ocean—and connected to the rest of New York and their burned-out past on a rickety trestle that crosses Jamaica Bay.

Today, as she awaits the birth of her seventh child, Kathy finds out just how important that train is to her life.

Anna Lans* has sat in an armored booth in subway stations every night of her working life, counting bags of money. Twice her booths have been robbed—but Anna can count herself fortunate, since other clerks have been burned alive for those bags of cash. Tonight her luck is tested again.

SONI, a.k.a. **Danny Gomez,** is very nearly the last of the graffiti tag kings. He lives in Bushwick, a rowdy, working-poor section of Brooklyn, the son of an immigrant Dominican, who arrives at work before dawn in the small bodega he runs seventeen hours a day.

Tonight, SONI is going to war against JA—**John Avildsen,** another tag artist, the son of a Hollywood movie director, who lives not in a hardscrabble section of Brooklyn, but in the fashionable Upper West Side of Manhattan. JA has "dissed" SONI by tagging the home of one of SONI's closest pals with his *nom de graffiti.*

Their battle will be fought in the perpetual night of the tunnels, as trains roar past, the scrawl of the combatants caught in the strobe of speeding headlights. Graffiti is dying, but SONI and JA intend to go out blazing.

The mortal enemy of both SONI and JA is **David Gunn.** A New England preppy who could have stepped from the pages of *A Separate Peace*, Gunn is president of the Transit Authority—and the man who declared that he would eliminate graffiti from the subway system. For his success, he has been declared "the man who saved the subways"

_____

* A pseudonym

by the *New York Times* and national business publications. In the all-guys game of railroads, he is a popular figure; in the press, he radiates candor and modesty—a carefully calibrated combination that provides him a catastrophe-proof aura.

Today, behind the scenes, he is fighting a far more important battle than the antigraffiti campaign: with the help of the governor and other state politicians, a powerful engineering and construction company is trying to wrest control of an important job from the system's own workers. Intrigue builds on intrigue: Gunn feels deserted by a key state official who is an old friend (and who also was a high-ranking CIA executive), as the politicians send veiled threats and messages.

The politicians want Gunn to give a $500 million contract for car repairs to the favored company—an act that will erode the Transit Authority's technical skills, its ability to heal itself. Gunn has spent his life watching the national railroad system shrink and vanish; for him, turning over this job to the construction conglomerate would mortally wound the subway system, the last vestige of the railroad system he has cherished from his boyhood.

The loss of those technical abilities over the last three decades has meant that even a rejuvenated subway continues to suffer from a low-grade terrorism that tilts the life of people such as **Joyce Bresa**. Born and raised in a rural upstate village, she is determined to make it to the top of the Manhattan retail race. Armed with an eye for elegance and style—and the orders of her family *not* to talk to anyone on the subway—she starts and ends the day by struggling against perverts, her own claustrophobia, crushing crowds, and a train that can be counted on to make a fifteen-minute trip last forty-five minutes.

Or even longer. Tonight, trapped in a dark, airless tunnel, she hears from other riders that the train may have been hijacked. Ridiculous, she thinks. After an hour, even the calmest heads around her have come to believe that terrorism is the only thing that makes sense.

In the company of these seven people, we will come to this place, if 700 miles of anything can be called a place, on a single spring day in 1989. In fact, their adventures did not take place on a single day. They are culled, with few exceptions, from several days in the late spring and early summer of 1989.

Alongside them, we'll view **the system**, in a series of snapshots showing how the world's largest and most untamed subway operated on May 12, 1989.

"They put the system together nearly a hundred years ago," says a transit ironworker, Joe Caracciolo.

> It's been out in winter, in summer, snow, sleet, rain, animals urinating all over it—the two-legged animals, okay? I should look that good at a hundred years old. The railroad was built eleven times its strength. You could get eleven of those train cars and put them on top of each other and that structure would still hold them. Now, it's a hundred years old, maybe it's seven times its strength.
>
> That structure is unbelievable. To me, it's the eighth wonder of the world. If I could go back in time, I would have loved to see when it first opened. The mosaic tiles. Everything. Had to be like the Eighth Wonder of the World.
>
> You're walking on the street, and you hear the subway underneath you. There's a hole in the ground and there's a big monster going—*rrrrhhh*—the damn thing is unbelievable!

The monster finished a makeover on May 12, 1989, the day the last train doused with graffiti was removed from the system. Nothing in particular happened to mark the event, other than a series of reports in the press. A ceremony was called off because the city's school chancellor died suddenly and was being buried that morning.

Still, it was an epochal moment of sorts, for graffiti in all their apparitions—from the desolate illegible signatures of kids with no talent and no daring, to the giant "burners," Day-Glo murals 10 feet high and 200 feet long—have epitomized the world's image of the New York subways.

A system out of control, in a free-fall interrupted only by catastrophe, it seemed to some. For others, the graffiti were joyous dances in a municipal graveyard, music for the fall of a bleak empire.

For everyone, their passing peeled away a layer of distraction and camouflage; the graffiti striptease left the subway system naked to behold in the eighty-fifth year of its existence.

New York recreates itself every fifteen years or so, when a new fiscal or social crisis announces itself as this generation's point of no return, and yet another tide of immigrants, hopeful and hungry, arrives to take the place of the departed fed-up.

People come and go. The subway stays as midwifery and mortuary to the city.

1 A.M., Rockaway Beach, Queens: Kathy Quiles

She isn't sleeping, so Kathy Quiles tries working the house. With six under the roof, one under the navel, a mother always can find something to do, even in the middle of the night. There is a light to turn off, a sock to throw in the hamper, a door to open, the soft tick of breathing to hear and hold as counterweight to a thousand worries beyond naming.

But, of course, this isn't a house, not even an apartment, and to check on everyone, she makes no ambling stroll down halls, poking her head in doors: they are in a single room, where she can sit up and see the three beds, and hear them, all eight people.

And maybe, by next week, nine. This is it, she thinks. We have to get out of this place. The baby had stopped kicking a couple of days ago. Now, at 1 A.M., there is something bothering her belly, a kind of burning. She does not want to go to the doctor now. Sabrina, the one-year-old, has just fallen asleep. The boys hadn't gone to bed until 10 and it was 11:30 before they finally were quiet.

"Another week," she says aloud to her husband, Ramiro. He barely grunts. "I got another week with this one."

She hasn't picked a name yet. No doctor tonight. The heartburn wasn't worth a $25 taxi. The C train? She doesn't want to wait on a dark platform for it to come. You could stand there a half hour. She sighs, pulls up the covers, and eases herself down in the bed next to Ramiro. He sleeps. She stares up at the walls.

Railroad clerk Anna Lans was patient but railroad cleaner Darrell Hawkes* could not wait.

He wasn't supposed to come see her until two o'clock. By then, everything would definitely be dead. And that would give Anna time to set up the bank in her booth, the tokens piled 20 high, 5 stacks to a row, 21 rows, 2,100 in all. But a few minutes past one, a rustling noise broke the stillness of the station. She glanced up from her counting and there he was, five layers of bullet-resistant glass away.

Anna could have left Darrell standing there. Much safer. After all, if she lets him in, Supervision might come by, want to know what he's doing in the booth, he don't work this line. They had rules for everything. No Walkman in the booth. No radio in the booth. No smoking in the booth. Sit there in the dark with your ass on the line and Supervision comes by to tell you you not sitting right.

Supervision was a bitch. But Darrell was hers, and she had to look out for the scrawny bastard, even if they would write up the pink form, G-2, the disciplinary sheet, and she would have to write a composition: I have been reinstructed in Rule 117(I), which says except in an emergency or when otherwise authorized clerks must forbid ALL persons from entering the change booth except the following properly identified: and then go on and list everyone from the chairman of the Metropolitan Transportation Authority on down who was allowed to be let into the booth. Everyone except Darrell. Shit. She was glad to see him. Even tonight. He kept coming back. She had to take care of him.

Now Anna hoists herself off the regulation green stool-chair and pads across the 12-foot booth to the fiberglass and steel door. A wooden block, the size of a deck of cards, dangles from a string, jamming a latch inside the door, making it impossible even for someone with a key to open the door from outside. She looks back through the five layers of bullet-resistant glass, double-checking that no one is coming down the ramp from the street, pries the block free, unbolts the latch, turns a key, and pulls open the door.

Darrell tries to brush past her, but Anna stands for a moment in

* A pseudonym

the doorway, and there is no getting by. Darrell kisses her on the lips, lingering just long enough to make her worry someone is going to appear in the station.

"Come on," she says. "Get in here."

1:05 A.M., Bushwick, Brooklyn: Danny Gomez

"I feel," announces SONI, "like getting up."

"Yo," says SLICK. "Yo, man, let's get up, but we got to take care of JA, man."

"Check it out," says SONI. "We dry."

The Bushwick night is howling to Danny Gomez and Rubin Fernandez. SONI and SLICK. Very nearly the last of the great Brooklyn graffiti writers.

Tonight, they face a critical problem: no respect and no way to regain it. They have no paint. They can't get up. You need paint to get up—to shoot your name across the blackstars, the subway.

A few days ago, JA had seriously dissed SLICK. He came by car to 320 Empire Boulevard and tagged up the walls of Slick's house.

JA JA JA JA JA JA JA JA JA JA JA JA JA JA JA JA JA JA JA JA JA JA JA JA JA JA JA JA JA JA JA JA

All over the walls.

Come down and fight, JA had screamed into the hallway.

Fair fight, JA had hollered. Come on, SLICK, you afraid of a fair fight?

Bullshit, man. SLICK wasn't afraid of no fair fight. He told his friends later that he stayed upstairs. There were, like, ten guys with JA, SLICK had said. In a car they came. From Manhattan. Fuckin' JA, man, think he rules the city. Man. Ten white boys he brings. Maybe it wasn't ten, but that was the minimum Slick could be outnumbered by and still keep his respect.

SLICK and SONI are members of the Bushwick graffiti posse, U5, which had been formed in the winter of 1986, a marshaling of the dwindling graffiti-writing resources of the largely Hispanic neighborhood. JA is John Avildsen, the hated ruling king of graffiti in the city, a white guy from the Upper West Side of Manhattan. His father is a big Hollywood movie guy—director of *Joe* and the original *Rocky,* he also produced *The Karate Kid* and *Lean on Me,* and even got JA a part in one of the *Karate Kid* sequels. Worse, JA has almost unlimited access to spray paint and is killing everyone's shit. Buffing over their work.

In plain language, he was scrawling on top of their scrawls, their tags, the nearly unreadable scribbles that wallpapered every public space in New York. Now he had come to SLICK's house and tagged it up.

The other fellows in U5 agreed that JA would have to be dealt with. But nobody was down for that tonight. People had school, people had work.

Yo, maybe the weekend.

For SONI and SLICK, that is too long to wait.

Tomorrow, after they went to the Door, their high school in Manhattan, they'd take care of JA. They'd go to one of his tunnels on the West Side.

"Yo, my cousin, OS, he's got some paint," says SONI. "We'll catch OS tomorrow. We'll hang out at the Door, then we'll go by my cousin's house."

"Bet," says Slick. "We gotta kill JA's shit."

1:15 A.M., Over the East River: Scene

The windows on the D train frame a view beyond price: the Manhattan skyline, a sleeping queen, jewels muted. The D train is rolling across the Manhattan Bridge, 200 feet over the East River, and across into Brooklyn.

But this is the middle of the night, and the two dozen riders in the third car of the train are dead to the glories over their shoulders. They are deep in subway glaze, the state of near-sleep that allows one to keep the eyes half closed until it becomes necessary to run for one's life.

The only activity is at the far end of the car, where a man sits, bent at the waist, as he works the zipper of a duffel bag. One stop earlier, he had boarded the train and spotted the duffel draped loosely around the shoulder of a rider who had toppled from subway glaze into sound sleep.

A knife glinted, and the bag's strap was slit in one fast motion. This was a class of thief known in transit police official statistics as a "lush worker." Any sleeping person robbed on a train is deemed a lush who has been worked.

The owner of the bag never stirred as the lush worker lifted it away. Kind of heavy. Lumpy. He carried it into the next car where he now works to assess the haul. On top of the bag is a towel, and he yanks it away.

Yellow, he can see something yellow and black maybe. He grabs to lift it out, and it feels very warm. Like, well, he doesn't know what. He pulls the yellow and black warm thing. It pulls back.

"Oh man!" he screams.

Mangrove, actually: a five-foot yellow and black mangrove snake, a mildly venomous native of Thailand, now slithering out of a duffel bag dumped on the floor of a D train just coming into Brooklyn.

2 A.M.
MAY 12

THE
AIR
THEY
BREATHE

Many are the fragrances of the subway. This morning, the Transit Authority is cleaning graffiti from the walls with 72 gallons of an orange juice mixture. Citric acid cuts the marker scrawl; the orange scent wafting through stations is merely collateral. Another 145 gallons of disinfectants—ammonia, bleach, and a lemon-scented concoction—are being used to swab platform decks. Their scents are definitely intentional. All but a hundred or so of the 932 subway toilet facilities were closed in 1981 because the Authority could not keep up with the vandals. The mouth of the tunnel has been used by thousands as the facility of choice, so that the wind of arriving trains turns certain platforms into mandatory no-breathing zones.

Years ago, the TA had an employee named "Smelly Kelly" with an excellent nose. His job was to track down suspicious odors. He once traced an odor of elephants in the subway beneath the main public library a block north. The Hippodrome Arena, long closed, often hosted the circus, and a water-main break had flooded a depository with elephant dung. Smelly has retired.

These days, the most sensitive nose in the subways belongs to Beau, a transit police dog. Beau is the only dog in the state trained to locate—there is no delicate way of saying this— rotting bodies. Beau was taught with a synthetic odor called "cadaverine" that smells like decomposing flesh. A brilliant dog, the police say. In an age of vanishing specialists, it is a privilege to ride the subways with such a creature.

Yet even Beau would have been stymied by the most mysterious air that ever whipped through a New York tunnel.

One day in 1967, a pudgy man with thick glasses boarded the A train in midtown Manhattan. He walked from car to car, pausing briefly at the end of each car to toss a light bulb onto the tracks. Poof.

About twenty other men and women just like him, many with thick glasses and earnest manners, rode the subways that day, pitching bulbs between cars. Each gently exploded on the tracks, sending an invisible cloud of chemicals into the dead subway air. But with each passing train, the fumes were blown blocks, then miles away. The results were measured by sensitive meters, strapped to the belts and carried in the purses and attaché cases of the very serious people in charge.

This was a top-secret test of the U.S. Army Special Operations Division. When Congress learned about it many years later, the scientists said they were using a harmless chemical to see if the subways were vulnerable to germ warfare. How harmless? More than two decades later, the contents of those bulbs is still classified information.

The subways "could not be safeguarded," concluded the earnest scientist in charge of the project, Charles Senseney, a gifted man who invented electric poison darts and a fluorescent light tube that showered death vapors when switched on.

"It apparently has not occurred to the CIA that New York subway riders have a natural immunity to lethal gases and diseases . . ." the columnist Russell Baker wrote in the New York Times *when the experiments were disclosed in 1975.*

Every subway rider knows he is marinated in anthrax from the moment he steps underground.

Do we worry about it? Of course not. Those who were going to die of it did so after their first few subway rides. The rest of us are immune.

. . . As for poison gases, we say "Fie!" Every subway rider worth his combat medals knows he can collapse at any moment in a cloud of poison gas, and plenty of us do. It has to be very powerful stuff, however, for most of us don't have lungs anymore. After six months in the subway, the lungs atrophy and people who don't die develop gas filters. The only thing we are really afraid of is oxygen.

2 A.M., New York City:
The System

Most of the world's rapid transit systems have gone to bed by now. In New York tropical sacrifices on the tracks must make way for trains, and exotic snakes are stolen by lush workers.

The lights, unseen by the subway-glazed riders on the D train, come from the office towers.

There, young men and women, baby lawyers, months out of school and priced to the most powerful corporations on earth at $175 an hour, their collars unbuttoned, their eyes bleary from nineteen hours studying in the canons of securities law, have phoned for the car that will take them home. They ride sleek black sedans, just shy of being limousines, driven by polite Russian immigrés. No cash. Just vouchers on a company account. In a single decade, the black-car business, 6,000 strong, was born on the principle that no one with money should have to ride the subway at night.

But the men and women who cleaned their offices are going home now, too. They have shucked the pale-blue or white smocks emblazoned with the name Allied or Ogden or the real estate company that hires them out.

Now they are heading for the subways, the cleaning ladies, cooks, the cellists, and the stagehands, into the honeycombed underworld that makes the great towers of New York possible.

Every few years, a politician runs for office in New York with the idea that he will make the trains better by shutting them down at one or two in the morning.

No other major subway system runs all night, the politician declares. Look at London, Tokyo, Moscow, Paris. They all close. It is only civilized. Maintenance will be better. The trains will be cleaner.

Why, only four percent of the ridership uses the system at night, he will thunder. Most *decent* people are home by midnight.

Then someone will explain to him about the A train.

The A train is the most famous subway line in the world because of the song Duke Ellington wore as the crown of his genius. When the route was built in 1932, African-Americans were able to move out of crowded Harlem to the great sprawling plains of Brooklyn, and still come back to visit.

Hurry, hurry, take the A train
The fastest way to get to Harlem.

The politician will be told the A train begins its journey in the Rockaway peninsula on the Atlantic Ocean, and arrives, ninety minutes later, in Times Square. (It still must go another 8 miles to the northern end of Manhattan before completing its route.)

To be in Times Square by 5:30 in the morning, which is when thousands of people head to work in New York, the A train must leave the ocean by 4 A.M.

In order for the A train to be ready to leave the ocean at 4 A.M., it must depart Times Square no later than 2:30 A.M.

Now, what times does Mr. Politician want the trains to stop? Two A.M.? Just thirty minutes before the first train must leave for Rockaway to be back in time for the morning rush hour? Even a politician can figure this one out.

The subways are too restless to sleep. Besides, at two in the morning, the trains are flooded with life: it is true, only 4 percent of the ridership uses them at night. But that means 170,000 people, more than most every other subway in America carries all day long. And that flood of life is tuned to the smallest nuances.

2:30 A.M., Under Broadway, Manhattan: Scene

Lila Kan, a tiny woman of mighty means, is a dead-of-the-night rider. She is an actress, matriarch of the Chinese-American dramatic community, and a brilliant chef. "I cook to support my acting habit," she often says. Arriving at midnight in the kitchen of the Charcuterie, a ragingly trendy SoHo restaurant—toting her own Chinese cleaver and boning knife in a shoulder bag, not to chance the aggravation of dull cutlery—she spends a few hours chopping and dicing vegetables, mixing custard for tomorrow's quiche, whisking salad dressings.

This suits the hours of her theater life just fine. By 2:30 A.M., the subway is bringing her home.

In the car she boards at Spring Street, there are a few people sitting in a cluster near the end. But Lila sits on a bench in the middle, preferring solitude, relaxing in the near-narcotic languor of an empty train barreling beneath the sleeping city.

But at Penn Station, three young people burst into the car. A woman and two men, decked in Big Night Out clothes, tailored suits for the guys, a low-cut gown for the woman.

Foxily dressed, Lila thinks. They are foxes.

They survey the car, note the people grouped at one end, and by herself in the middle of the car, tiny Lila, serene as a cloud.

With yards of vacant seats to choose, the woman drops into the seat next to Lila, jostling her shoulder. One of the men sits to the woman's right. The other man settles into the seat opposite Lila, and they all take up a loud, profane discussion.

Not even a flicker of awareness, of acknowledgment, crosses Lila's face, even as the young woman rocks against her. Why do I have to be subjected to this? Lila wonders. All I wanted was to take a quiet ride home.

She does not waste a glance at them. Her right hand creeps into the shoulder bag, and finds the cleaver that had served so well on the broccoli and scallions in the restaurant.

Slowly, in pure harmony with the rocking of the train, she slides the cleaver from the bag. She begins to clean the thumbnail on her left hand.

The woman next to her cannot see what Lila is doing, and neither can the man beyond her. But across the aisle, the man opposite Lila sees the gleaming blade flashing. He stares in shocked silence for a moment before speaking.

"Oh shit!" he hollers, jumping to his feet and pointing across the aisle at Lila. "It's Lady Kung Fu!"

His foxy companions look at the tiny woman with the giant cleaver and scramble up, clearing to the opposite end of the car. Lila continues to work on the nails of her left hand. The train comes to a stop and the three people run out the door and up to the next car. Lila turns her attention to her right hand.

"I'm an actress," she said later. "Balance is very important."

Lila lifts her head from her paring, and notices a man at the other end of the car who had watched the entire episode. Their eyes meet. He nods. So does Lila.

2:35 A.M., DeKalb Avenue, Brooklyn: Scene

On board the D train, the snake has fully escaped the duffel bag. And who knows what first roused the other riders from their late-night trance? Is it possible that the ears of these subway riders, delicately tuned to pick through the roar of the train for most subtle irregularities, had heard the snake slithering along the linoleum?

At DeKalb Avenue, the first stop in Brooklyn, the motorman sticks his head out the window and sees his riders fleeing from the third car. He goes back to investigate.

"D train to Command."

"Come in, D."

"We got a snake in the third car."

"Come back to me again, D. What's that you say?"

"I say we got a snake in the third car."

"Is that a live snake?"

"Very much so."

"All right. Make an announcement that the train is going out of service. Evacuate the passengers."

"The snake already did that."

"Stand by."

Every day for the last few decades, a third of the 6,000 trains sent out through the New York City subway system have been delayed or taken out of service. To keep track of the causes, the city's Transit Authority has 132 computer codes explaining the delays. Stuck doors, 0111. Bad brakes, 0501. Overheated motors, 0312. Year after year, the TA manages to reduce one cause of the breakdowns, only to find another source of problems increase; the number of stuck doors goes down, for example, but low power problems increase. And so on. No matter what, a third of the trains always go out of service.

The dispatcher searches through the list of codes to explain the D train at DeKalb Avenue.

Finally, he settles on 0230, Interior soiled/dirty, and 4013, Police action.

3 A.M.
MAY 12

HOW THE SUBWAYS CIRCULATE

The water table of New York rises fractionally every year, thousands of forgotten springs burbling below the skyscrapers. The streets were called Spring and Canal for a reason. Fresh water was everywhere on the island when the colonists arrived. It still is, although much of it's visible only in the subways, where 13 million gallons a day infiltrate the walls and tunnels. Seven hundred pumps push out the water. The next day's tides or heavy rains send it back. Pumps in the old IRT tunnels were bought second-hand; their previous employment was in the construction of the Panama Canal. They were retired in 1986.

In Brooklyn, when the Flatbush Waterworks Company shut down a few years back, ground water rose dramatically. The subway at Nostrand and Newkirk Avenues was being inundated. The Transit Authority drilled a 90-foot-deep well—one of thirty-four around the city—and now pumps a thousand gallons a minute, twenty-four hours a day to lower the water table and keep the structures from washing away. When the state built a large office building at 125th Street in Harlem in the 1970s, the foundation displaced several underground streams. These backed into the Lenox Avenue line. A huge apparatus is being installed there—400 "well points" where water will be drawn into a pump and then moved into the storm sewer system.

The subways themselves are the sewer of last resort, often saving city basements from hydraulic disaster. When water mains break—like aging vessels in a high-risk patient—the street storm drains cannot handle the deluge. With no regard for turnstiles or gates or token booths, the water runs downhill—into the subway. The pumps are waiting.

3:15 A.M., Washington Heights:
Anna Lans

The night dragged on without a soul buying a token. A few people got off trains and glanced at the booth as they passed, but Anna did not want any eye contact. Not tonight. Soon, the trains were on twenty-minute headways, and the station utterly still.

Darrell is a crazy man, wanting to do it right then.

You crazy? she asks. Just wait.

A moment later, as if to prove her point, the emergency phone rang.

"Station Command calling," says the voice on the other end.

"Yes," says Anna.

"Please identify yourself."

"This is Railroad Clerk Lans." She looks at Darrell and points to the door. He makes a face and sulks out.

"Your booth number?"

"Nancy Six-A."

"We're doing a check on the equipment. Would you please call us back on the hot line?" Anna sighs, relieved. No one had snitched out her Darrell.

Every token booth was equipped with an emergency phone, a regular phone, a microphone in the glass, and a hands-free alarm system. All that stuff was there with good reason. Token booths were miniature banks with full-scale cash bundles in them: every day, nearly $4 million in small bills is paid to the clerks for tokens that can be used either in the subway turnstiles or on the city buses.

Unlike the average Chase Manhattan branch on the street, with its guards and video cameras, the token booths, bursting with cash, are secured only by an unarmed clerk who has to leave the confines of the booth twice a shift to empty the turnstiles.

Perhaps this was reasonable in a more innocent age. Until 1972, the clerks sat in wooden kiosks, behind simple barred windows. Then, the Transit Authority started to replace them with sturdier versions, but not fast enough to keep pace with the holdups; in 1974, there were 1,145 booth holdups, three a day, the most ever.

By 1978, every clerk had been moved into baby-blue fiberglass and steel fortresses, and were now visible through five layers of bullet-resistant glass. (In 1989, each booth cost $250,000 to build, the Transit Authority said.) For this 6- by-12-foot space, a mere 72 square feet, the equivalent of a restaurant lavatory with two stalls, the city thought it was getting a citadel to stand for the ages.

Until a cold January in 1979, they seemed to be impregnable.

That day, three dim white teenagers—a girl and two boys—from an isolated community on Jamaica Bay called Broad Channel, walked by the row of turnstiles and pushed through a gate at the Broad Channel station. The clerk, an African-American woman, watched them and, exasperated, gave out a yell.

"Pay your fare," she hollered over the loudspeaker. A transit policeman in the station heard the ruckus and gave each of the kids a summons. This was no bother, since 90 percent of tickets for fare beating are thrown out, anyway, but then the cop ejected them from the subway. Stuck on an island in the middle of Jamaica Bay, they would have to walk three miles to the next station.

The next day, they returned with a five-gallon container. This time, they saw two black women in the booth. They doused the booth with gasoline and poured it through the change slot. Then one of them threw a match. Something was said about showing the niggers. The two black women died. The young men pleaded guilty to murder and were given fifteen-year prison terms; the young woman, who was cooperating, pleaded guilty to attempted manslaughter and was sentenced to a year and a half. (Neither of the victims, by the way, was the clerk who had reprimanded them; she was off duty when they came back.)

At that moment in 1979, before crack cocaine had driven a new generation madder than the previous one, the crime seemed to define a new rank of urban terror.

There was a way into the token booths, after all. More than armor was needed.

Infantry tanks, with all their protections, were vulnerable to rockets, which could set off fiery explosions inside the cab. To protect the tank and crew, the army installed an automatic fire extinguisher that would stifle the flames with a gas called halon. Halon replaces oxygen in normal combustion, effectively snuffing out fire.

After all, what was a token booth but a tank that couldn't move? Transit officials began to experiment with halon extinguishers. A contract was let in November 1986 to install the extinguishers in 433 booths. In theory, after the heat reached 135 degrees, a detector would open a valve on a canister, releasing a 6 percent concentration of the gas into the booth. Six percent was enough to smother the fire and still allow the clerk to breathe.

Installation of the halon canisters started while the Transit Authority was in the midst of a major capital overhaul program. Although the Authority was spending more money than it ever had, the number of people on the engineering staff that designed, oversaw, and tested its contracts remained more or less the same. (The only job titles of the Authority that grew during this period were for cleaners, who were battling graffiti, and nontechnical managers.) To improve efficiency, vendors were ordered to provide warranties that their products met the Transit Authority's own specifications.

In the case of the fire extinguishers, this saved the Authority from having to assign transit engineers to test them. A clause in the contract demanded that the vendor check and certify their worthiness.

Jeanette Butler, mother of two, working at the best job of her life, was the first to discover that the new extinguishers weren't all they were cracked up to be. Butler worked from midnight to 8:00 in a token booth at Livonia Avenue, inside a wheel-less tank set in one of Brooklyn's poorest neighborhoods. When you were new on the job, you got last pick on job assignment. But she wasn't complaining: the job "meant I'd be able to provide for my children, get them out of the neighborhood, and provide a better environment. It was security for my children."

She remembered it was 3:15 A.M., April 3, 1988, because she had just moved the clock ahead for daylight saving time when a man walked up to the booth. He started pouring something into the change slot.

"What are you doing?" asked Butler. Then she smelled the gasoline.

"Oh my God."

"Don't press any buttons."

Jeanette backed away from the slot and slid her finger onto the emergency alarm.

"I told you not to press any buttons," said the man.

"No, I didn't—I didn't touch anything," she said.

In the dim light of the station, the flare of the lighter startled her. The smoke was dark and foul. She thought about the door. What's he going to do to me if I go out there? she wondered. The line of fire was getting hotter, and the smoke heavier. She pushed open the door and the man, ignoring her, brushed past her, walking in. She ran to the public phone and dialed for help. The man with the lighter grabbed a single bag and stalked away; his own fire had thwarted him from reaching more riches.

From the pay phone, watching the booth, the black smoke and the flames licking at the structure, Jeanette started to cry into the telephone. "The whole booth is going up," she said.

As the police were arriving, there was the sound of a pop—an explosion without the bang—and suddenly, the flames vanished. The halon had, at last, discharged—after most of the booth had been consumed. Ten days later, the chief safety officer for the subway system got around to writing a memo to the transit executive in charge of the token clerks. The halon didn't come on in time, he said, and the clerks had better be warned.

"[The] System Safety [Department] recommends that all railroad clerks be instructed not to rely on automatic operation of the system and, if attacked, to manually activate the halon system." He said a warning sticker should be sent to every booth. He included a facsimile of the notice.

On June 3, 1988, seven weeks after that attack, the stickers still had not been issued. A further test was conducted that night, at another booth, two stops down the line in the same desperate neighborhood. A Haitian immigrant, Mona Pierre, also new on the job, also raising young children, was set afire.

"The only parts of her body that weren't burned were her armpits and the soles of her feet," said Harry Harris, a transit police detective. Mrs. Pierre died within hours.

Noting that the booth was not destroyed in the attack, officials later announced that the halon had worked well.

However, the warning stickers were issued at last. Then the TA did its own tests: a booth was moved to Randall's Island, where the city fire department has a training center, and it was set afire. The Authority came up with a new device to trigger the gas, an ultraviolet sensor that worked so well a passenger smoking a cigarette in the station, or a welder's torch, could set it off; the system discharged more than nine hundred times accidentally in its first year.

By 1989, token booth clerks were being robbed about once a day in New York, and only the most gruesome attacks were deemed worthy of notice by the city's jaded press corps. Most were prosaic: a clerk taking the count off the turnstiles would be yoked from behind, menaced with a gun, faced by a razor.

Then, if the thief was afraid of being interrupted, or just stupid, he'd settle for the pail of tokens carried by the clerk. They were easily exchanged on the street for crack cocaine, or sold at a discount for cash.

The more ambitious criminals led the prey back to the booth, where there was often a few thousand dollars. In the end, most of the clerks got away with bruises and a bad case of fear in the bones. If reporters even learned of the robbery, they'd shrug it off. What else could you expect when someone, the equivalent of a bank teller, completely unprotected, was walking around a subway station in the middle of the night? (In fact, for most of the 1980s, there were more token booth robberies than successful bank robberies in New York City; and the token booths yielded much higher takes.)

In her booth at 181st Street, Anna Lans knew the risks. Twice she had picked up the emergency phone and announced that she had been robbed.

No clerk in her right mind would complain about headquarters checking on the emergency equipment.

She made her call. The system worked well. They weren't checking why Darrell was in the booth. He was leaning over a rail, looking down from the mezzanine to the tracks below when she finished the phone calls.

She tapped on the window to get his attention, and waved him back inside.

3:30 A.M., DeKalb Avenue, Brooklyn: Scene/The System

The mangrove snake has the entire car to itself. The crew has shut the doors, definitively. The transit police have arrived en masse. The first supervisor on the scene is a Sergeant Raymond Alston, who decides that the matter is best turned over to the Emergency Services Unit, which is the kitchen sink division of the transit police. Let them handle the snake.

As he awaits their arrival, he calls his headquarters and gives an update. A clerk in the Criminal Intelligence Section prepares a memo to the chief of police:

"At time and place of occurrence Conductor Alexis observed one three-foot black and yellow reptile snake on southbound D train car No. 1065.

"Sergeant Alston classified this an unusual event."

Sergeant Alston is correct: unusual, but not unique. Snakes have been used to hold up token booths by directing them through the coin slot; at other times they have been found wandering through the stations.

Animals of all sorts turn up in the subway. One afternoon a monkey rode the 42nd Street shuttle for several hours. The police gave chase, but the monkey was clever as well as cute. At the Times Square station, the police searched the train but could not find him. "You'd look around for him but he wasn't there," said TA police Sergeant Joe Sede.

> Then the train would leave the station, and you'd see him hanging on the last car. You go on the radio and notify Grand Central the monkey's hanging on the last car. The

train would get to Grand Central and there'd be no monkey on the last car. The cops over there couldn't find him. Then the train would leave, and they'd see him inside.

They'd put it on the radio: Notify Times Square that he's in the third car. This went on for two, two-and-a-half hours. Finally, the monkey decided, "I'm tired of entertaining these people."

Sergeant Sede was asked if this was a direct quote. "Well, he literally just sat there in the car, and we picked him up and brought him to the ASPCA exotic animals unit."

A story was told several years ago of a penguin that had gotten loose in Grand Central, but even Sergeant Sede says there is some doubt as to the bird's-eye accuracy of that one.

There was, however, the avian incident on the R train one fine afternoon some years ago, and a witness who survives to testify. "I was sitting on the R, out to Astoria, when all of a sudden this chicken was running down the aisle," said Doris Gonzalez Light, a former MTA official. "An older Oriental woman was running after the chicken with a bag. She was hollering at it in Chinese, I think, or some language. They ran into the next car."

Pigeons are frequent flyers on the subways. They are a particular hazard in the narrow corridors outside the turnstiles at Grand Central, where they swoop low in carpet bombing raids. Rats, which are thought by a few of the wildlife geniuses in New York to be the wingless cousins of pigeons, can regularly be seen cavorting along tracks of the station at 42nd Street and Eighth Avenue. Teenagers, squatting on their haunches, make coochie-coo noises, as though dealing with Garfield or Snoopy.

Once in a while, a cat who lives in the tunnels will come to the attention of the ASPCA. The rescue efforts often are tricky. Cats tend to have badly jangled nerves after a stay in the subways, which generally costs them seven or eight of their nine lives. The cats are lured down there by what must seem at first glance to be a twenty-four-hour cat restaurant, with pigeons, rats, and other bountiful delicacies for the feline palate. When the harsh reality of fourteen-inch rats and thundering trains shatters their dreams, some cats gratefully chow down on the doped bait left by the ASPCA.

Dogs, in their oblivious, goofy way, can be especially interesting visitors. One mutt trotted through a tunnel ahead of a Lexington Avenue train that crept behind, with the motorman blasting the horn. Eventually, he was asked to leave by the TA police, who have syringes and dart guns with tranquilizers that work to excellent effect. A case in point is the Doberman who was trapped by himself inside a car.

"He was trying to eat his way through the glass," said transit cop Lou Falsetti. "We gave him a shot and he turned into a toy poodle. In fact, he came out smiling, saying 'I like that stuff, give me another one.' "

3:45 A.M., New York City: The System

By reputation, by acclamation, the subway is a most sinister place and never more so than at night. This, after all, is a public space built at the start of the century, in an age when a 36-watt bulb was considered an adequate light and was installed by the millions in stations and tunnels.

Someone did a study in the 1960s and found that the mean temperature of the subways was rising one degree every two years, which could be explained, in part, by the great machines stopping and starting thousands of times a day.

But more than machine exhaust raises the temperature. There is the radiance of the cargo, the accretion of 4,472,000,000 BTUs of heat released, week after week, from the 167 million pounds of human flesh that are the workday haul on the New York subways, a heat source surpassed only by some nuclear power plants working at full capacity for a few hours, enough energy in one week of rush hours to heat forty houses in the northeastern United States for a year. Including their water.

Today, the rapid transit system of New York carries only half the riders it did during the boom after World War II, before traffic jams replaced the subway crush. Over a year's time, riders make a billion fewer trips on the train than in 1946.

By 1989, with the loss of all those 98.6-degree bodies, the subway should be a much cooler place.

But it is not, at least not spiritually: all those BTUs have been replaced by a mean annual rise in subway terror, measured in the absolute refusal to enter it except when necessary for transport to a livelihood, and in the dwindling comfort of the 36-watt bulbs, the standard light of the subway, some million and a half of them—each, by the way, wired to throw off just 30 watts so as to last longer and require fewer changes and less labor.

High-voltage crime arrived in the second half of the twentieth century. The chart on page 34 shows the crime reports generated by 2 billion riders in 1946 and by 1 billion nearly half a century later.

The subway of May 12, 1989, is a far more dangerous place than the subway of 1946. Even so, there is nothing more peaceable than a train rattling below the streets at night. No car trip, on rural highway or ten-lane interstate, compares to it for safety—even at night.

Crime is at its low tide between midnight and 6 A.M., at least by strict numbers: only 19 percent of the serious assaults and robberies take place during that quarter of the day. Of course, robbers have less opportunity; after midnight, only 4 percent of the riders are on board, so the odds of encountering crime increase dramatically. But a postmidnight rider on a subway train, taking the train every night, in 1981 had a one-in-forty chance of being the victim of a felony crime, a study found; that is, in forty years of midnight-to-dawn subway trips, a rider was guaranteed, statistically speaking, to be the victim of one serious crime.

A person driving a car, on average, has an accident every eleven years.

Oddly, at night, the subways are a refuge and haven.

3:55 A.M., East New York, Brooklyn: Scene

No one has a phone on Doreta Campbell's block. Lots of things they don't have in East New York, never had, going back to the days

CRIME	1946	1956	1966	1976	1986	1989
Bookmaking	3	13	1	3	1	0
Assault	87	189	236	396	959	1,107
Homicide	2	1	1	5	11	20
Robbery	78	184	315	3,231	5,686	8,267
TOTAL CRIME	6,147	17,286	18,100	33,891	38,816	40,102
Ridership (IN MILLIONS)	2,002	1,363	1,296	1,010	1,030	1,073

Eastern European Jews and then Italians lived there, in the decades before the Puerto Ricans moved in. But none of them was ever short on babies. And they always have the subway.

In the middle of the night, here comes Doreta with her arms full of Nodoria, a two-week-old baby who has stopped breathing. There was no way to call from her apartment, and the street phones had been pummeled into silence.

She ran along the streets, to the corner, to the first sign of life: the subway station at Rockaway Avenue, open around the clock, with working pay phones. With a live clerk, someone hoping to stay that way through a lonely shift.

Doreta ran to the two pay phones near the booth. She dialed 911. That connected her to the city police.

"My baby is not breathing, I need an ambulance, she's turning blue," she screamed.

Where are you, the dispatcher asked.

"I'm in the A train station at Rockaway Avenue."

Let me get you transit police, said the dispatcher. (He was the dispatcher for city police. They don't handle subways. Transit takes care of that, so they waste a few seconds forwarding her call.) Doreta waited for the transit police operator to come on.

"I'm at Rockaway Avenue. My baby is turning blue. Please . . ."

She was still on the phone when Vinny Giordano and Tom Paccione, from a transit police office four blocks away, ran down the stairs at a full gallop. The clerk, silent in the booth, stuck her head out the door when she saw the cops.

"Help the baby!" shouted the clerk.

Giordano grabs the baby from Doreta and cradles her in his arms. He begins the little breaths that must be used in infant resuscitation, and together they run to the squad car, two cops and an infant girl named Nodoria, all hope and hurry and odd little reflexes, and a mother, who came to the subway in the middle of the night and found the tiny puffs of air that would keep her baby kicking.

4 A.M.
MAY 12

THE
TRASH
BASH

A diesel engine snorts into Grand Central, towing six flat-bed cars behind it. They have come to mine the mother lode of garbage, trash by the ton that could close the subway in two days if it were neglected. A hollering cast of cleaners leaps onto the platforms. Working in pairs, they shove big canisters of garbage onto the flatbed while another team rolls an empty canister onto the platform. Ninety tons are pulled from the subways every night, six thousand pounds of that from Grand Central. The per-capita trash left by each rider: less than three-quarters of one ounce.

What a marvelous place for a tidiness-obsessed man, ready to wage a mad holy war. In 1983, the year before David Gunn arrived, there were 172 news-stands in subway stations. Today, 52 remain. For Gunn, their sole function was the issuance of gum and papers that end up on the platforms and tracks. For riders, "they are like a campfire on the prairie when no one else is around," says straphanger Kevin Hayes. With lights, people, action, the news-stands made the stations feel safer.

When Gunn started knocking

them down without ceremony, the protests were loud. He responded by assigning a "concessions committee" to create guidelines: not surprisingly, the guidelines eliminated virtually every concession, including an all-night hot dog stand in Times Square, "about the only legitimate thing going on in the station at three in the morning," noted Joe Rappaport, a transit activist. Gunn is winning his intifada. In Grand Central today, the busiest rapid transit station in the country—130,000 passengers a day—there is no place to buy a magazine.

4:05 A.M., 240th Street Yard, the Bronx: The System

The subway moves to tidal rhythms, so that even at the moment of its lowest ebb in one place—say, any platform before dawn, when a rider waits twenty minutes for a train—the system is rising, lapping furiously at the distant shores of that industrious, nocturnal New York where things are being readied for the morning to come: the unseen city where newspapers are printed and bread is baked, pipes laid and milk boxed, roads paved and shirts washed.

Here, at the 240th Street yard, it is high tide. Built in 1906 below the ridge of a cliff in the northwest Bronx, the yard is the nighttime home of trains from the city's oldest subway line, the No. 1. By day, No. 1 trains run from near the northern border of the city, south along Broadway for 14.73 miles to the tip of Manhattan Island.

In the hours before dawn, seven trains move along the route on twenty-minute headways. Also assigned to the line are twenty-six other trains, but at the moment these are out of sight: they are being beautified, rectified, and rested in the 240th Street yard.

Darrell Williams sits in the tower, master of the yard below, ordering a half dozen trains ferried to an automatic car washer a mile south. There they are doused with water and chemicals that relight the gleam of their aluminum skins.

Just last weekend, Williams had been in Atlantic City, and he struck up conversation with a Maryland man at the blackjack table. He had something to tell Darrell about the New York subways.

"I vowed," said the man, "never to go on the trains in New York City. But my car broke down when we were up there last time."

"Where were you?" asked Darrell.

"Uptown somewheres, I don't know exactly. Near to Broadway."

"And?"

"I jumped on the train and we got downtown, no time at all."

"The Number One, right?"

"That's right—and the amazing thing, it was clean. No, it was more than clean. It was shiny."

Back in his tower, Williams smiles at the memory. You forget how bad they were. You get used to them not having any graffiti, filth all over the place. Part of the routine now: get them down to the car wash, and then give special attention to any of the cars that had been tagged by the kids.

He looks over his hold sheet:

2425	#6	d/o	c/o	H/G/L
2310	#2	d/o	c/o	slow door

The shorthand is telling him door-operator motors on two cars need attention. They are on separate trains. Williams instructs a motorman in the yard to "drill them out" of the trains they are attached to.

A New York subway train typically is made of ten separate electric locomotives, making it a mechanical palindrome, the same machine in either direction. Moreover, a car in the middle of the train is as capable of moving the other nine as the ones at either end. All of them are bound to each other electronically, linked through fifty-two separate pins that resemble a much enlarged version of the connector cables in the back of a computer. These pins carry messages along the entire 513-foot length of the train: Close the doors. Turn on the lights. Bring up the air conditioning.

These two cars on Williams's hold list are having garden-variety door problems: on one, a little bulb ("H/G/L" for "hanging guard light") was telling the crew that the doors were open, even when they were shut. And the other door was slowing down—no doubt a result of the time-honored practice of people racing for the train and holding it open for trailing slowpokes while the conductor was pushing buttons to shut them. The result was a failing motor on the door. About a third of all the train delays in the city are caused by door problems.

These cars have to be removed and working cars inserted in their place. A key was used to uncouple the bad cars so they could be moved aside and into the barn.

And this had to be finished by 5 A.M., for then, the tide would go out: instead of a train every twenty minutes, there would be one every twelve. The trains would be lined up on the yard tracks, waiting for crews to arrive and move them to the terminals.

In the tower a long board, dimly lit with yellow and red bulbs, shows the progress and movement of the trains.

4:05 A.M., Ronkonkoma, Long Island: Thomas Thomasevich

The alarm rings and Tom Thomasevich bangs it and is out of bed before his wife opens an eye. Brooklyn born and bred, he is living in the suburban house of civil servant dreams, bought on his $30,000 conductor's salary. He pads down the hall, a handsome man with neat beard and a full head of salt and pepper hair, past the bedrooms where his eight-year-old daughter and five-year-old son are sleeping.

In the bathroom, he turns on the shower and waits for the water to come out hot.

Turning his face to the spray, he wets his face, slowly rotates under the water, and begins to tap his toe to some inner beat. He sings:

> *Well, it's one for the money,*
> *Two for the show,*
> *Three to get ready,*
> *Now go cat go!*

4:25 A.M., DeKalb Avenue, Brooklyn: Scene

Police from all over the city have stopped by to see in person what they have been hearing about on the radio. The snake has been lifted with a pole into a five-gallon can and the lid has been fitted on tightly. Two officers put it in the trunk of their radio car and head for the Brooklyn ASPCA. But they are told upon arrival that this is a matter for the exotic pet unit based in Manhattan. The officers return to their car with the can of snake.

4:45 A.M., Washington Heights: Anna Lans

Through the thick glass, Anna can barely hear the A train arriving, a flight of stairs below her. But at this time of night, the system runs on a regular schedule. Every twenty minutes, a train will arrive.

When they come up the stairs, the two men have grim faces. Baseball caps, pulled low on the brow, nearly cover their eyes.

Anna knows. They are here for the money.

Revenue agents come once a night to pick up the cash leavings of the 3,760,000 people who rode the subway the day before. Most of these people pay a one-dollar fare. (A quarter-million students ride free. A quarter-million senior citizens pay half fare. These reduced-fare groups alone could fill up every train on every other rapid transit system in the United States.)

In each booth is a safe that must be emptied every night to make room for the next day's take: in total, an average of three tons of cash, 365 days a year.

At 181st Street in upper Manhattan, where Anna and Darrell were conducting their idyll, the clerk collects $3,300. But at Grand Central Station, twelve token booths handle $130,000 in daily fares; at Brooklyn's Dean Street, where most riders routinely hop over the turnstiles without paying, the take is a mere $122.

The two men in the baseball caps walk up to the side of the booth, barely nodding to Anna inside, not acknowledging Darrell at all. Whether he's supposed to be there or not, it's none of their business.

Ordinarily, night transit workers are especially friendly to each other, welcoming the chance for any crumb of communion in the solitude of the postmidnight hours.

But the guys from the money train and the people in the booths aren't friends. For the sake of all those hundreds of pounds of cash, they're not meant to be. This is about business: a missing dime comes out of someone's paycheck, the clerk's or the revenue agents'.

Each group tells stories on the other: clerks have been known to slice open the bags of money and slip a few twenties out, say the agents.

The people on the money train were razoring the bags open, to slide out a few bills, say the clerks. Someone heard that they even had a hand-held sewing machine to stitch the canvas bags back together.

Eventually, the missing money, whether lost to a miscount or to a diabolically clever thief, is docked from someone's pay check.

In this endless drizzle of mistrust, the two revenue agents arrive at Anna's booth. Their first order of business is to drop a case of tokens inside the booth, a week's supply. Anna rips the seal and counts seven white boxes, all sealed with a clear safety tape stamped NYCTA to show they are as pure as a bottle of Tylenol. In each box are 100 plastic bags of 10 tokens each, making the case worth $7,000.

A sheet is presented to Anna for her signature accepting responsibility for the tokens. She looks at the number, then at them.

"Only seven thousand? You guys are getting cheap!"

One of the agents smiles. The other asks, "How many you supposed to get? We got seven thousand on the list."

"I don't know," says Anna. "I'm doing a relief on this booth."

The agents never enter the booth: they hand over the tokens to Anna at the door. And they are able to unload the cash from the booth through a half door at the rear, nearly out of the line of sight of the clerk. One squats and unlocks the half door. Behind it, there is a safe with no knob, a ritual precaution. The knob is in the revenue agent's pocket. He attaches it to the safe door, twirls the combination, and opens the vault. He drags out a half-dozen sealed canvas bags of coins and bills.

Inside the booth, Anna and Darrell are pictures of nonchalance. Against a list that has been stored in the safe, the agents tick off the bags, rolling them over for telltale slash marks, ensuring that the bag's serial number lines up with the log. The whole procedure lasts about six or seven minutes.

"Take care," the agent mouths at the glass.

"You too," Anna lips back, not bothering to flick on her microphone.

The agents really do need to take care: now they are going down to stand on the platform with six lumpy gray bags of cash while they wait for the money train. To get to the station, they had grabbed a regular A train. While they performed the rites at the token booth, the money train was lumbering up the line, picking up other agents at stations along the way.

The two men stand on the subway platform with the gray sacks at their feet, peering down the tunnel in search of a glimmer of headlights like every other commuter. The subways are ever the great equalizer: dragging around $40,000 or $50,000 in small bills doesn't make their train come sooner than it does for any one else in a hurry to get home.

If the money trains stood at each station for the agents to finish logging in the cash, they'd never get through the whole subway system in one night.

After a twenty-minute wait, the money train rattles into the station. The two men board a battered old car whose seats have been torn out to make room for metal bins that resemble laundry hampers, bolted to the walls to keep them from rolling around. Inside these, the sacks of money are laid. The windows are painted black.

When they had gone downstairs to the platform, Darrell opened the door to the booth and watched them from the mezzanine.

Darrell walks back to the booth.

"They're gone," says Darrell. "I'm ready."

" 'Love me tender,' " sings Tom Thomasevich as he walks into the crew room, " 'love me sweet. Make my life complete.' "

Three other conductors, waiting for their trains to depart, barely look at Tom, familiar with his nonstop balladeering. "Let him keep it up, some days in the street would make his life complete," says one, suggesting a suspension.

" 'Oh my darling, I love you,' " croons Tom, " 'And I always will.' "

Every few minutes, another crew arrives. Their starting times are geared to the train schedule, which picks up steam as the morning progresses. Tom is on the first wave of early morning arrivals. He greets the train operator he is paired with, and together they inspect the train they will be running from the eastern Bronx down the East Side of Manhattan.

Tom strides through the cars, checking that the destination signs are accurate: on top, the signs show Brooklyn Bridge, in Manhattan, the last stop. Below that, they list Pelham Bay Park, for this was the train immortalized in *The Taking of Pelham One Two Three*, a novel by John Godey and movie starring Walter Matthau. Pelham was the terminal; 1:23 was the departure time. A train full of typical New Yorkers was hijacked for a million-dollar ransom. (For more than a decade, no transit planner dared schedule a train leaving Pelham at 1:23, morning or night. That departure time was unofficially banned. Finally, in 1987, the transit executive in charge of the schedule told the planners to forget the ban—they could send a train out at 1:23. Thanks, boss, the schedulers said; still, between noon and 2 P.M., the schedule does odd contortions, with headways jumping from six to eight minutes and then to ten—to avoid a 1:23 departure. To do otherwise, the schedulers believe, would be an invitation to trouble; there is no shortage of nuts with strong appreciation for literary landmarks in New York.)

The movie and book were set in an era when the subways already were thought to be impossibly dirty and chaotic. No one could have dreamed, in 1974, when the film was released, of the greater collapse to come.

There was a fair chance then, for instance, that whoever was doing

Tom Thomasevich's job—ensuring that the destination signs were in place—would have seen to it that the signs really did say where the train was going.

In the decade that followed, the roll signs would be ripped out by roving vandals or train buffs searching for souvenirs. Or the ancient gears that turned the signs would be cracked, so that a train's destination on the day the sign broke would forevermore be its published destination—no matter where the riders ended up. If you found someone who cared about fixing them, he wouldn't have the parts or the money.

That was institutionalized vandalism. Riders could watch as a train pulled into a station, and the signs on every one of the eight or ten cars would list different destinations: NEW LOTS. PELHAM BAY. FLATBUSH. SOUTH FERRY. WOODLAWN. WHITE PLAINS ROAD. For the passengers, it was subway roulette: get on the train, then find out where it was going. These were the signs of a train patched together with cars from different barns serving routes at opposite ends of town.

And these were the signs of a system falling apart, of the lethal, silent mischief of the city's power establishment when it stopped paying the cost of running and repairing the trains. New York in the 1970s abandoned its maintenance of trains and bridges and schools and streets, depleted its fire and police corps, stopped inspecting buildings for safety. This was done in the name of keeping a good credit rating so that the city would be able to sell municipal bonds. The city succeeded. Bonds were sold.

Between 1975 and 1979, thirty subway maintenance programs were eliminated, cars no longer were overhauled, track inspection was all but eliminated, and the electrical cables were left to rot. As a result, the cancellation of scheduled trains doubled, a report by City Council President Carol Bellany found in August 1979. The useful life of hundreds of millions of dollars' worth of equipment was cut short.

Meanwhile, train yardmasters faced morning rush hours without enough cars capable of lumbering into service. So the yardmasters would raid other lines, borrowing equipment, returning it somewhere else the next day. Before long, no one knew where any car had come from, and no one had the time or the interest to change the 12,400 signs on trains. They just might have to be turned again tomorrow.

Mayors and government people made loud noises about graffiti—about what a terrible symbol graffiti were. The chaos of mixed signs was more than symbol: they were symptoms of the deeper, more lethal problem of nonmaintenance.

But as Tom Thomasevich walked through the cars, humming to himself, that era lay behind him and the city. He didn't have to adjust any of the signs. All of the cars had come out of the same barn, dedicated to service for the Pelham Bay line. And all of them read (6) PELHAM BAY–BROOKLYN BRIDGE.

Now it is time to test the public address system. Tom walks back to the middle of the train and opens the door to the conductor's closet-sized compartment. Fingering the P.A. button, he pushes his face next to the microphone that is built into the wall. He sends a stream of *pffffts* at it, then draws a breath and sings:

> *Who knows where*
> *We'll meet again*
> *This way?*

5 A.M., Washington Heights: Anna Lans

Alone in her booth, Anna Lans tries to bring her breathing under control before reaching for the emergency phone. There are two in the booth: one for emergencies, and one that rang at the transit Command Center and was rarely answered.

"Yes," she says into the emergency phone. "This is booth Nancy 6A. The booth was just robbed." She pauses.

"No. He's going up the ramp now. A black male. With a ski cap. Two of them. A Hispanic also . . . I'm okay. Tell Supervision I have to go to the clinic. I think I have high blood pressure . . . The booth? It is secure. They got me when I was pulling the wheel."

"The wheel" is the collective name for the turnstiles—and every clerk must venture outside the booth near the end of the shift to register the count, open the vault at the bottom of each turnstile, and carry out the tokens, nearly $4 million in cash and tokens every day, all of it hauled by clerks and collection agents through unguarded stations, handled the way it was forty years ago when the money involved was just a few hundred thousand dollars and the city—the innocent, vanished city of memory—could be shocked by a token booth holdup.

5:25 A.M., The ASPCA, Manhattan: Scene

The transit cops have arrived at the brick building on 92nd Street, by now bored with their haulage. They tote the can down a long hall as dogs howl and yip through the cages.

"What do you got, fellahs?" asks an attendant, prying open the lid.

"Snake from the D train," says one of the cops, Ron Reale.

"D like Dead snake," says the attendant, lifting the beautiful, still form out of the can. "This one is gone, gone. That subway will get you every time. Course, this is a tropical snake—can't take weather much below eighty, eight-five degrees. Night like this—fifty degrees out—the snake freezes right up."

The police stare at their dead cargo. Case closed.

5:30 A.M., 240th Street Yard: The System

Train crews are arriving every five minutes, the pace at which they will be launched from the yard starting at 6 A.M. While the conductor checks the inside of the cars, as Tom Thomasevich did, the train operator—the unisex term that replaced "motorman"—must look over the exterior of the train, checking the electrical cables for gross abnormalities.

Then they rock and roll—the train.

Normally, subway trains are stopped by a combination of friction and electrical power reversing itself. The juice that propels the train forward also can act in the opposite direction, reducing the speed of the train by about 90 percent, to less than 10 miles per hour from a top of about 45 or 50.

The last 10 percent of the speed is eliminated by friction brakes, which work like ordinary brake shoes on an automobile—equal, deliberate applications of brute force.

Until 1960, the friction brake provided all the stopping power for the train. It also created tons of steel dust—so much that a vacuum train was purchased to run through the system and suck up the filings. To this day, the transit police run an annual golf tournament called the Steel Dust Open. But over the last three decades, all the trains have been modified to rely on electrical slowing of the train, "dynamic braking" rather than friction, a vital adaptation for a railroad whose trains must stop hundreds of times every day.

The brakes have an ingenious fail-safe design. To move the train, the friction brakes must be released. This is done by pumping air, under pressure, through the pipes beneath each car. The air provides the power to lift the brakes from the wheels, allowing the train to move.

This makes excellent sense: if an air pipe should be ruptured and lose the compressed air inside, the brakes will automatically apply and stop the train. Air pressure lifts the brake; absence of air pressure applies them. Without air pressure, the brakes engage and stop the train automatically—a safe failure.

This system has many practical applications. For instance, a train that runs over a large object on the trackbed—a piece of wood, a tool left behind, a person—is liable to derail if it does not immediately slow. So hanging underneath each car is a valve that flips open when it's touched by something on the trackbed. This valve releases all the air in the pipes, and the train automatically slows and stops.

Now, in the 240th Street yard, these systems are being tested in the "rock and roll" formation. First, the train operator turns on a compressor that pumps air at about 40 or 50 pounds of pressure through the system.

Then, while the train is standing still, the operator moves the brake handle back and forth. Next, a small amount of power is given to the train, and it is moved forward at 1 or 2 miles per hour, and stopped. Finally, the train is pushed to about 15 miles per hour, and stopped.

Then the train operator tests the radio. "This is the 6:03 Van Cortlandt to South Ferry on eleven track. Radio check, please."

"Radio check loud and clear," responds the dispatcher.

When these tests are finished, the train pulls up to a signal in the yard. In the yard tower, the train is a single light on the model board—a 20-foot-long layout of the twelve tracks in the yard and six others in the barn, as well as the main-line network for 5 miles south. The board is used to steer trains onto the correct track for service.

As morning breaks, the lights at 240th Street twinkle with a gentle urgency.

5:30
A.M.
MAY 12

KEYS
TO
THE
KINGDOM

The subway system is a colossal sieve spread along hundreds of miles: until recently, it could be entered from 1,950 stairways in the streets, leading up or down to its 469 stations. Another 85 flights of stairs are cozyed inside private buildings. It seems people always wanted a subway nearby. Then they started changing their minds. As ridership dropped, the people running the transit system started chaining the stairways and closing down token booths.

Around 1968, a key known as the "400" was developed for a lock of that same name, which was installed on gates across stairways, on swinging exit doors on platforms, and on fences pulled across turnstiles. In time, 3,972 "400" locks were placed across the mouths of the system.

The "400" locks are the motif for a prematurely shrinking subway. Of those 1,950 staircases, about 600 are now locked for all or part of the day. At stations along upper Broadway a few years ago, the TA closed entrances where the passenger volume, a couple of hundred or so, didn't pay the token clerk's salary. At those places, the Authority placed a special revolv-

ing door that could be operated by a token. These broke so often that the few hundred riders quickly dwindled to none. To go uptown a rider had to go downtown and turn around. The locks work. They keep people out.

By 1989, the public forced the system to expand.

How many "400" keys were duplicated? No one knows. The number is surely in the tens of thousands. A Brooklyn hardware store in walking distance of TA headquarters sells the key for a dollar. To anyone.

Private enterprise heard the demand for more ways into the subway. The subway is being unlocked, by hook and by crooks.

5:40 A.M., Greenpoint Avenue, Brooklyn: Scene

Paul Franklin is in high gear already, collecting fares, dispensing greetings.

"You have a nice day now," he says, saluting the people of Greenpoint, a hard-working Brooklyn neighborhood where the street signs are in English, Spanish, and Polish.

"Have a flier about the new fares," says Franklin.

In a city where everything is extravagantly overpriced—then marked down slightly to provide the illusion of a good deal—Franklin provides an authentic bargain.

He charges half price, 50 cents, to get into the subway. At least, he did until today, when he raised the price a nickel, to 55 cents.

Franklin's low prices are a tribute to the private enterprise system, because he doesn't work for the Transit Authority. He lives in a shelter for the homeless down the street and has somehow obtained a key to part of the station that's normally closed until 7 A.M.

Not only does Franklin save his customers money, he also spares them a two-block walk to the official station entrance, which is operated around the clock by a transit worker. More than a hundred people every morning throw change into Franklin's cardboard box.

He is nothing if not punctual: Franklin opens the south end of the Greenpoint Avenue station by 5 A.M. By the time the first brace of hardworking Greenpointers arrives, Franklin has unlocked the bolted gate and is ready for business.

A few times, the police have arrested Franklin and a team of cohorts. But the city jails barely have room for violent criminals, much less someone stealing quarters from the subway system. Franklin is back on the street the same day. And his precious key to the station, always squirreled in a hiding place right after he unlocks the gate, is waiting for him when he's ready to resume business.

Though the arrests have failed to put him out of business, they are adding to his overhead costs. Today, Franklin is distributing a flier to his loyal customers, announcing that, as of today,

FARE FOR RIDERS WILL BE 55 CENTS.
NO PENNIES WILL NOT BE ACCEPTED NO MORE.
PEOPLE WHO DON'T PAY WILL BE TERMINATE
FROM THIS SIDE OF THE STATION AND WILL
HAVE TO WALK 3 BLOCKS TO THE FRONT OF
THE STATION PAY $100 FARE. WE LET YOU GO
FOR THAT REDUCE FARE OF 55 CENTS.
PEOPLE WE HAD RUN-IN WITH TRANSIT POLICE
SO THAT WHY WE RAISE IT.
WE COULD NOT AFFORD OF GETTING BUSTED.
WE OPEN FROM 500 AM TO 645 AM.
CATCH THAT FARE SPECIAL.

5:45 A.M., Park Slope, Brooklyn: David Gunn

Screaming in unison, the phone and kettle demand the attention of the man. He is just starting his own morning engine, but he works methodically, deliberately. Ignoring the phone, he reaches first for the kettle and fills his tea cup. One noise quieted. Then he picks up the phone.

"Gunn here."

"Good morning, sir. Pearson, Command Center calling. How are you today?"

"Yeah, fine. What do you have for me?"

David Gunn has opened for business, which is running the world's largest and most untamed subway system.

Over the phone, he gets a report on the only major incident of the night—a flagman, steering trains through a construction site, was grazed by an F train.

Comedy is not on David Gunn's early morning menu: he doesn't hear about the snake that had tied up traffic in Brooklyn, and the report of the robbery at Anna Lans's booth is just now being logged in at Command Center, so he'll get word of that later in the morning.

The worker brushed by the train was not seriously hurt, although he was badly shaken and taken to a hospital.

As Gunn dresses, it is still dark in the streets of Park Slope, an old neighborhood of Brooklyn Irish that is giving way to young New Yorkers priced out of Manhattan.

In many ways, the neighborhood is a perfect fit for Gunn. His wardrobe appears to have been lifted from an L. L. Bean catalog, although the tailoring is custom. A born and bred New Englander, he comes by his taste for tweeds and pinstripes naturally, a fifty-two-year-old preppy out of Andover and Harvard. Every other weekend, he flees the city for a camp in New Hampshire, where he climbs rocks and hikes the woods.

His duplex apartment—a co-op in an old clock factory that was converted at the height of New York's 1980s real estate boom—is meticulously tidy. On the walls are pictures of old steam engines. He also collects oil lanterns and lights them on special evenings when he entertains guests. He lives alone, and always has, with his railroad stuff.

This devotion to the business, and the obsession with cleanliness, had, by the end of the 1980s, won him praise as the most successful president in the history of the New York City Transit Authority. In some ways, the accolades were a tribute to the amnesiac nature of New York commentators. Forgotten were men who had built the system and run it for decades at a time, opening 20 to 30 new miles of subway in a few years while carrying twice the riders. New York had a chronically short memory, and it just about reached back to 1980, when the trains and buses had been staggeringly bad. Gunn arrived almost simultaneously with $12.27 billion in funds for new equipment and rebuilding the old stuff.

As a passionately tidy man, living in New York, he was bound to be frustrated. But he beat a retreat out of the city just about every other weekend.

This is one of those weekends. Between sips of tea, he packs his overnight bag, because he will leave directly from the office for the trip north, up to Crawford Notch, an ancient piece of the White Mountain range that had been sliced open by glaciers, and since then, left largely untouched by nature or man. To Gunn, it always seems a long way from the city.

5:50 A.M., Washington Heights: Anna Lans

Anna Lans, waiting in her token booth at the 181st Street station for the police to arrive, is set in a notch left by the same glacier that shaped David Gunn's hiking territory.

Until the twentieth century, the most powerful shaper of the New York landscape was the glacier that crept through New England and into the Hudson Valley more than 18,000 years ago, spending itself at last in the formation of the archipelago and splendid natural harbors that today are called New York City.

Almost immediately above Anna Lans is the city's highest natural point, a rock shoal in a playground, reaching 267.75 feet from sea level. Here, and for several miles north, the city's natural geology is most visible and dramatic: along the rocky crests of Fort Tryon and Inwood Hill Parks, there are magnificent prospects.

From the east, slanting between the orderly rows of Bronx apartment houses, the first long rays of morning sun play across the park. Joggers shuffle along the paths. In a meadow, beneath a great copper beech tree, a woman moves through the ancient Chinese exercise regimen of t'ai chi, holding her hands and feet in the most delicate and deliberate poses as she readies herself for the plunge into the daily frenzy.

To the west, the stately walls of the New Jersey Palisades soar high above the Hudson River, and a stream of cars, every three minutes lengthening by a few hundred yards, urge their way along the top of the cliff toward the George Washington Bridge, anchored in the firm grip of the rock.

On the Manhattan side of the river, buried in a rock wall that is a twin of the Palisades, the subways are the deepest in the city, 180 feet below the street. Through most of Manhattan, the subway tunnels are just a few feet below the street level, but in the north, the island ascends steeply from sea level, reaching its peak in this ridge that formed 180 million years ago during the Jurassic period.

"The land merely gets higher and the tracks—at least relatively—lower," explain Elliot Willensky and Norval White in the *AIA Guide to New York City*.

Of course, the most famous aspect of New York's geology—if rock can ever be thought famous—is not the cliffs, but the Manhattan schist, the billion-year-old bedrock on which its midtown skyscrapers sit, as every New York school kid knows. In fifth-grade civics classes, they are taught that this great plate of rock, so close to the surface, made possible the 60,000-ton steel fingers that tickle the clouds, a thousand feet up.

But that schist bedrock was there from the dawn of time without colossal buildings. Until the subways.

The opening of the first New York subway in 1904 was the dawn of an instant new geological age, for mass transit was as potent a sculptor of the cityscape as the glaciers that preceded it by two hundred centuries.

To understand the influence of subways on physical New York, it helps to think of the Jack Nicholson film *Chinatown*: in California, bloody battles were fought over water rights, not for the sake of water but the land that it would make developable. Without irrigation, most of California's arid land would not be worth anything. It couldn't be farmed, and worse, couldn't be built on.

Subways are to New York what water is to the West. Around 1800, nearly all of the city's population was locked into a tiny fraction of its land, clustered at the southern foot of Manhattan island, near the excellent harbors around which the colonial trading village of Nieuw Amsterdam had been built. For most of the nineteenth century, no one dreamed that the neighborhood around the 181st Street station would ever exist.

In fact, a city commission confidently—and reasonably—predicted in 1811 that the edge of Trinity Cemetery in Harlem, better than a mile south of where Anna Lans now sits, was the point beyond which New York "could never grow." Many scoffed at the grid drawn by the commission, which covered miles of farmland and wild forest in the northern part of the island.

After the Civil War, development was pushed uptown, to the edge of Harlem, by the Tammany Hall group led by William Marcy Tweed, who later became journalists' and historians' most valuable all-purpose villain of nineteenth-century New York politics. But the group didn't get very far: Tweed's development schemes did not outlive his power, which came to a crashing end by 1872.

Tweed did leave New York with the best water supply in the country: pure springs in the Catskill mountains, collected in reservoirs and then fed, by gravity, to the thirsty city a hundred miles to the south. Of course he made a fortune on the land. Why shouldn't he do well while doing good?

(Some of the nation's most famous families were in high dudgeon over the corruption of the Tweed Ring. Of course, Tweed also had bad manners: expanding the boundaries of the city to the north was an affront to such as the Roosevelt family, which captured plump fortunes from the high-density squalor of lower Manhattan, on streets named James, Catherine, Henry—after Roosevelt children. Tweed and his ilk were not only corrupt—they were inconvenient.)

With an explosion of immigrant arrivals in New York through the last part of the nineteenth century, pressure grew for a rapid transit system. Manhattan's population in 1850 was 696,115; by 1890, it had doubled, to 1,441,216, and would nearly double again in the next twenty years.

For reformers such as Jacob Riis, subways were the sweet chariots that would deliver the suffocating masses from the tenements of the Lower East Side. On its streets in the late nineteenth century, nine hundred people were housed on a single acre, the highest-density population in the history of the world.

Along the dreamed-of subway lines, working people would live in houses, not apartments, and they would commute quickly and economically to the central city.

Of course, there were other visions of what could be built alongside subway lines. And they certainly didn't count on one family to a lot.

"By the time the railway is completed, areas that are now given over to rocks and goats will be covered with houses," said William

Barclay Parsons, the chief construction engineer of the subways in 1900. "Plans have already been drawn up by every property owner for the undeveloped real estate at the northern confines of the city which the rapid transit railway is projected to reach."

While the route of the subway was still on the drawing board, a loosely held secret among the private entrepreneurs who were building it, real estate investor Henry Morgenthau learned the location of several stops in upper Manhattan. One of those stops was 181st Street and St. Nicholas Avenue in Washington Heights.

Wasting no time, Morgenthau, a German immigrant who had become a business partner with the financial barons Cornelius Vanderbilt and Charles Schwab, assembled a syndicate of investors to buy 140 vacant lots around the site.

Then they sat back and waited for the trains to get there. Many of the lots were quickly turned over, undeveloped, to other speculators, who threw up tenements and then sold them, quickly, to still other investors.

All over New York, the process was repeated, as subways opened to the Bronx, then Brooklyn and Queens between 1906 and 1918. The modern city followed, defined by high rollers and men of property.

Thus the apartment houses of lower Manhattan spread through the city, up Broadway, and into the Washington Heights section, where Anna Lans is working on this day most of a century later.

It turns out that a neighborhood of tenements wasn't the only thing Henry Morgenthau developed. With a solid fortune in real estate speculation, he went on to become national secretary of the Democratic party. His son, Henry Morgenthau, Jr., was Franklin Roosevelt's secretary of the treasury. And on the day Anna Lans's token booth was robbed, the grandson of Henry Morgenthau, Robert Morgenthau, was also in politics. He was the Manhattan district attorney. His office would be prosecuting the culprits of the token booth theft—if they're caught.

6:10 A.M., Jay Street, Brooklyn: The Money Room

When he glances up from his work and squints at the window, Keith Edwards can see the streets of downtown Brooklyn. But he has to look hard, past the steel grates and the puffs of soot, for these windows are never opened, never washed. This is the money room.

Edwards sighs and fans a bundle of $20 bills: no one has slipped a five into the pack. He stacks them into a Brandt currency counter, a machine that counts 25 bills a second, all the while scanning the paper to be sure magnetic ink is embedded in it, a mark of authenticity. The machine is sharp enough to read 1,500 a minute and pluck out the phonies—as much as $5,000 worth a month has been fielded, mostly charged back to the clerks—but it can't distinguish among denominations: an authentic $5 bill in a stack of twenties would not draw an electronic second glance.

The money room of the New York City Transit Authority is the world's busiest private currency-processing enterprise, receiving, counting, double counting, packing, weighing, and shipping upward of 800,000 "pieces" a day. Most of them are singles. On an average day, 46 percent of the work is one dollar bills; 22 percent is twenties; 20 percent is tens; 12 percent is fives.

Other banking operations count greater amounts—including fares from both buses and subways, the TA handles only $5 million a day, while Citibank, Chase Manhattan, Wells Fargo, and Brinks move between $12 million and $20 million. But they deal in big bills. The subway token booths don't accept anything higher than a $20 note, and their customers rarely have anything larger anyway. "Whether you count $50 or $100 bills, the effort is the same," says Alan F. Putre, the transit executive who oversees the money room.

Eight hours a day, five days a week, the bills spin through the currency counter under the eyes of cashiers like Keith Edwards, who handle more money before their first toilet break than they make in a year, which is $19,000 to $25,000.

No cashier enters the money room until he or she has stripped down in a locker room and donned the only permitted clothing—brown and beige uniforms. With no pockets. They pass through double interlocking gates controlled by a police officer inside a bulletproof booth. They cannot carry so much as a pack of cigarettes into the counting room, so outside the second gate are lockers where all personal property must be stored.

The money room actually is not a single space but a series of identical counting rooms, a staging area and weighing station. The complex is a few yards down the hall from the transit police headquarters. Closed-circuit cameras, perched on the ceiling like crows on a telephone line, record time-lapsed videotapes of the clerks. The cameras caught one woman who fingered a $20 bill into her waistband. Another, who made frequent trips to a coffee machine, was found to be tonguing bills inside her cup. "The most effective security, people in the business believe, is closed-circuit television," says Putre. "My cameras are out in the open. I don't want to catch crooked employees. I want to keep honest persons honest. The philosophy is to keep putting obstacles up. Without them, given enough time and temptation you can turn a good, honest person into an evil one."

After pickups are made from 750 token booths, spread over the 238 route miles of the system, a prodigious effort in itself, notes Putre—"I've worked in armored car companies, and there isn't a collection operation like it"—the money arrives at Jay Street in the small hours of the morning on trains that park along a special track area in the basement of the building. A sliding door is opened, like a zipper, and cans of money are wheeled into a freight elevator that runs directly to the money room.

With this starts a daylong, intricate ritual prescribed in a 35-page policy book. Money is weighed, logged in, and custody is passed from the workers on the train to another set of agents in the building. They parcel it into smaller cans for the cashiers. Everyone must sign for his or her piece of the action. A dollar that slips away is lopped off a paycheck.

Besides the bills, there can be as many as half a million coins arriving on a Monday morning, most of them pennies. (A fare increase in January 1990, from $1 to $1.15, instantly eased the nation's perennial penny shortage; New Yorkers, who had used folding currency for their token purchases from 1986 through 1990, rifled forgotten drawers and started unloading hoards of change on the token booths. Suddenly, the Transit Authority was delivering a million pennies a week to the Federal Reserve.)

The coins are counted and sorted by a single cashier in each counting room, who operates another Brandt machine. This one can sort 5,000 per minute, but is fed them at a much slower pace, because the cashier first spills the coins into a tray and picks through them for slugs and foreign pieces. For a while, the Connecticut Turnpike was selling tokens for 17.5 cents that worked fine in subway turnstiles, and the TA was doing a brisk business in underpriced fares from out-of-towners. That problem ended when Connecticut stopped collecting tolls. Certain pesos also fit the turnstiles. A visitor watches as the cashier nudges these bad ones aside with her right hand, all the while using her left to slide quarters and pennies and nickels and dimes into the throat of the machine.

She sends to the reject pile a shiny, brassy piece that obviously did not originate in the United States mint.

What country is that from, the visitor asks.

"Peepland," says Putre, with a numismatic eye. "Peep shows in Times Square take these things. Somehow, it got into a turnstile."

And they wind up in this room of sooted windows, where workers sort out slugs from the Connecticut State Turnpike Authority and the Republic of Peepland and during the course of a year count better than a billion dollars of the money of the working people of New York.

All those singles and millions of pennies add up to more than two-thirds of the operating costs of the subway system. In 1989, a subway token pays 68 percent of the cost of the ride.

The rest of the cost is provided by tax revenues, most of them levied on the same people who provided the pennies; the city has an 8.25 percent sales tax on everything from a Coke and hot dog to a Porsche and a fur coat. The last quarter percent of the tax goes to transit. (Many more hot dogs are sold in New York than Porsches. And high-end retail dealers are famous for shipping goods out of town for wealthy customers to evade the local tax.)

On few other public transportation systems in the country is so much of the cost of the trip borne by the individual rider. Suburban train passengers in Long Island and Westchester pay just under half—about the same share paid by riders in Philadelphia, Atlanta, and San Francisco. These governments tax land, income, and cars for the remainder.

But in New York, public transportation always has worked as a plow for developers—a device, provided at little or no cost, to harvest the rocky streets of Manhattan into skyscrapers that would paralyze any system of roads if their inhabitants arrived by automobile. Mile for mile, the subway is the single most vital improvement ever provided to real estate in the United States. Only the federally funded irrigation system in California comes close; there, a huge public works canal carries water from the mountains to the arid Central Valley, converting it into thriving farmland for giant agribusiness concerns. The snow in the mountains of California is called white gold because the soil irrigated by the spring melt produces, in a single year, more wealth for the landowners than all the yellow metal scraped out of the rocks and rivers during the California gold rush.

The subways, too, have been gold—a grimy gold. At the turn of the century, as New York grew at a fierce pace with immigrants from Central and Eastern Europe, all of the newcomers were met by the subways and carried to the frontiers of the city.

The success of the IRT operation led to the development of the Brooklyn Rapid Transit Co., later called Brooklyn Manhattan Transit, or the BMT. In the first five decades after the rapid transit lines opened, the population rose from 3.4 million in 1900 to 7.89 in 1950. "All of the net population growth between 1910 and 1940 occurred in the communities opened by the [IRT and BMT] lines," Peter Derrick, an MTA planner, wrote in 1986. "By 1940, more than half the city's population lived in the areas that first received rapid transit service as a result of the [subways]." Between 1913 and 1927, the assessed value of city land increased 50 percent.

Despite this, from the beginning, the subways were meant to be "self-sustaining"—a code phrase meaning that only those who rode them were to pay for them, not those who built fortunes in real estate atop them.

The idea that the subways would pay their own way entirely has never, in fact, worked out to the satisfaction of the real estate interests; even on the very first subways, which were extremely profitable—aside from the precious buildable land they brought into reach—the city lost money to the private companies running them, which essentially suckered the city out of a share of revenues, and forced the municipality to assign a portion of its land taxes to subway expenses.

The principle of taxing land supported by subways is unassailable. But the city always awaits a crisis before doing it. There is never a shortage of those.

Starting in the 1920s, every decade since has seen a transit emergency of some sort or another. Every one of these "crises" was traced—either by contemporary power brokers or by historians—to an alleged shortage of money because fares were too low. In fact, the nickel fare was set under the first contracts at the insistence of the private companies. They feared that the city would try to lower it once the riders started paying.

This was a poison pill the operators had to swallow when the first inflationary cycle of the century hit in 1920, and their costs began to eat into their profits. A new subway car that had cost $14,000 in 1914 was, six years later, $40,000. In addition, the companies were laden with a very 1980s-style illness: too much debt from acquiring new businesses. To buy up elevated lines, which were owned by other private concerns, the subway companies had bought their stock at stiff prices, borrowing heavily.

Of course they screamed poverty—which, in view of then-Mayor John Hylan, was too good for them. As a young man, Hylan had operated a train on the Brooklyn elevated lines but was fired—unjustly, he said—for nearly running down one of his bosses. Hylan had nurtured a bitter grudge against the "traction interests." And no one has ever lost votes in New York shaking a fist at the people in charge of the subways.

The public grievances were precise: the trains were horribly crowded, carrying the same number of passengers in 1918—a billion—as they would in 1990, in a fourth of the space. Moreover, the builders of the IRT had wrapped the tunnels in a waterproofing material that kept them dry but also trapped heat in the stations and tunnels, instead of allowing it to radiate into the earth. On top of these impossibly hot and crowded trains was a substantial body of evidence that the people who ran them had been getting good and rich, and there was little sympathy extended in 1920 when the companies looked to increase the nickel fare.

The terms of Contract One, for the original subway, help explain why the public had no appetite for a fare increase.

The original IRT line was built by the Interborough Rapid Transit Company for a fee of $35 million paid by the city. In addition to laying the tracks from City Hall to 145th Street, the company would provide the cars and operate the system for fifty years. The company demanded that a nickel fare be set for the entire life of the contract. Although it seems hard to believe now, at the turn of the century the country experienced a "deflationary" period: between 1899 and 1914, prices actually dropped. So a mandatory 5 cent fare seemed like a good idea.

The city borrowed the $35 million with the agreement that the interest would be repaid by the IRT company out of its operating revenue—the nickels it was collecting, by 1917, at the rate of a billion a year. In the meantime, the demand for more transit to develop more land and to ease the crowding in the tenements produced additional schemes, the most important being the Dual System, approved in 1913. It called for the IRT and Brooklyn Rapid Transit company to more than double the miles of track, from 296 miles to 619.

Under the Dual System, and all the contracts with the private companies going back to the first, the city ended up with the debt and the companies with all the profit. The fares paid off the companies' share of costs and gave them profits. The city just paid back the interest with whatever money it could cajole from the private operators.

"The IRT rapid transit system always produced a substantial operating surplus, never any 'profit' as contractually defined," explained Joshua Freeman, author of *In Transit,* a history of the Transport Workers Union.

"Between 1910 and 1940, the city received, in addition to $80 million rent for the lines built under the first two IRT contracts, only $19 million, not enough even to cover the debt service on the $188 million it had invested in IRT construction. . . . The company, on the other hand, made a real cumulative profit of over $90 million."

The city had an even worse deal with the Brooklyn Rapid Transit, the other early subway developer, Freeman writes. The city invested $208 million and got nothing back; the company, on its investment of $116 million received all of its operating costs plus a cumulative "preferential" of $94 million and $131 million for debt service.

(These sweetheart bargains were replicated seventy years later by the New York Yankees. The team leases its famous stadium from the city, then pays "rent" based on attendance—minus maintenance costs. Even in years when two million people came to watch the team, the city didn't see a nickel, because the team claimed its maintenance costs exceeded any share the city might be entitled to. And by the way, the stadium, known as the House that Ruth Built in honor of its greatest star, could be more accurately known as the house the IRT built—the ballpark didn't open until 1923, six years after the Lexington Avenue line reached the then-pastoral Bronx.)

The outcry against the original transit arrangements came loudest after World War I, when there was even less profit to share. Those who devised the deals said, in their defense, that no one could have foreseen the inflation. Nevertheless, the issue flared when a city of miserable riders was governed by unhappy former train driver John Hylan. Backed by William Randolph Hearst, whose newspapers, the *American* and the *Journal*, had long and loudly complained about the dealings with the transit company, Hylan staked out a line against any fare increase that has affected all transit politics since. And when the transit establishment sent an envoy to City Hall to present a detailed plan on orderly expansion of the subways, Hylan called a policeman to throw him out.

The mayor had his own ideas about how the subway should grow. He proposed and pushed a third system that would have the creature comforts the older lines lacked. In many places, Hylan's lines—which came to be known as the Independent Subway, or the IND—would run alongside the older IRT and BMT. But the IND offered bigger cars, spacious stations, and straight tracks for faster rides. When the first sections of the IND opened in 1932, the system's ridership figures were in a Depression crash; many of the riders who remained were siphoned from the existing routes onto the Independent.

The Depression, riders lost to the new Independent lines, the high debt that the companies were carrying, and the frozen fare all contributed to the financial collapse of the private subway companies during the 1930s, when they went into receivership.

In 1940, after eight years of negotiations, Mayor Fiorello La-Guardia acquired for the city the stock to the two private lines operated by the IRT and BMT companies. He paid $326,248,000 and was buying trouble. The argument over the 5-cent fare was then entering its third decade. And most of the system's equipment was at least that old, and at the end of its useful life.

Unification of the three lines would be the salvation of the subways, LaGuardia and others had declared. It would reduce costs, eliminate competition that wasted money by having several lines stop within a block or so of each other, and generally improve the life of the beleaguered straphanger.

So it was thought. For a while, it worked.

During World War II, the subways actually produced a surplus the city was able to capture since the cash no longer was being filtered through the fine mesh terms of the private contracts. "There was a six-day workweek, which meant you had people taking the subway an extra day a week, and there were very few automobiles," said Daniel T. Scannell, who was to join the transit system as counsel shortly after the war.

But subways acquired in 1940 had been ravaged during the Depression. Maintenance was not deferred, it was ignored by companies that were interested only in unloading their stock on the city. And now, when politicians turned to their favorite whipping boy, they'd be belting their own backsides. At the end of the war, when practically no automobiles had been manufactured, travelers within the city had no choice but to return to the subways. They arrived at the turnstiles in fantastic numbers, there to board decrepit cars in suffocating crowds. On December 23, 1946, the all-time record for passengers was set when 8,872,244 riders were carried in a twenty-four-hour period. (A very busy day in 1990 saw about 3.9 million.)

While transit nostalgists look back on this period as a golden age, it was, by contemporary accounts, an era of interminable suffering.

At the same time, a movement rose in the city, led by a Republican lawyer named Paul Windels, to save the huddled masses—by doubling the fare. Windels headed the Committee of Fifteen, a group of real estate owners and business executives, who argued that the city was inefficient and corrupt. It was time to take the politics out of the transit system, they declared—politics having tainted the process since John Hylan had led the charge against the fare increase in the 1920s. People would be willing to pay an honest fare for a decent ride, they argued. Double the cost and expand the system.

Their position was not without merit, nor was it without a healthy dose of self-interest. But it did lack the merest specifics on what was needed to enlarge the subways. And despite the roaring return of the customers, so much money was needed for repairs of the forty-year-old plant that the property tax—then the only source of revenue for the city—was sure to ache under the load unless there was a fare increase. In 1947, even though the trains carried more passengers than in any year in its history, the city had to eat its first operating deficit of some $17 million. It cost the city 6.3 cents to carry a subway rider who was paying a nickel.

Yet powerful voices argued that the fare should not go up merely to expand the system. That was the burden of the property owners, argued Stanley Isaacs, the most eloquent of those speakers—a real estate lawyer who also happened to be the Manhattan borough president.

"The subways were built under pressure from real estate interests and added tremendously to real estate values in the city . . ." said Isaacs. "It should be remembered that those who want it changed are the very real estate men who profited most by unloading their property because, as they advertised, it was within reach of the very heart of Manhattan for five cents."

But not only the real estate men wanted the hike. Master road builder Robert Moses had designs for the money that would be freed if the subways covered their own costs. To Moses's argument for the rise, Isaacs made a prophetic response:

> The whole program is clear. The straphanger is to pay double the present fare so as to carry the full interest upon and amortization of the capital cost of the subway. Why? So that the city will be able to borrow more money to build parkways, expressways and highways, which are to be furnished free of charge for the capital improvements to the man who can afford his own car, doesn't travel on the subways and doesn't pay even a nickel toward construction of the speedways furnished him.

In 1948, the fare went to a dime, and five years later, 15 cents. At the same time, a Republican state legislature extracted the transit system from direct control of elected officials. It created a body known as the New York City Transit Authority, which was ordered to balance its budget annually.

Under the new laws, explained Scannell, "that authority could not accept any operating subsidy, and they had to charge a fare that could cover all the costs of operation. The city was always pleading with Albany they needed money, and the legislature did not want one of the reasons to be that they were subsidizing the fare. When the Authority came in, that 15 cents fare lasted until 1966."

The Committee of Fifteen's work was complete. Real estate values were protected from the mass transit system that had made them.

There were a few minor concessions from the city in the decade that followed. All transit police costs would be picked up by the municipality, since policing is the city's function; the TA would be reimbursed for the reduced fare afforded school children; and the city would provide some money for the purchase of electricity, since it had pressured the TA to sell its own electrical plants to Con Edison, a power broker in more ways than one.

On a spring evening in 1981, a bright young man named Daniel McCarthy wandered into a talk given by Victor Gotbaum, a municipal labor leader. Gotbaum had been a major player during the fiscal crisis of the 1970s by agreeing to lend portions of a pension fund he controlled to the city. He had become close with some of the key financiers of the era, including Felix Rohatyn, an investment banker who shaped the city's fiscal policies.

Now, as McCarthy sat in the audience, he heard Gotbaum discuss the city's recovery.

"All my rich real estate friends are telling me how much money they are making," said Gotbaum. "They're making more money than they know what to do with." At that moment, a light went on in McCarthy's head. The latest transit financing crisis was occupying the front pages of the city's newspapers several times a week.

HELP, screamed one *Daily News* headline. Another said, "TA

Plans $17M Cuts—More Delays for Trains, Longer Waits for Buses, Dirtier Subway Cars."

The transit deficit was put at $348 million by Richard Ravitch, the MTA chairman. Not only was money desperately needed to rebuild the system, Ravitch warned, but the fare was almost certain to climb from 60 to 75 cents and then a dollar within the next few months.

Not long after hearing Gotbaum, as McCarthy chewed over his offhand remark about the real estate windfall, he read another headline: the Pan American building, a midtown landmark, was sold for $400 million, dozens of times the original cost for the building. The city's real estate community was entering a decade-long frenzy. A single room in a co-operative or condominium apartment had cost $51,500 in 1980; by 1989, it was $108,040, an increase of 109 percent.

McCarthy wrote a short paper that he distributed to politicians and the press, proposing that the city impose a 10 percent tax on the gains made in all real estate sales above $1 million and devote the money to transit.

"The fastest growing source of wealth in New York City is real estate," he wrote.

> The recent $400 million sale of the Pan Am Building and the $100 million offer for the St. Bartholomew Church property reflect the spectacular gains in local property values. The city's extensive mass transit network provides a direct benefit to local real estate operators and it is only fair that they should bear some of the increasing costs of maintaining the system. Without mass transit, the intensive development that we are now seeing on Manhattan's East Side and elsewhere would not be feasible.

It was, Mario Cuomo would later say, "a nearly perfect tax." An assemblyman from the Bronx, Oliver G. Koppell, held a press conference at the Pan Am building to announce he would champion the McCarthy proposal, and he secured the backing of the Speaker of the Assembly, Stanley Fink.

With a package of other taxes for support of transit, the measure went to the legislature on the night of July 8, 1981.

Loudly opposed to the taxes were some of the most powerful people in the city. David Rockefeller issued a statement opposing all the levies in the transit proposal, noting that "the real estate tax will have a chilling impact on this vital industry in New York."

The property tax will "be a sure way to scare people away and a major disincentive" to real estate investment, Richard Rosen, the president of the Real Estate Board of New York, told the *New York Times* on July 4, 1981.

And Mayor Edward I. Koch? With the subway system having returned for its once-a-decade peek at the abyss, the mayor had little choice but to support the proposals, and so danced around the questions of which taxes he supported, and which he opposed.

On the morning of the vote, Koch hosted a breakfast at Gracie Mansion, his official residence, with a group of business leaders. It "is a package which I would not be urging if there were alternatives acceptable," Koch told them. The *Daily News* reported that "he wished the business leaders success in their efforts to change specifics of the tax package but said that if they fail, they should urge legislators to support the original plan."

And, in fact, Koch had something in mind to help out his business friends.

Long into the night and early the next morning, the State Assembly wrangled and debated the terms of the package. Watching from the gallery was Gene Russianoff, a young lawyer who grew up in Brooklyn and upon graduating from Harvard Law School had devoted himself full-time to improving the city's transit system. He was the driving force in a group called the Straphangers Campaign, which had strongly promoted the tax on real estate profits.

"It passed at two in the morning," said Russianoff. "I made the mistake of going home before they adjourned. Took the four A.M. bus home to New York City, the red-eye. The next morning, the Koch administration called the Speaker's office and said they needed a slight amendment to the bill. Instead of going into effect on August 1, they delayed the start-up until October 1."

In New York, the mayor hailed the act's passage by citing heavy pressure against the package from the business community. "However," said Koch, "the people prevailed."

At the moment he was speaking, the mayor's legislative representatives were ensuring that the business interests, not the people or their transit system, would triumph. They told state officials that they needed more time to come up with the tax forms, that two weeks wasn't enough. Thus the "enactment date" was changed from August to October.

The two-month delay in the tax set off the greatest spurt of big real estate sales ever recorded in the city. SAVE A BUNDLE: CLOSE BY OCTOBER 1, advised the lead story in the *New York Times* real estate section. During the period before the tax became law, the American Express company sold its downtown building for a $180 million profit—which would have yielded $18 million in transit taxes without the Koch loophole—and promptly moved into a site in lower Manhattan where the real estate taxes had been abated under another Koch program.

The two-month loophole sewn into the tax fabric by the mayor helped the Manufacturers Hanover Trust Company escape $7 million in subway tax on a $70 million profit the bank made on the sale of its 350 Park Avenue headquarters, a two-minute walk to Grand Central Station, where there was subway service every four or five minutes. On property directly above three separate lines that reached into Queens, the Bronx, and the East Side of Manhattan, Citicorp made a clear profit of $35 million. Thanks to Mayor Koch's sleight of hand, none of the profit could be diverted for the subway.

But delaying the law wasn't enough for the mayor and his real estate pals.

A week after the legislative action, Koch announced that he would seek to repeal the law and replace it with a tax that would apply to all sales, large and small. His deputy mayor for economic development, Karen N. Gerard, argued that property owners would find ways around it by artificially lowering sales prices, and that it could suppress real estate values.

Few in the Koch administration really believed that.

Nearly a decade later, the chief economist for the city Department of Finance during the period explained how he saw the tax:

"From an economist's perspective, this [boom] was a sort of windfall in the real estate industry," said James Suarez, now a professor at Manhattan College.

There was nothing [real estate owners] did to make the property go up 150, 200 percent in three or four years. And it's logical to tax that profit, because the value of the property is so tied into the subways.

We [in the Koch administration] never really did an analysis of the tax—the first time they came to me was to ask for reasons to oppose it. There weren't really any valid ones, so I came up with this usual stuff about it distorting the market. It was really bad policy making.

In effect, the administration submarined the law. Why?

"There were real political considerations in this," said Suarez. "The people with big access at City Hall are the Lew Rudins, the Larry Silversteins, the big real estate owners. They are major contributors. The mayor listened to them."

Silverstein sold a twenty-story office building at Madison Avenue and 30th Street during the Koch loophole.

The mayor has always insisted that he was not swayed by the hunks of money thrown to him by the real estate industry, that he only operated with the best interests of the city in mind. The major property owners may not have liked putting their easy-earned profits into the subways, but they were delighted to invest in Edward I. Koch: in each of the three campaigns he mounted between 1981 and 1989, Koch turned to the real estate industry for fully a third of his campaign money. Two of the individuals cited by Suarez, Larry Silverstein and Lew Rudin, contributed $129,000 between them to Koch's campaigns from 1981 to 1989. Richard Rosen, the head of the Real Estate Board, which had argued strongly against the tax, was Silverstein's partner.

A sampling of the contributions during Koch's golden age, from 1981 to 1989, reveals substantial support from real estate interests: Hanover Companies, Gerald Gutterman, $50,000; Sylvan Lawrence, $43,500; Peter Kalikow, $102,000; Reuben Glick, $61,000 (Glick Development Affiliates); J and D Realty, $125,000 (Donald Zucker, construction magnate); Helmsley Spear, $147,000 (real estate managers and owners); Leonard Litwin, $31,000; Leonard Stern, $11,500; Fisher Brothers Management, $47,500; Real Estate Board of New York, $46,000; Sterling Equities, $70,000 (Fred Wilpon, who is also the owner of the New York Mets); M. J. Raynes, $17,000; Rudin Management Co., $66,000 (Jack and Lew Rudin); Silverstein Properties, $63,000 (Larry Silverstein and Richard Rosen); Swig Weiler and Arnow, $41,000; Milstein Properties and Milstein Ventures, $43,000; Shearson American Express, $52,000.

Only the mayor knows if these treasures made him too cozy with the property owners. But when the tax law finally took effect that October, the colossal sales period died—and property owners waited for the levy to go away.

"Koch had announced he was going to repeal it, so all the real estate people held off until he had it repealed," said Suarez. "If the city had held on just five or six months longer, they would have had to start making those deals. The city would have gotten a lot of money."

The law was repealed, but Mario Cuomo rode into the governor's office in 1982 on the promise that he'd restore it. He did, in 1983—but now it applies statewide, not just in the city, and the revenues aren't dedicated to mass transit but to the state's general funds.

In the years since the tax was promoted, the city has seen the value of its real estate increase by 100 percent, from $35.18 billion in 1981, to $71.08 billion in 1989. It has seen that 109 percent jump in the price of a room in a Manhattan apartment. Some 45 million square feet of commercial space has opened—more than that of the entire cities of Dallas and Boston combined.

And how much is the tax on real estate profits worth?

In 1988, big real estate deals in New York State—almost all of them, actually, in New York City—meant profits of $8 billion. The state collected 10 percent of them: $800 million.

And the subway fare went up 15 cents. And New York rediscovered the missing pennies: a million a week, out of the drawers in tenements and apartment houses, ending up in the barred room on Jay Street, where the windows never open.

6:30 A.M., Astoria, Queens: Joyce Bresa

Three years in New York City, and Joyce Bresa just now is getting used to the idea of wearing dark glasses into the gloomiest place she'd ever been. "Don't make eye contact with anyone down there," Reno had told her. "Wear sunglasses."

A tall, striking twenty-six-year-old blond from a rural village in upstate New York, she'd listened to her boyfriend give her this first piece of city smarts when she moved to Queens and started using the subways.

That was good advice—as far as it went. But there were other, worse kinds of contact. One day recently, she had pried her way onto the R train, heading back out to Queens, and found a place to stand. After a minute, she felt the man move in behind her. He was about fifty, swarthy. Breathing in heaves. Worse, he was leaning heavily against her back. She shifted her weight to edge away. He pressed. She looked for more space, but the passenger in front of her, a businessman in a suit, was reading the *New York Times* with one hand and holding the overhead bar with the other.

There was no room. In the small of her back, she could feel the swarthy man behind her, moving down and back up.

The words for what he was doing had just formed in her mouth when a scream piled onto them, stuffing her mouth with so many sounds that she was gagged and uttered none. Her limbs would not, could not move; she felt like a frog, pinned to a dissecting tray. How could someone shuffle toward her in a public place and do this?

In front of her, the man with the *Times* moved to turn another page of the financial section.

Moving the *Times* from a standing position in a typical New York subway car could qualify as an Olympic event: closed and folded, the paper is 1.28 square feet; spread fully opened, it is 4.3 square feet.

In an ideal world, the average subway rider would be entitled to 3.0 square feet of room, according to Transit Authority loading guidelines. In fact, on a train such as Joyce Bresa's, people actually have 1.641 square feet of standing space—well into what psychologists called the scream zone, the F level on a rating scale that runs from A to F, with A being the most comfortable level of space. "Level F allows two square feet or less of space per standee and no movement is possible. This level of service can create a panic situation and causes the standee 'physical and psychological discomfort,' " a transit planner wrote in 1987.

Now then.

Stockpens must "have sufficient space for all the livestock to lie down at the same time," by decree of the United States Department of Agriculture. While in transport, federal regulations require that animals weighing 150 pounds be allowed 5 square feet of space.

That was more than three times as much room as Joyce Bresa had. She could not move, could not speak. Her eyes screamed. Plying the pages of the *Times*, the man in front of Joyce was, for an instant, face to face with her. He moved the paper back in front of his eyes. Then he peeped out at her. She *was* staring at him. Those *were* tears. He lowered the paper to below his nose and stared into her pleading eyes, then over her shoulder to the swarthy man who was now lost in his assault.

"Get the fuck away from her."

The man pushed away, quickly, without comment. For Joyce, it was the end of her skepticism about the terrors of the subway. People had talked about it and had warned her, but she'd never really believed them until this stranger would walk up behind her in a train and press his body up against her.

It had been a quick, nasty lesson: dressing for work and dressing for the subways are two opposing, contradictory notions. Today, for work, she has to dress at the height of style, to look of a piece with the fine goods she sells at Henri Bendel's in midtown Manhattan, where she is training to be a buyer. For the subways, she needs a suit of armor with central air conditioning. The day promises to be mild, which means the subways will be hot. She picks out a cotton top, and a pair of palazzo pants. "Very light, very flowy, very soft," she says to herself, almost as if she is choosing a line for Bendel's. A pair of high heels.

Reno is away on a business trip. She takes a deep breath, and steels herself. She is off to the subway station at 46th Street.

If the physical city was shaped by the subways, the soul of the city just as often was racked by broken promises and pilfered money. The typical Queens transit rider, Joyce Bresa, boarded trains that were criminally crowded for cattle, and everyone knew it.

And any time modern New Yorkers had been asked to do something about the trains, they had, by voting more money, approving new transit schemes, backing the support of subways with tolls paid by automobile users. None of this worked. Since 1940, the year subway expansion in New York City stopped, the borough of Queens had gained 800,000 inhabitants.

By 1989, four decades of plans for transit improvements had come down to a pile of rocks in Central Park. Rebuilt rocks.

When the city announced in the early 1970s that to build a new subway line to Queens it would be drilling a tunnel through the southeastern corner of Central Park—the esteemed earth of the city, precious specks of tranquillity in a cosmos of madness—the locals rebelled. Mothers picketed with baby strollers.

Oh come on, said the Transit Authority, we'll put it back the way we found it. So boulders were cut into pieces, marked as if they were antiquities for museums, then stored in a warehouse somewhere to await the day they would be reassembled. By one nasty rumor, when the time came to put them back, the bureaucrats couldn't find the rock horde stashed away years before and had substituted forgeries. Not so, said the TA: these were the rebuilt originals. "A few were lost," concedes George Ziegler, the chief engineer at the TA for many years.

But they were lost to a public works project that Nelson Rockefeller, the governor of New York, had declared, two decades earlier, was as important to the state as the construction of the Erie Canal. Strong stuff—at the beginning of the nineteenth century, the Erie Canal had connected New York to the rest of America, opening the western frontier of the new nation.

Rockefeller was on top of his history: new subway lines, including this one sweeping the southern end of Central Park, were a major step for the city. He was wrong only about what the future held for this tunnel and the rest of the grand vision of expanded transportation in the city.

Rockefeller spoke in the mid-1960s, the end of an era of road building that had been masterminded by the brilliant tactician Robert Moses and backed by the federal government and the Regional Plan Association, which represented the city's banking and real estate establishments. In the twenty-five years after World War II, Moses had built 627 miles of highways, an achievement that "possibly . . . is history's greatest feat of urban construction," wrote Robert Caro, the Pulitzer Prize–winning biographer of Moses.

In that same era, not a single mile of new subway track was laid. The fare tripled. The cloggery of the automotive commute was poisoning New York.

For a city that grew around rapid transit lines, this was an astonishing change. Between 1900 and the early 1930s, the city of New York built, on average, 73 miles of subway lines every decade. Money dried up during the Depression, and nearly completed routes had to wait a few years for the final touches. But by 1940, the New York City subway system, as it exists today, was virtually complete. After the war, Moses was appointed the city's coordinator of construction, and he drove ever harder on the road-building plans outlined in the Regional Plan of 1929.

To general applause from the press and political establishment, he created mile after mile of expressways, at times bulldozing and boulderizing neighborhoods that stood in his way. No matter: Moses also created semipublic authorities that insulated him from accountability to the general public and allowed him to butter up politicians and influential journalists by wining and dining them in splendid style. Until the Moses era, Long Island was a sandy enclave of farmers and millionaires' mansions, set along fine seashores. The suburban tracts of Nassau and Suffolk counties were sculpted by Moses's parkways and highways as surely as the modern city of New York was wrought by the subways of an earlier generation of planners.

Moses monopolized city capital construction funds, borrowed money against the tolls on the bridges he controlled, and formed alliances with the federal government. During the age of the highway, he seemed to have cornered the market on municipal ingenuity.

"One of the things I suspect happened is that in the period of the late forties, fifties, early sixties, the people coming out of college looking for jobs, interesting jobs, ignored [mass] transit which was widely viewed as dead as a doornail," says Robert Kiley, chairman of the MTA during most of the 1980s. "So there's a missing generation there."

The same story was told across the country. Some 40,000 miles of interstate highways were built after the war, 90 percent funded by the federal government; these were roads to the suburbs. The old cities tore up their efficient electric trolleys, like aging matrons shucking their practical shoes, in favor of the high-heeled sexiness of the expensive and polluting motor bus.

That the Moses solution wasn't working for New York—that the volume of cars instantly surpassed the capacity of the roads that carried them, producing longer backups every day—was grimly evident by the mid-1960s. Jobs remained in the central city. The highways were choked morning and night. Mass transit was, once again, on the lips and minds of the forward-looking.

In 1967, a massive transportation bond issue was put forward. The voters of the state authorized borrowing $2.5 billion for a menu of schemes and improvements.

Even in an era of rising disillusionment with the auto, the road remained king: of the $2.5 billion, less than a quarter, $600 million, was devoted to new subway routes, with the remaining going to highways and bridges. (This reflects a standing fact of life in New York State politics—the fee for the support of rural and semirural upstaters for city transportation projects in the urban southern tip of the state is the building of costly roads that serve, on average, far fewer people at far greater expense than mass transit projects.)

With just a fraction of the 1967 bond issue, planners in a new agency went to work. The Metropolitan Transportation Authority was handed $600 million of the bond money and, in effect, was asked to do for the subway system what Moses had done for the roads. In fact, the MTA was created by Governor Nelson Rockefeller, in large part, to shelve Moses by assigning his power base—the Triborough Bridge and Tunnel Authority—to the role of a subsidiary of the MTA. Moses had survived six decades in public life, but was at last bested by this new authority. The ouster of Moses would remain the MTA's single accomplishment of note.

Planners for the new agency declared they would use that $600 million—plus another $451 million from the city—to build eight new subway routes. Another five would be designed.

The vital elements of the scheme could be traced along the axis of a map of the city: North and south would be served by the Second Avenue subway, which would run from Wall Street to 180th Street in the Bronx. East and west would meet in the 63rd Street tunnel, which would deliver passengers from a "super express" and ultimately to regions of Queens no train had ever seen.

Both of these routes engaged the hopes of a public then crowding the existing lines on Lexington Avenue and Queens Boulevard well beyond the most optimistic livestock-cargo rating. The New Routes project would carry 150,000 riders a day, the planners declared.

But no one in the agency had done any engineering to figure the true costs. Incredibly, not a piece of paper existed to say how much "tunnelling or auxiliary trackage" would cost, a 1980 audit by state comptroller Edward V. Regan found. "The initial plan was developed without any knowledge of the exact number and locations of stations. . . . [One Transit Authority official said] the early estimates were predicated primarily on past experience . . . the cost patterns and ratios experienced in the construction and development of the IND system more than 35 years previous."

In short, no one had a clue how much these eight subway lines would cost, or even, precisely where they would go. Moreover, the work was in the hands of a new and untried authority, the MTA, which was given a wide mandate to control and organize the transportation of the region. While separate agencies still would run the buses and subways of the city's Transit Authority, the Long Island Railroad, and other suburban transportation outfits, the MTA would sit over them all.

The MTA started in 1968 with zero employees and no office space. By 1970, it had a staff of eighty-three.

On paper, the MTA was built on the Robert Moses model: the public authority, its board members appointed by the political structure, but independent of it, capable of raising money with tolls, user fees, or by borrowing money, able to get things done in the arenas where traditional government failed or was too slow. And best of all, it was a political foxhole.

The MTA "was specifically designed to insulate the politicians from responsibility," said Mario Cuomo, who became governor of New York in 1983. "So were many other things. This state practically invented that game. What Moses did was introduce the Authority. You can argue that there are advantages to it. There are advantages to autocracy. There are advantages to kingdoms. There is no question that the democratic process is not always the most efficient. [But] when you created the MTA, you did it specifically to insulate the politicians."

The MTA soon would cure any reputation for efficiencies on the part of public authorities. Its performance in the execution of the New Routes program—aided and abetted by poisonous expediencies of other politicians and the city's financial establishment—can only be likened to a berserk tycoon who could fill two freight elevators with cash, ride to the top of the Empire State Building, and then spend the better part of twenty-five years scattering the money into the swirling winds. Which is precisely what the MTA did.

By 1989, when the New Routes Plan had spent every dollar it could find, all that remained was a tunnel under 63rd Street, under Central Park and the East River, where New York kids played on many a night for two decades. It was a tunnel that went nowhere.

John V. Lindsay, the mayor when New York last dared to dream out loud, had issued one of the great studies in 1965 calling for the construction of a new Queens tunnel. In "A Modern Transportation System for New York City," candidate Lindsay said that if elected mayor, he would "see to it that there are no further delays in the construction of the East River tunnel."

That tunnel first appeared in a transit planning document in 1940, but Al Dellibovi, a former federal transit official, has a newspaper clipping of his father speaking in favor of a new link as far back as 1923. There certainly was a consensus for it—people in Queens were overpacked into their trains every morning—and Lindsay was even able to find a good piece of the money to build it.

The first problem was especially delicate.

The proposed route of the tunnel, 64th Street, cut across the southern tier of what was then called the Rockefeller Institute, now the Rockefeller University, a research facility on the banks of the

East River that was founded and funded by the oil tycoon's heirs. Big stuff goes on there—test tubes, electronic gadgets, fellows in long white coats ready to fix the world but good, as soon as they get the go-ahead.

One of those Rockefeller oil heirs with his name over the door was Nelson Rockefeller, the longest-reigning governor in the history of the state. And so plenty of people heard about it when the Rockefeller Institute's hierarchy said its delicate instrumentation would be rattled beyond reading not only by the blasting necessary to excavate the big tunnel, but also the constant rumble of the trains beneath.

"We finally decided to settle it by hiring the seismologist from Fordham, Father Joseph Lynch, and the Rockefellers hired the fellow from Columbia, who immediately said he would accept Father Lynch's findings," according to Daniel Scannell, then a commissioner of the Transit Authority.

> Father Lynch found that there already were greater vibrations from the tankers that were passing up and down the East River every day than would ever come from the subway. I wanted to pay him a fee as a consultant, but he said he had great fondness for the city and didn't want money. "All I ask," he said, "is that you give me a pass each year for the subway." We arranged a luncheon where we gave him the pass, and the mayor gave him the Medal of the City of New York.

Despite Father Lynch's findings about the innocuous effects of blowing a subway tunnel under the streets, the site finally was moved a block south to 63rd Street, as a stop to the Rockefeller Institute and to make it possible to connect with the busy subway intersection at 59th Street, below the Bloomingdale's store. (The transfer connection was never built.)

Then Lindsay ran into problems of a more personal nature. If 64th Street was bad for the Rockefellers, 63rd Street was terrible for the Whitneys. And John Hay Whitney was the millionaire horseman and newspaper publisher whose *New York Herald Tribune*—and whose money—had done more to advance the Lindsay candidacy than anyone else. Whitney once told the writer Jimmy Breslin that in his entire life, no alarm had ever woken him. He got up when he had slept enough.

The 63rd Street subway changed all that. The first charges of dynamite went off below the Whitney townhouse, nearly knocking the tycoon out of bed. He immediately placed a call to his man in City Hall, only to learn that the mayor personally had approved the new location to avoid the conflict with the Rockefeller Institute.

Lindsay, caught between a Rockefeller and a good pal's place, told friends that Whitney barely could bring himself to speak with the mayor for a long time.

It goes without saying that the cost of building in New York is inflated by the needle-in-a-canyon delicacies of heavy construction along streets loaded with life. Not only does every sidewalk abut some mammoth structure, but a single block covers hundreds of miles of telephone, electric, gas, steam, water and sewer lines to connect, warm, light, and bathe the inhabitants of buildings. Not to mention subways.

For this tunnel, there was an additional factor: the East River, which it would cross at a particularly treacherous point. The labor for traditional tunneling, a deadly job, would be exorbitant, and many of the city's sandhogs—the miners—already were engaged on a major water project. Scannell had been to Rotterdam where he'd seen a tunnel being laid across the harbor. It had been prefabricated and dropped into a trench.

A scale model of the New York harbor and its waterways is maintained in Vicksburg, Mississippi, by the Army Corps of Engineers. Transit engineers practiced dropping the tunnel into the swirling waters. They were able to get a direct hit. Calculations were made that showed a three- or four-day window, when the tides would be at their gentlest.

In Port Deposit, Maryland, four steel shells of the tunnel were fabricated, then floated to Norfolk, Virginia, where concrete reinforcement was added. Then they were pulled up the Atlantic coast by barge to the East River.

The East River is not a river at all: it's a branch of Long Island Sound which is also under the sway of the Hudson River estuarial tides. Part of it is called Hellsgate, a tribute to the voracious appetite of the waters. Rikers Island, the city jail, is secured by the insane currents far better than by electric fences and killer dogs.

Now the Transit Authority was dropping a tunnel into the bottom of the river. Not only that, it was actually dropping four sections—each 385 feet long. They were secured between two barges and loaded with stone until they started to sink.

"A fabulous undertaking," says Scannell. "Even in a six-knot tide, they could sink the precast sections. It came in under budget and right on target."

Hard as the East River was to navigate, digging up the streets of midtown Manhattan was like sailing the Bermuda Triangle. Construction in New York is also a sadistic orgy of whippings by organized crime, by purposeful government corruption, by bumbling and delays that would hospitalize a saint. One giant engineering firm, Bechtel, was interviewed for the project in 1970, but then backed off, frightened by what one insider called the "political scene" in New York—code for shakedowns.

The builders also organized themselves so that the costly efficiencies of competition could be ironed out. Rather than have two or three bidders seeking the same work, only one might come—with an understanding that he would stay away from the next job. Production of concrete, the principal structural material of the tunnels, was controlled in the city by a cartel of hoodlums who charged the highest prices in the world for this mix of sand and water.

There was, however, one moment of accidental grace for the city, a memory that many years later warmed the engineers in charge of the project.

On a spring day in 1977, when 63rd Street was being torn up, two contractors took an elevator to the eleventh floor of the grim transportation building at 370 Jay Street in Brooklyn.

They were bound for one of the most sacred and profane rituals of civic life: the opening of bids for public works. From the fording of great rivers by the federal government down to a little school district that wants to install new bleachers in the gymnasium, the process is not much different.

An educated guess is made as to what the job will cost, and in what range the bidders are expected to land. Work on the 63rd Street project had been divided into eight sections.

"I had figured this section would come in under $200 million if we had three bidders," said Mel Levy, a transit engineer who prepared an estimate. "They—the higher-ups—told me to put the estimate at $225 million, figuring we'd only get two bidders. They were worried that the job might come in at $300 million."

As was the custom, an advertisement was placed in the newspapers and trade journals, announcing the project and inviting interested parties to submit prices for the work.

The companies also review the project to make two guesses. The first, in an educated way, is what the job will cost. Then they try to divine how much profit they can squeeze from the job, given the state of the competition. In New York City, there often isn't much guesswork involved. The contractors set up cartels that divide up the work. No bothersome competition. It takes away the element of surprise. And it inflates the cost of building in New York to the highest in the country.

The two contractors strode past the cubicles and the battered gray furniture to the office of the engineering department on the eleventh floor, and they went into the conference room of the chief engineer.

They sat in the room, bantering mildly with transit workers. All parties pointedly avoided staring at the white envelopes on the table in front of them as they awaited the witching hour: 10 A.M., when the doors would close, no one else would be permitted in the room, and the envelopes would be handed over to the head procurement officer, the secretary of the Transit Authority, who had not yet entered the room.

At 9:58, a Japanese man walked into the room, and pulled out a chair at the table.

"Hello," he said. "This is room 1100?"

"Yes," said one of the workers.

A look of great consternation crossed the faces of the two contractors. Their pas de deux was being ruined by this short man in a business suit. A Japanese contractor!

The white envelopes went back in their jacket pockets. Each removed a second white envelope. At that moment, the procurement officer strode into the room and took his place at the head of the table. A court stenographer sat next to him.

"Good morning, gentlemen," said the procurement official. "We are here to accept bids pertaining to Route 131A. All those wishing to submit bids, please step forward and submit your bids. Identify yourself to the clerk."

The contractors handed over the envelopes to the clerk, who stamped them front and back, and recorded the names of their companies.

Finally, the Japanese man stepped to the front of the room.

"Excuse me, sir, you are Stan Kottick?" he asked the procurement official.

"No," he said. "Kottick's upstairs."

"Thank you very much," said the Japanese man, and he left the room.

The two contractors looked as if they were going to be sick. By the calculations of engineer Levy, the arrival of the Japanese man saved the city $40 to $50 million by provoking the two contractors to reach into their pockets for lower bids. The contract let for $184 million, $41 million below the official estimate of $225 million.

Price-gouging chicanery aside, the years following the New Routes bond issue marked a time of spiraling inflation radically unlike the years before it: during the first eleven years after the 1967 bond issue was passed, the cost of building in New York increased by 133 percent. In 1971, for instance, the index used to measure building costs went up 21.6 percent.

Right around that time, people in Manhattan began to catch on to exactly what the Transit Authority had in mind for their neighborhoods. It seems that the TA was ready to proceed in the bulldoze-'em-down style that years before had made Robert Moses the envy of constipated public works administrators around the country. There were plans to blast a bird sanctuary, a playground, and a pond clear out of Central Park. The politically savvy Manhattanites rose up to protect their park—and after delaying the award of the contract by two years, won concessions that included rebuilding the boulders blown from the park. And a rule was created about the destruction of trees: if a reasonably mature tree of, say, nine inches in diameter was removed, the TA would replace it with three trees of three-inch diameter.

In the two years in which these details were negotiated, the cost of doing anything had jumped by nearly half. By 1971, the tab for the New Routes program was up to $1.7 billion—a 70 percent increase from the figures given the public only four years earlier. (The increase was due not only to inflation, but also to more focused cost estimates.) Eleven routes were reduced to seven.

The federal government stepped forward. Starting in 1971, it would provide 80 percent of the construction costs for new mass transit projects. This kept the project alive for a while.

Then there was the concrete.

Every morning, four cement trucks were supposed to deliver their loads to the job sites. They were checked in by the team of "resident inspectors"—engineers hired by the city to make sure it got its money's worth. Then the same trucks would be used to remove the muck and debris that was being cleared away to make room for the cement.

"A funny thing would happen before that fourth truck of the morning arrived," said a transit engineer familiar with the process. "The inspectors would leave the job site. And instead of concrete, a product called blue stone would be delivered and pumped down the length of the tunnel. Blue stone is worthless, of course. So the workers would just shovel it into the muck piles. And the next day it would be carted away—often by the same truck that had delivered it the day before."

On top of this scam, no one in government could find the delivery receipts for some 44,000 cubic yards of concrete—enough to build a good-sized apartment house—which had been paid for, a federal audit would find over a decade later in 1985. Industry standards call for strength tests of concrete on every day that it is poured. An audit of one section of the 63rd Street tunnel found that on the 724 days that concrete was poured, tests were performed on only 308 days—fewer than half.

Eventually, tests were performed that found the concrete to be adequate to hold up the tunnel. Those who built the tunnel scoffed at any worries. Redundancy was part of the design. "This wasn't just belt and suspenders," said engineer Mel Levy. "We had belts and three pairs of suspenders."

If chicanery was rampant, so was brilliance. A tunnel-boring machine was used for the first time in midtown, drilling through the famous schist bedrock of Manhattan, which is excellent for supporting skyscrapers, but very unpredictable when attacked head-on with drills. It develops seams, holds water, and is colossal trouble.

Moreover, as the tunnel crossed 63rd Street on the East Side, it would be moving through one of the most congested blocks in the world. The new tunnel would pass under an existing subway tunnel at Lexington Avenue, which ended up being pinned like a ceiling light fixture to the rock above it. The excavation was just shy of 60 feet wide, so it ran from building line to building line, across 63rd Street, with a 6-inch margin at one side. One of the sidewalks that was to be jackhammered up was in front of the home of the designer Halston, who had embedded special decorations in the cement. When he realized what was afoot, he hired private guards to protect his patch. They eventually were told that the construction workers would drill through their feet if they didn't move.

At some points, this hole went 130 feet down. An elevator was built just to bring trucks up and down for muck removal. The contractors devised new noise-abatement gimmicks that changed construction: shrouds for jackhammers, special mufflers on compressors, even extraquiet trucks. All this tiptoeing around did not mean that the 63rd Street tunnel was not an endless pain to its neighbors. But few of them checked into asylums, as they would have without the efforts at quiet.

A quarter century later—and four mayors, four governors, five MTA chairmen, and five Transit Authority chief executives later—the 63rd Street tunnel has come to nothing. Or more precisely, nowhere: it crosses the East River and barely reaches into Queens before dead-ending at a housing project in a factory neighborhood.

The first IRT line, from City Hall to Harlem, was built in under four years, from drawing board to opening day, October 27, 1904. As the subway system approached its diamond jubilee, things had slowed down considerably. Then-City Council President Carol Bellamy wrote in a 1979 report to the MTA board, "Planning and approval procedures alone take no less than three and one half years—for projects encountering no significant delays."

In the decades that the city talked about—and then half built—a Second Avenue subway and a 63rd Street tunnel, it went ahead and tore down elevated tracks that were perfectly useful, if ugly to some eyes.

The els were demolished to make way for subways that were never built. As a result, after 1940, "New York gained the dubious distinction of being the world's only city with a shrinking rapid transit system, even as world [subway] mileage grew over 40 percent a decade," a Regional Plan Association study noted in 1986.

For the 63rd Street tunnel, once priced at $157 million, New York spent $968 million dollars. The city that had led the world in its mass transit facilities could not fasten this single tunnel to anyplace or anything useful. The tunnel stopped 1,500 feet short of the packed Queens Boulevard lines, and in the geometry of New York politics, not even a crooked line could connect the two. None of the original thirteen routes of the 1967 bond issue has been completed, and there is almost no prospect of that happening in the twentieth century. "The time for action has passed," an MTA planner declared in the 1970s. "Let's have another study."

"There are two tunnels under Roosevelt Island," a *Daily News* editorial said in 1985. "One is a water tunnel, ten years behind schedule and dry. The other is a subway tunnel. It has five feet of water in it."

The MTA didn't foul this up by itself. It had aid and comfort from many parties. In the city, protests over the construction work by everyone from Rockefellers to mothers with baby carriages delayed the line by at least ten years. Having moved the tunnel a block south in 1964—and delaying the project a year—the Rockefeller University resurfaced in 1976, along with neighbors, to object to a ventilation shaft on York Avenue. This tied up work until October 1978, a two and a half year delay. (The shaft eventually was used as planned by the Transit Authority, which had failed to file an environmental impact statement with the federal government.)

Finally, every one of the New Routes contracts that was let had to go through seventeen levels of government approval.

The worst blunder of all involved the handling of the federal government's grants, a program created as political atonement for years of highway funding while mass transit systems were neglected. In 1971, an act of Congress provided 75 to 80 percent of the costs of the New Routes construction project. For every dollar invested locally in mass transit, the federal government would add three. (This helped build transit systems in Washington and San Francisco, to name two places where the money was not squandered.)

The federal grants might have bailed out the MTA from its guesstimates of 1967 if the Beame shuffle hadn't been created. The official name was Section 3H of the National Transportation Assistance Act of 1974, but "the Beame shuffle" is how it's described in official reports of the era. The shuffle involved an amendment to the federal law to allow the city to borrow construction grants for ongoing operations, such as running the trains and paying the salaries of transit workers. The city had lobbied for the law to take pressure off the fare.

It erased a subway route from the map.

Part of the 1967 bond issue was to have built the Second Avenue subway. Holes were dug in the ground at widely disparate points— one near the southern end of Manhattan that stretched from Confucius Plaza to Manhattan Bridge Plaza, and two other sections uptown, in East Harlem, between 99th and 105th Streets, and 110th and 120th Streets. Transit executives were seeing their construction money being eaten by inflation, and they realized the desperate need for the line. By building portions of the tunnel, miles apart, the hope was that the money to connect the dots would be supplied from the federal grant program.

In 1974, when it came time to extend the lines, the city crashed financially. The local banking cartel cut off all short-term loans, which traditionally had helped the municipality make ends meet before taxes were collected. In a search for gestures to convince the investment community that the city was creditworthy, the subway fare was abruptly raised from 35 cents to 50 cents—apparently on little or no rational basis.

Abraham Beame, then the mayor, was desperate to keep the

subway fare from going up yet again—the people urging the fare increases, after all, were generally bankers and unelected financial officials who didn't have to face the public—but the mayor had almost no sources of city revenue to subsidize transit operations.

Alone among the nation's mayors, he turned to the federal construction moneys, to Section 3H, to hold down the price of the token.

The Beame shuffle meant no federal funds for the Second Avenue subway, which was indefinitely deferred—for all practical purposes, abandoned. It also was quite possibly the most expensive legal loan in history.

From 1975 through 1978, the city diverted $280 million in federal grants from construction to transit operations under the Beame shuffle. Because they were intended by the federal government for construction purposes, those moneys had to be paid back—some from the original bond issue, others from the city's own funds. Had the city and state used the $280 million to trigger the federal construction grants—instead of borrowing them to keep the fare down—it could have gotten close to a three-to-one payback. The $280 million "had the potential to generate . . . a total of $906 million in additional Federal funds," the state comptroller concluded in 1980.

If Beame and the MTA had used the farebox to raise $280 million over four years, it would have required a single 5-cent fare increase, which would have yielded about $70 million annually. This was the Beame shuffle, and it didn't even keep him in office: in 1977 he was voted out and replaced by Edward I. Koch.

For a nickel saving on the price of a token, the city lost nearly a billion dollars in federal aid. It lost the possibility of the Second Avenue subway, a route that had been promised for nearly half a century. It lost a train line that would have driven up Bronx land values, instead of watching acres of the borough burn very nearly to the ground.

The federal government, by the way, did not notice until 1986 that work on the route had been shut down: the Second Avenue subway was carried as an ongoing project on the books of the Urban Mass Transportation Administration for eleven years after the plug had been pulled.

What was left of the 1967 bond issue, the thirteen new routes, the 150,000 new riders? A 3.5-mile tunnel that went nowhere, and a squiggle at the end of another route in Queens. At best, 6,000 new riders.

Oh yes, there also was the MTA, which did manage to oust Robert Moses. While its building projects have flopped, the agency has prospered. From 83 employees in 1970 it had grown, by 1982, to 295. In 1989, the MTA has 465 on the payroll, dozens of consultants, a network of drivers and gofers and analysts. Altogether, it fills an entire twenty-story office building at 347 Madison Avenue and seven more floors of 345 Madison. Its cousin fungus, the TA bureaucracy, has enjoyed similar growth in its headquarters staff.

And the 63rd Street tunnel turned out to be a spectacular place for teenage boys to hold graffiti-writing parties. Young John Avildsen once played softball there with some pals, including a pal named REAS, who remembered a fine graffiti gallery the city had built him.

"Excellent," said REAS. "We brought our beers, we had time to work on our pieces. It was warm, modern and safe. Excellent."

7 A.M., Washington Heights: Anna Lans

When Anna Lans hit the alarm, the transit police dispatcher put the word out in the telegraphic prose of emergency broadcasters everywhere: a booth holdup, one minute in the past, perps, one black male wearing a ski mask, one Hispanic male, believed to have fled through the Bennett Avenue, 184th Street exit.

At transit police District 3, in an office a mile south, a lieutenant looks down at an assignment sheet and swears. A young cop is on a "fixer" in that station: since 4 A.M., he has been on a fixed post there. He is to go nowhere unless ordered.

"District Three to Callahan."

"Callahan, 'kay."

"There's a booth robbery at Nancy 6A. Where are you?"

"I'm in the station."

"Where the fuck have you been?"

"I been here the whole time. There was no booth robbery, 'kay?"

"The clerk just reported that she was grabbed by a black male wearing a ski mask and a Hispanic."

"When?"

"One minute in the past."

"I'm the only male that's been through here since four A.M., 'kay?"

"Were you cooping, Callahan? Never mind, stay there."

Callahan drops the radio to his side and walks up to the booth.

"There was just a robbery?"

Lans nods.

"Which way did they go out?" There is an elevator up the 180 feet to Fort Washington Avenue, and a ramp out to Bennett Avenue.

Lans points to the ramp.

"When?"

"Just now," she says, shrugging her shoulders.

7:05, Rockaway Beach, Queens: Kathy Quiles

All through the 1950s and the '60s, in the years of its gritty prime, the Lawrence Hotel of Rockaway Beach rang with summer glee, the joy noise of kids who had come in the glory of youth to face an ocean. Every step on the linoleum floors of the Lawrence crunched with sand traipsed from the beach, and the perfumes of fried-food stands on 116th Street trailed through the halls, and transistor radios, between the games of now-vanished baseball teams, banged out the hit songs of treasured, not fancy, vacations.

As Kathy Quiles wakes on this spring morning in 1989, the air of working-class holiday has long vanished from the halls of the Lawrence.

She rises in a single room where three beds hold eight people. Clothes are mashed into giant black trash bags and stacked against a wall. Atop one rickety dresser is a hot plate with two burners and a few dented aluminum pots.

For anyone who cares to sit on something besides a bed, there is a plastic milk crate. The toilet and bathroom are down the hall.

To house Kathy Quiles and her family in this single room, the city of New York was paying $2,400 a month to the owners of the Lawrence Hotel. The sum was astonishing, even by New York standards; for a like price, the family could stay in a fine hotel on the Upper East Side of Manhattan. Or carry a $262,000 mortgage on a nice house. Or rent a comfortable three- or four-bedroom brownstone, complete with den, in such fashionable neighborhoods as Park Slope in Brooklyn.

Until 1986, Kathy had never received any form of public assistance. Then the family and the city embraced and fell into a spiral of disaster, each of its own making.

Kathy Quiles met Ramiro Casiano in 1975, when she was eighteen and working at the corner of DeKalb Avenue and Broadway in Brooklyn. She was the receptionist in a doctor's office; he was the postman who brought the mail, ever slim and handsome in a uniform. Her dark eyes flashed and her thick black hair flowed down the white medical uniform. The children came along: Jason in 1976, Shereen in 1980, Jillian in 1981, Jonathan in 1984, Alexander in 1985, Sabrina in 1987.

For most of those years, it never seemed to matter to Kathy and Ramiro that New York was burning down. Between 1970 and 1987, some 355,000 units of housing were lost, nearly all of it in poor neighborhoods, torched for insurance or abandoned as an irredeemable loss. In this era, the New York Yankees played in a World Series, and the network television blimp, between innings, would float away from the stadium and film the flames bringing whole blocks of the South Bronx to an end. In the living rooms of the nation, people shook their heads and rooted against the Yankees and the decadent city they represented.

There was no occasion to bring a national television blimp to Brooklyn, for the team that had once played near the corner of DeKalb and Broadway had moved to Los Angeles the year before Kathy was born. Out of the national line of sight—not that the notice had made much difference to the Bronx—the streets of Brooklyn fell around Ramiro and Kathy.

"I was making good money in the post office," Ramiro would explain years later. "But you don't see it, you know, because you get paid every two weeks. So you don't got enough, so you try to make even. Messing around, selling whatever."

Trouble was much more exciting than the post office, he decided.

So what if he had been there for thirteen years by 1978 and was being paid $20,000? "I said, I make myself three thousand a day [on the street]. You don't want to get up at five o'clock in the morning, tired, to go to work. You understand what I'm saying? I say to myself, I don't feel good, I'm sick. I made my mistakes."

Kathy bore the children and bore with Ramiro. When he was inclined to honest labor, his hands were clever, and he could make a few dollars working on cars or painting. They lived six years on Grant Avenue in a house owned by her mother. Then Grandma sold and moved to Florida, but helped Kathy buy a home far from the streets of Brooklyn, in Mastic, Long Island.

The living was good. Ramiro was working. Out of sight, behind the kitchen walls, a wire was losing its insulation. Ramiro and Kathy were there less than a year when the fire, following them from Brooklyn, destroyed the house and every possession they had accumulated in a decade together.

As Long Island is famous for people who moved away from welfare clients, Ramiro and Kathy returned to the city, where no one is ever denied housing. Not in so many words, anyway. The welfare department offered a maximum of $300 a month for an apartment. This was in 1986; that year, $300-a-month apartments were vanishing at the rate of 372 every single day.

Thus was born the $2,400-a-month welfare hotel room.

In the city welfare bureaucracy, no one expects people to find any shelter in New York for $300 a month. And there is little expectation that the families can or will pitch in to raise more cash for rent.

Instead, the city draws on emergency housing funds supplied by the federal government. The use of this money is restricted to "temporary" shelters—such as hotel rooms.

Kathy and Ramiro and their five-going-on-six kids moved to the Brooklyn Arms Hotel in the Fort Greene section. This was a highrise chamber of horrors, twenty floors of children sitting atop terror and crushed beneath poverty. At one point, the hotel held six hundred housing violations, issued by the same city that was making its owners very wealthy.

The Casiano-Quiles family were assigned to a room on the fifteenth floor. The rats were bold, the drug merchants worse, bartering openly in the halls. Tormented, Kathy went to bed crying at night.

"My wife has always been a very straight lady," says Ramiro.

One day, Kathy was forced into a stairwell by two crack fiends. They took the few dollars in her purse and threw her down the stairs. Two-year-old Alex was with her.

"Alex caught eight stitches," she said.

The next day, the family was moved to the Lawrence on Rockaway's 116th Street. Here was peace. The children loved the beach, among the world's finest municipal shorelines. Kathy relished the remains of a middle-class shopping strip. Ramiro was a safe distance from the streets of East New York. The family had been moved onto a peninsula that was the most easterly point in the city, a long train ride across a bay before reaching Brooklyn.

The Lawrence was a step into a smaller, safer world. Most of its residents knew each other. They'd keep an eye on the children in a pinch. But it was a temporary space, meant only to hold them for a couple of months, until the city could find a large apartment, decently outfitted, in its inventory of eight thousand buildings acquired through tax foreclosure.

But Kathy's family had arrived in the city's arms at the intersection of historic trends that made their chances of finding something large enough to live in nearly impossible. Mass transit, the chariot of the poor envisioned by Jacob Riis and other turn-of-the-century housing reformers, had built a city that was impossibly crowded.

Ever since World War II, when rent control was instituted in New York, housing vacancy rates have been under 5 percent. When the population dropped, as it did from 1950 through 1980, so did the housing supply. For those who couldn't find or afford the few vacant apartments, the city had large and relatively decent public housing projects that were home to a half million poor and working class people. The projects had a waiting list of 176,761.

Private apartments were just as hard to come by—at least the kind that poor people could afford. Rents rose 43 percent in 1986 and 1987. And during the first six years of the Reagan administration, between 1981 and 1987, federal funds for new housing declined from $33.4 billion to $5.4 billion. (Much of this was ladled out to Republican power brokers connected with the U.S. Department of Housing and Urban Development, a traditional gravy bowl for both major political parties—but one that, until the cutbacks of the 1980s, at least allowed the poor to lick the bottom.)

By August 1988, a year after Kathy and her family arrived in Rockaway, they hadn't seen or heard of a single place that would have been adequate for the eight of them. No wonder: that month, 5,200 families were living in welfare hotels or city shelters, the most ever. The cost, between $25,000 and $30,000 a year for each family, was well beyond the means of all but the most privileged Americans.

That summer, Edward I. Koch had been mayor for eleven years. Public outrage was rising over the millions spent on keeping children in such squalor. Ronald Reagan himself fueled this by citing as folly the exorbitant rates the city paid the welfare hotels. He did not mention that the practice had been devised by his own administration, which refused to shift the funds from emergency housing—the hotels—to permanent homes.

Koch vowed to move every family from the hotels. He said he would rehabilitate the thousands of city-owned abandoned apartments so that families could move into them.

Every morning or week, it seemed, another kid would knock at the Quiles door, room 203, to say So long to one of Kathy's children. A place had been found for the other family. They were moving on.

By the spring of 1989, Kathy and her family are the most senior residents of the hotel. The welfare authorities have not been able to find an apartment or house large enough to hold the brood. Which, on this fine day, is not far from increasing.

Kathy shakes Ramiro.

"I don't feel too good. I got, like, heartburn."

"You want to go to the doctor?"

"I think so. I'm supposed to see him today anyway. Get my eyes checked."

"I'll come with you."

The older kids are packed off to meet the school bus. The young ones are left with a neighbor.

Kathy and Ramiro walk to the end of the street, the terminal of the C train. The train will carry them off the peninsula of their limbo, across Jamaica Bay, and back to Brooklyn where Kathy's doctor is located. It is more than a jaunt—this trip is a long haul. But the C is the only way out for Kathy and Ramiro.

7:10 A.M., Park Slope, Brooklyn: David Gunn

Of the 9,860 people who use the Seventh Avenue station in Brooklyn on an average day, only one makes the news for doing so.

Seventh Avenue, in the Park Slope section of Brooklyn, is David Gunn's stop, a short walk from the former Ansonia Clock Factory.

Newspaper stories often mentioned, with a measure of surprise, that Gunn himself rode the trains—a rare practice among powerful government figures in New York. Gunn's own boss, Robert Kiley, the chairman of the board of the Metropolitan Transportation Authority and a man with a national reputation as an advocate for mass transit, almost never took the subway to work. Kiley was met every morning at his Upper East Side townhouse by a government car and driver, who could spend twenty-five minutes creeping along the clogged streets to MTA headquarters in midtown Manhattan. A subway ride would—should—have taken no more than 10 or 15 minutes. (No complaints from Kiley's driver, who made about $50,000 a year—of which overtime alone accounted for $20,000, a sum equivalent to the mean annual income of the average New York City household.)

Kiley's car and driver was the rule among government officials, high and low: one of his neighbors, Ed Koch, the mayor and city mascot, traveled in a convoy that was never shorter than three cars—a police car for protection, a backup car in case of breakdown, and a car for Koch himself, who had ridden a city bus to his first inauguration in 1978, vowing to be a regular user of mass transit. The promise withered the next morning. His successor, David Dinkins, said he had no intention of regularly riding a bus or subway.

Other members of the MTA board, which was charged with overseeing the mass transit system, also used personal and government vehicles to be chauffeured about town. One day in November 1989, nine board members came to a public hearing near City Hall on raising the fare. Of the nine, seven—including chairman Kiley—arrived by car. In the hour before the hearing, at least 150 trains, coming from all over the city, had stopped within four blocks of City Hall.

No wonder, then, that Gunn's modest claims upon his arrival in New York in 1984 were greeted with skepticism.

At the time, breakdowns were part of nearly every New Yorker's daily commute, so old and patched together was the subway fleet. A few new cars were arriving, the first of a big order of gleaming trains from Japan. On their first run in passenger service, kids went through the brand-new trains, wielding spray paint and kicking out windows.

This made the new Japanese cars just like every one of the other 6,200 in the system: blanketed with filth and graffiti, end to end, 13 linear miles of equipment covered with black marker scrawls on top of Day-Glo murals on top of more black marker scrawls.

Gunn was introduced to the press on February 1, 1984, in a press conference at MTA headquarters, where the floors were carpeted with two decades of broken promises about subway improvements and new lines—promised by officials who dealt with the transit network in abstract, but often grandiose terms.

"It's a very troubled system," said Gunn. He promised little. First, he told the reporters that he was hoping to cut back on the amount of graffiti. Reporters wisely pointed out that this had been promised by three mayors and numerous transit executives since the graffiti had first appeared, in 1970.

In one burst of heroic folly, officials stripped and sandblasted a few hundred cars, then painted them white. Special efforts were made to secure them in the yards from night vandals. The cars did not make it through the night.

Gunn could plead ignorance of past failures, having just arrived from Philadelphia, where he ran the commuter lines of the Southeast Pennsylvania Transit Authority. But Philadelphia's entire system could fit handily into any one of the twenty-six lines that snaked through New York—many of which were mysteries even to native New Yorkers. And Gunn, of course, had only vague ideas about where they all ran.

But that would be fixed by his second promise: he would learn all the lines soon, because he planned to use the subway system every day. For a New York public official, this was the same as declaring a log cabin birth: By God, I know the people; I ride [or rode] the subways. When Ronald Lauder, heir to the Estée Lauder cosmetics company fortune, ran for mayor in 1989, he was asked if he used the trains. He spoke proudly of a regular commute, one hour each way, that he'd made on the Bronx's Woodlawn line—twenty-five years before, as a student in high school.

So the press, hearing Gunn's promise, was skeptical. And so was the new transit president's would-be staff. As soon as the press conference was over, a functionary from Gunn's Brooklyn office approached him. "We can take the elevator right down to the garage," said the aide.

"I'm not going to the garage," said Gunn. "I want to get down to the subway level."

"But your car is waiting downstairs."

"You take the car," said Gunn. "I'm taking the train back to Jay Street."

"It's not direct from here."

"So I'll walk a couple of blocks. What's the big deal?"

"Sir, the riders, they can be very unruly at times. It's not very safe for you to be riding the subways. During these breakdowns, the passengers get upset. If they learned that you were the president of the Transit Authority . . ."

"I'm taking the train."

He stuck with his rule. Five years later, he guessed he had ridden a car in New York City only a few dozen times—with the exception of a three-week period in late 1984.

Nine months after arriving in New York, Gunn came down with testicular cancer; he underwent treatment that appeared to be successful. In follow-up tests, though, doctors noticed a suspicious shadow in his abdomen and performed major exploratory surgery, which found that Gunn was in perfect health. But climbing subway steps was tearing at his incision. He decided to travel by car to the office until it was healed.

One morning, his driver called. "Mr. Gunn, the car is gone. Someone has stolen it. I'll get another one out of the motor pool, but it doesn't open until eight o'clock."

To hell with it, Gunn decided. He'd make the stairs. It would get him back in shape for the rocks up in New Hampshire.

Some months later, the stolen car turned up in Virginia. It was being used as a taxicab. By then, Gunn was back on the F train. Four stops, two miles, ten minutes. He'd be crazy to go any other way. Heck, he even had a free pass.

Rene Ruiz could have a free pass, too, but the people who teach him think he would be better off using a token—for the practice of standing in line, paying for it, and counting the change.

A twenty-year-old man cloaked in the innocence of a boy of seven, Rene is heading for the Broadway train. This is the first morning since he was five he is not boarding one of the yellow buses that have taken him to one special education program or another.

Not that he has stopped going to school. Today, he is bound for the Manhattan Occupational Training Center, where he is learning the rudiments of holding a job, and riding the subway is very nearly the final lesson. Macy's has its corporate eye on Rene and a few of his classmates for positions in the stockroom. But Macy's does not run school buses for any of its employees; nine train lines stop underneath the World's Largest Department Store.

"Walk up the steps . . ."

Half a block from home, Rene climbs the stairs of the Broadway el and makes the purchase: a dollar drawn from his purse, fed into the notch in the glass of the booth, the token drawn back with his stubby, deliberate fingers. He drives the token into the turnstile and walks along the platform so he can be seen from the seventh-floor kitchen window of 130 Post Avenue. For his mother, Grismelda Ruiz, it is very convenient to have an el down the block. She rests her elbows on the ledge of the window as she watches her precious, perpetual baby embark on his first solo flight. From 207th Street to his school on Houston Street: one end of Manhattan to the other.

". . . Then I put in the token . . . and I walk to the conductor . . ."

Rene has been taught to stand near the point where the conductor's car will stop. To go directly inside and to sit down. To carefully count the twenty-six stops between home and school. To keep to himself, and not to socialize, which is his gift and which the family regards as a possible curse on the train, for Rene would never suspect that someone might do him harm.

". . . I was inside the conductor train and I was sitting down. I was being quiet on the train . . ."

Just as Rene cannot shuck his blank-check trust of the world, ncither can the people who love him most be sure that they will be at his side in the days to come, forever reaching into the bottomless purse of their affections. Grismelda is getting older. His sister hopes to keep him, but she is a young woman. One day, Rene's family may not be able to take care of him.

If a decent adult group home is to figure in Rene's future, he must prove himself capable of commuting to work in a stockroom, mailroom, or print shop. If he cannot master the subway, his future could be a custodial program of crafts and droning televisions.

The No. 1 pulls in. Without hesitation, Rene walks to a seat, taking his place among the commuters of New York, an innocent abroad, holder of the freedom of the city. At the window, Grismelda watches until the train pulls away.

"*. . . And then, move train, the train is moving. Right? The train keeps moving, all the stops.*"

7:35 A.M., South Bronx: Tom Thomasevich

By the time Tom Thomasevich's local has hit the southern end of the Bronx, there are no seats left. In fact, he can barely move outside the conductor's cab, although he must push his way through the crowd of standees because the train platforms, depending on the station, are on the right or on the left and he must switch cabs. He sticks his head out the window.

"Good morning, good morning," he says, grinning, defusing stares or glares at the show of good cheer. "All right, all right, we're gonna have a good day. Step lively. Watch the closing doors. This is the Number Six local, next stop, 138th Street."

The train runs along the edge of the richest neighborhoods in New York, home to people who are among the most powerful and influential in the world. Chairmen of big corporations. Wall Street bankers. The mayor. University presidents. And, of course, thousands of the near important and possibly powerful.

The only reasonable expectation is for these people and their neighbors to get the city's best subway service. This is, in fact, the opposite of the truth.

Due to freak historical accidents—and skulduggery by the local government—there is a strange imbalance in the island's subway service that leaves the East Side the city's most crowded.

To understand this, a little geography and history are necessary. Manhattan is a long, narrow island, 12.5 miles from south to north, and just 2.5 miles at its widest point from east to west.

The West Side of the island is served by lines on Eighth, Seventh, and Sixth Avenues, as well as Broadway. But the East Side, the gold coast of the city, has only one, known as the Lexington Avenue line.

"Between 40th and 60th Streets in Manhattan is the largest concentration of jobs in the country," noted the Regional Plan Association in 1963. "Seventy percent of the jobs are east of Sixth Avenue, 30 percent are west. Yet subway track capacity is just the reverse: only 28 percent is east of Sixth Avenue and 72 percent is west."

Once, the East Side had three lines: elevated lines on Second and Third Avenues, in addition to the subway. Famous for noise and shadows, the els became the target of real estate interests, who argued that it would be better to sink the trains and their racket underground. Much of the Second Avenue el was closed by the start of World War II.

What remained was the Third Avenue el and the Lexington Avenue subway, both of which were jammed. In 1951, with an eye to getting rid of the el and easing congestion, the city fathers proposed a $500 million bond issue to build a new subway along Second Avenue and other projects. The voters duly approved it. Immediately, the money was diverted.

The subway system, buffeted by postwar inflation, had just seen the first two fare increases in its history—in 1948 to a dime, and in 1953 to 15 cents. But it wasn't enough to sustain operations. The politicians were unwilling to raise taxes or fares to balance the books.

Thus was started an official policy of deferred maintenance. This was a fine-sounding title for a system of guaranteed failures—waiting until something broke down before fixing it, rather than replacing a part in advance of its breakdown. In short, it was a program that got every last minute of life from a piece of equipment and assured that trains would run worse.

To ease some of the financial pressures of this program, the money from the 1951 bond issue was grabbed away from its original purpose of building new routes, including the Second Avenue subway. At the same time, the Third Avenue el was being torn down—leaving the East Side with one remaining rapid transit route, on Lexington, which remained crowded beyond endurance.

A second bond issue for new subway lines was put to the voters in 1967. This time holes *were* dug. A few blocks of tunnel were built. In 1974, the city entered a fiscal crisis. Construction was, as then Mayor Abraham Beame put it, "deferred."

Having bought and paid for the Second Avenue subway twice, the people of the East Side continue to cram into the remaining line on Lexington Avenue.

What else can Tom Thomasevich do but keep grinning? He feels like singing, but that will have to wait. It's too crowded.

8 A.M.
MAY 12

A
STICKY
QUESTION

An assault team of jackhammers rattles against the tile floors at the 51st Street Lexington Avenue Station, which are one year old. The glue is no good. Tiles are popping up or being chipped by women's high heels. The Transit Authority has been removing acres of new tiles all over the city. Having endured bare concrete floors for eight decades, the city decided to improve the ground in 1981. It was done wrong.

When money was plentiful in the early 1980s, modernizing stations, gloom palaces of the subways, was an ambition. The plans were scaled down a few years later when someone calculated the rate of the improvements: 102 years to finish all 466 stations.

Once, glass-bricked street sidewalks cut the dimness in the stations below. Then the glass bricks went away and the stations darkened. The sordid flavor is the residue of a fast, inexpensive design. The subway is basically a box in a shallow trench: the roofs of the oldest subways are just 5 feet below the street, and the box is held up by lines of columns along the train platforms that reek of lurking danger. A *place defined by humans defies their spirits at every turn.*

Most stations had been painted twice in eighty years. Until the misbegotten tiles, the station floors were done in chewing gum motif: when attacked with high pressure machines, special solvents, and even quick freezes, it took a team of ten people six weeks to remove the ancient tar. "Then we got to Times Square, and gave up," said Carol Meltzer, the chief station officer.

Subway rider Barry Meier pondered the twin problems of tiles that won't stay down and chewing gum that won't come up.

"Why not use chewing gum to hold the tiles?" he asked.

8:05 A.M., In the Subway: Scenes

The big Friday crowds don't stop Bhakta Leo, the *nom de commute* of Leo Jiminez, who must make his move before the weekend. By Monday, people will have spent all their money in nightclubs and have none to give him.

In his polka-dot robe and big rubber nose, Bhakta Leo pushes into the car and flicks a switch on a tiny bullhorn. John Philip Sousa's "Stars and Stripes Forever," engraved on a micro chip, plays through the car.

Heads pull up from newspapers.

"Da-da-*ta*-da-da-da-daaa," blares the song for three seconds. Then Bhakta Leo takes over:

"The clown that you see is from the ISKCON Food for All program, which has provided fifty million meals to needy people around the world," he begins. Contributions will help feed the hungry in New York. "Thank you for your attention and have a healthy life."

Who would have guessed that ISKCON stands for International Society for Krishna Consciousness?

Leo is a Hare Krishna, and the leaders of his Brooklyn temple have targeted the Lexington Avenue line because its new cars are quieter than most, and because it plies the rich waters of Manhattan between Wall Street and the Upper East Side.

Jiminez sidles through the swaying car with his bullhorn and a paint bucket that is labeled with a yellow leaflet from ISKCON Food for All.

He smiles at everyone, whether they drop money in the bucket or not.

Leo has performed careful calculations to arrive at Friday as a good day for begging. On weekends, he fronts as a singer in a salsa band, and so he knows well how a patron's money vanishes as music heats up, and the night, the greedy night, seduces and calls for more. Monday is too late for a clown begging in the subway. By Thursday or Friday, though, payday will have rolled around again, and Leo can count out $200 or $300 after a good morning begging on the Lexington line, all of it—he swears—going toward the vegetarian meals the Krishnas feed three days a week to all comers, and to the upkeep of eighty celibate students—including Leo—and for printing more books that feature the bejeweled four-armed deity of the Hare Krishnas on the cover.

Why the clown outfit?

Truth is, Leo's a bit shy.

"Myself, I don't have the lines," says Jiminez, bemoaning his lack of glibness. "The clown, it's easy for me to do it. Everyone gives, blacks, bums, blind people, whites. Sometimes they say make sure they [the needy] get it. If you don't do it, you're going to get a lot of heavy reaction for that. It's cheating. Even though this whole society is cheating everyone. People take a chance."

On the chances taken by the great spill of subway souls, there are steady bivouacs of Muslims and Krishnas and Dianetics in train stations around the city, the religious ramble side by subway rumble.

In the Grand Central subway stop are paperback stacks of *Dianetics* by L. Ron Hubbard.

"Repent! Jesus Says Earthquake Is Coming!" proclaims a sign tacked to a broomstick and borne by a Bronx minister who climbs aboard the D train every morning.

"Beelieeeeeve," hollers the Reverend Exree Walton of the Full Gospel Tabernacle in Full Subway Voice. Reverend Walton spends an hour every morning at 179th Street, a station in eastern Queens, preaching—no, bellowing—the Word to the daily rush of 31,000 riders. Anyone in arm's length is handed a Bible tract.

On the walls of the cars, next to advertisements for roach poison and hemorrhoid remedies, the New York Bible Society preaches via poster the gospel of Jesus in English, Greek, Hindi, Chinese, Spanish, and French. "But God demonstrates his own love for us in this: while we were still sinners, Christ died for us."

To the Atlantic Avenue stop in Brooklyn come the white-robed Black Muslims, there to unfold tables and set up rows of jewelry, sticks of incense, and small books that ask large questions, such as *What Is the Real Meaning of Valentine's Day?* In neat lines are tiny bottles of scents, the reds on the left, violets in the middle, the yellows on the right.

Subway religion may run from the prophets of doom to the profits of perfume. But many straphangers manage private, interior journeys along with their daily commute.

Today, a woman boards the downtown A train in Washington Heights, and finds the last seat. She settles in, which is to say she tightly gathers her hips and legs into the seat to avoid the strange knees on both sides. She reaches into her handbag and pulls out a small black book. Then she folds her arms across the bag, and in one hand holds the book, which is filled with prayers.

A few pages are loose in the binding. In the book, little cards have been stashed, souvenirs of wakes and novenas, pictures of Christ or the Virgin on one side, and terse, specific prayers on the other.

The woman picks a page—at random, it seems—and her lips purse and close along a tiny aperture. In the dark tunnels beneath the city, those who pray silently can be found by the nictitating flicker of their lips. She fingers the pages, the way beads are fingered by some people, the way cigarettes are fingered by others.

By the time the train has reached 145th Street, her eyes have closed. Her lips do not move. As the train clacks smoothly downtown, rocking and swaying below Harlem, the silence and heat of the crowd weigh heavily on the car, and the woman with the prayer book dozes off.

At 59th Street, she jolts awake, blinks and looks at the station sign. She jumps to her feet and joins the push toward the door. Suddenly, she feels a hand grab her arm. She pulls away, instinctively.

Then she feels something pushing at her arm. That hand, reaching through the crowd, is tapping her with the black prayer book, which had slipped from her sleeping hands onto the floor of the train. Snatched from the trample of rush hour many blocks before by a stranger who had fingered its pages, waiting for its owner to awake.

8:10 A.M., Houston Street, Manhattan: Rene Ruiz

Now, Rene says to himself. Twenty-six stops. He stands up and holds with two hands onto the pole of the train. Intent on their books and newspapers, no one pays any attention to him.

"Houston Street Watch the Doors," the loudspeaker calls out.

As the doors of the train open, Rene takes a deep breath. He must find the stairs. There. He pushes the gate open and looks over his shoulder to see if anyone is behind him.

He walks up the stairs. A big brick institutional building is straight ahead, maybe 50 yards. His eye is on the prize. Don't look at Blimpie's. Mmm. Smells good. Don't look. No curbs to cross. A driveway past the printing plant. Don't mess up. Walking, walking, walking, walking.

There.

8:15 A.M., 46th Street Station, Queens: Joyce Bresa

Joyce Bresa only has to turn a corner to see the world. She lives in Astoria, one of the greatest of all New York neighborhoods. The cafes serve coffee thick and black, the way the Greeks like it. Yugoslavian soccer clubs dribble and feint along grassy strips beneath the approach to the Triborough Bridge. Venerable Armenian ladies stoke their ovens for rich savories, awaiting a visit from their up-and-coming grandchildren. Church signs are in at least four languages and three alphabets.

Sometimes, Joyce Bresa would meet a friend from upstate, who was in the city for a visit. How was she adjusting, they all wanted to know. She'd tell them, "I can't believe how *ethnic* it is here. Upstate, if you had a black family living there next to you, their father worked at IBM too. They weren't your New York City black family. We all were the same class. Middle class. Nobody was any different. Here, I've got people around me speaking in different languages and people smelling different than I am accustomed to them smelling, and people living differently than I am accustomed to them living."

Her husband, for one: he was born in Trieste, the son of an Italian-Yugoslavian couple, and they all live in a big comfortable house. An elevated train line runs overhead, throwing perpetual shadow—but a roaring shadow, for the train connects Astoria to the city.

The city. That is the name for Manhattan for the people of Queens and Brooklyn, a holdover from a century ago when those boroughs were separate cities, before the consolidation of the five boroughs into one entity. And long after the people who lived in those nineteenth-century municipalities had died, the name holds, for the distinction is part of life: You go to the city to work. You take the train to the city. Then you come home, to not-the-city.

For Joyce Bresa, of Hopewell Junction, New York—a tiny town near Poughkeepsie, 90 miles north of the city—Astoria was the home of her love, Reno, the ponytailed electrical engineer she'd met in the Hard Rock Café and eventually married. Before she moved in for good, she'd spend weekends in Astoria, alternately amused and shocked by city habits.

"Why do the men *spit* in the street?" she asked Reno. He laughed.

Now, standing in the 46th Street station, she can see the ancient signs that warn the riders:

NO SPITTING
NO SMOKING
or carrying an open flame

By order of the Board of Transportation

---

a now defunct body that had ruled the subways when civility could be governed by warnings against spitting.

YEAR	Total Summonses (SPITTING, LITTERING, FARE BEATING, ETC.)
1946	56,261
1956	16,544
1966	16,780
1976	230,256
1986	375,817
1989	240,218

Let's see, if the Board of Transportation was still around, it could add a few rules. The papers had a story the other day about a woman walking through Grand Central with her hair on fire. A definite no-no—but one probably already covered in the open-flame clause.

Then there was the fellow who went into a station on 125th Street and blew himself up. Well-dressed, with battery wires running from his wrists, under his arms, and across his chest, where he had strapped some gun powder. No bombs allowed.

And then there was the poor fellow who had his heart broken over a love affair and went up to Dyckman Street with a machete and cut his fingers off—delaying trains along Broadway for the afternoon rush hour. What rule could cover that? Don't fall in love, badly?

The noxious, the miserables, the badly mannered, the troubled and puzzled: They lined up down under as if the subway were their hall of fame.

People pile into the station, and while she recognizes them, and no doubt they recognize her, greetings are not offered. A few years before, she had commuted from Scarsdale, a suburban town just north of the city. Lots of people, meeting each other day after day, would nod and say hello, then settle into their seats on the commuter train. In the subways, she'd notice the same people heading to work, taking kids to school, but no one spoke. It was one thing to say Hi to someone waiting for a commuter train that promised plenty of seats and space; quite another to strike up conversation with someone whose face might be in your armpit for the next thirty minutes. This coldness charged to New Yorkers could, in fact, be attributed to exquisite manners.

One day, she had spotted a heavyset woman carrying a Bendel's bag waiting for the R train. Ignoring all the interdictions against speaking to strangers, she chatted with her.

"I see you shop at Bendel's?" Joyce opened.

"I don't shop there—I work there," said the woman.

"Where? I've never seen you," said Joyce. Renee Guttierez, it turned out, was a part-time switchboard operator. No wonder Joyce never saw her in the store; operators are always behind an unmarked door somewhere.

This morning, just like every morning, to go with the familiar faces on the platform are familiar odors. Joyce always can smell the coffee and bacon from the diner on the street, home of a remarkable New York phenomenon: the $1.50 breakfast special, offered by every corner diner—two eggs any style, toast, potatoes, juice, coffee, 75 cents extra for bacon or sausage, a meal impossible to produce for a cheaper price at home. There are doughnut shops and short-order joints above and below just about every train station, and they all serve some version of the breakfast special, the description scrawled with a black pencil on the back of a paper plate. People often carry their coffee and fried egg sandwich into the station.

Not Joyce. She can't risk a mess on her Henri Bendel clothes.

8:25 A.M., Washington Heights: Anna Lans

Talk about a headache. A token booth robbed under the nose of a uniformed cop. Ranking officers descended on the scene to figure out how it happened. The young cop, Callahan, recognized he was in trouble and stood to the side, glaring across the station at Anna Lans in the booth, which was getting crowded.

The day clerk had arrived for duty, and of course could not use Anna's account sheets because there was nothing left to account for. A fresh supply of tokens and currency had been rushed to the station by a revenue supervisor to replace what had been stolen.

Now, another supervisor, bent over the turnstiles, writes numbers off the counters; then she'd have to empty all the vaults at the bottom of the turnstiles and bring the remaining tokens back to the booth. There, the supervisor would spill them into a contraption that looked like a big mixing bowl with a crank on the side. This was a counting machine; each turn of the crank sent the tokens down a chute and through a register. When this was finished, the supervisor toted the loss from Anna's logs: 7,000 tokens. The cash had survived.

And still another boss is taking a statement from Anna, who holds her head in one hand.

Meanwhile, the station regulars are arriving to the unlikely throng of transit workers and cops. The newsboy, pulling bundles of papers, worries that he can't make his normal deal with the clerk: she gets a free paper and he is able to change a $10 bill for coins. But this gang of officials and bosses might find a rule against it.

And passengers are coming, each minute another ten or fifteen, in their normal morning frenzy for tokens: *Fast right now ten please hurry it up the train's coming.*

"What's all this, a murder?" asks one man, pushing through the turnstile.

"A robbery," says another policeman.

"Here?"

"No, Times Square. We decided to do the investigation up here because we like the quiet."

"Smartass."

Glowering over all, arms crossed, is Callahan, the cop who missed the robbery.

"What's the deal, Callahan? Where were you?" asks a lieutenant.

"I'm not saying anything till my rep gets up here," says Callahan. Like all the other officers, Callahan is a member of the strong Patrolmen's Benevolent Association, which advises its members in trouble to keep their mouths shut.

"Have it your way," says the lieutenant, shaking his head and walking back to the booth. He takes the phone and calls the transit detective bureau.

"Tommy? Can you get up here? We got a problem."

"What's the story?"

"A booth robbery here at 181st on the A. There was a kid on a fixer, but he claims he never moved."

Tom McGurl puts down the phone. He turns to his partner, Jim Christie, and says, "We got one up in Washington Heights."

8:45 A.M., On Jamaica Bay: Kathy Quiles

The C train out of Rockaway Park—the official name for the neighborhood in which Kathy Quiles and her family reside—rides tracks that cross Jamaica Bay on a stretch of fifty thousand piles and two islands made of sand dredged from the bottom of the bay by the Transit Authority.

Through a bird sanctuary, hard by a national park, the C train crosses a 3.5-mile causeway. In rough weather, waves lap across the tracks. For the first half of the century, the Rockaway line was operated by the Long Island Rail Road, and the trip into midtown Manhattan could be made in thirty minutes.

But fires on the creosote-soaked trestle were so common that the railroad gave up in 1950 and turned it over to the city subway system. If fire or water do not stop the trains—and they often do—the subway cars may not run, anyhow. The equipment assigned to the line is famously unreliable. Four decades of municipal operation had transformed the half-hour trip to midtown into a ninety-minute crawl.

There are other ways off the Rockaway peninsula. A city-regulated bus comes along every twenty-five minutes or so, and drops riders at stations in Brooklyn that are served by faster express trains. And there is a ferry to Wall Street—but that costs $6 each way and Kathy and Ramiro have no reason to go there.

And then there are the vans.

In April 1980, Local 100 of the Transport Workers Union of America struck the city's bus and subways. This led to two permanent changes in the lives of New Yorkers. First, women—New York women, the most stylish in the world—gave up their miserably uncomfortable pumps and high heels and started wearing running shoes. Droves of working women, part of a contingent of 30,000 walkers, strode across the city's 2,098 bridges, business-garbed down to their ankles. On their feet were Reeboks and Nikes and Pumas—shoes made for pounding the pavement. After the strike was over, the running shoes stayed on.

The second change was the entry of vans into New York's commuting life. Overnight, the vans, carrying a dozen or so passengers, emerged to ferry riders from distant parts of the city during the strike. They never left. As train performance slid through the early 1980s, the vans were beating subways and city buses every day.

In Rockaway, where the middle class was still an Irish-American stronghold, an outfit called Erin Tours provided van service by appointment. In middle-class black neighborhoods in Queens, West Indians took to the road. They ran along established routes, scooting in and out of traffic while the city buses lumbered behind. City officials huffed and boiled as they saw ridership decline on bus routes served far more efficiently by vans. The police launched ticket blitzes. But the vans stayed because people kept paying. (A big part of their efficiency was discrimination: the elderly and the handicapped, for example, had to wait for the city buses, especially if they needed help climbing on board. City buses "knelt" at the curb. The vans were fleet but not open to all comers.) The Transit Authority called for greater enforcement efforts against the vans, which often evaded licensing and insurance rules. In response, the Queens Van Plan set up a radio network that warned of traffic obstructions—and police on the prowl.

Through the bureaucratic wars, the customers were loyal to the vans—and often put it in terms that cut home.

"Do you know how black people have been criticized with the vans?" testified one Queens man during a public hearing on van use. "But in white neighborhoods, they have the same thing, with private cars. The white people call it carpooling."

White people also called them vans. By 1989, perhaps ten thousand vans were running along bus routes and subway lines. But for people such as Ramiro and Kathy, not working commuters savvy to the ins and outs of the vans, it was far easier to rely on the subway, clunky but familiar.

Though they have left most of their Brooklyn life behind, Kathy still trusts her doctor in the Ocean Hill–Brownsville section and goes back to him for her checkups. Today, she rides the seventeen stops to the doctor's, staring out at the water of the bay, at the dancing glint atop the waves, glad to be moving. She holds Ramiro's hand.

9 A.M.
MAY 12

WAKE UP, GET OUT OF BED

The subway system peaks in the IRT 72nd Street subway station at 9 A.M.: more people will pass through less space in the next fifteen minutes than anywhere else in the subway and probably the world. The people of the Upper West Side start their commute a half hour later than their colleagues in Queens, Brooklyn, or the Bronx because they are just ten or fifteen minutes from work—but it's an intense journey.

Their trip begins in a station that has been the system's most crowded express stop from the opening day of the IRT subway, October 27, 1904. Designed by George Heins and Christopher LaFarge, it took most of its inspiration from the architects' triumphant work at the Bronx Zoo. The two staircases are single-file-wide and if they weren't lifted directly from the chimp house, then they were made for a shorter species of human.

Though the subways carry only half the customers they did during the 1940s—people no longer work a half day on Saturdays, and many no longer take discretionary rides—the trains are as crowded as ever during rush hours.

At 72nd Street, during each

of the next fifteen minutes, 66 customers will spin through the turnstiles—close to 1,000 whirring people in one quarter hour. At day's end, the total will be 22,076. Every car on the local trains that leave the station will be filled to its "crush load" capacity of 180—and then, the records show, another 3.42 people will pry themselves in. Somehow it happens, Monday through Friday, fifty-two weeks a year. And the riders who mutter under their breath that the place is a zoo don't know the truth they speak.

9:10 A.M., Union Square, Manhattan:
Tom Thomasevich

A downtown train that reaches 14th Street is a train about to sigh with relief. Here, around Union Square, is the last big commercial district before the civic center, and here, a Lexington Avenue local that has been crowded to the very limit of any mammal's ability to perform aerobic respiration is leaving the bulk of its passengers.

In deference to a major squawk raised by property owners along the line at the turn of the century, the railroad has a perilous curve just as it enters the 14th Street station. Trains bank heavily to the side; riders are thrown by centrifugal forces toward the wall and their fellow travelers. The platform itself is curved, which makes it incompatible, geometrically speaking, with the straight-line subway car. The practical result, discovered shortly after the station opened, is that people getting on or off the train face gaps of 18 inches between the fixed platform and the door. A moving extension platform was installed. After the train enters the station, the metal grates push out from under the platform and against the cars.

The real estate power struggles of the nineteenth century not only bent the subway platform, but also caused an unnatural pause in a subway train's "breathing" cycle: normally, doors open the instant the train has stopped, and people are up on the balls of their feet, leaning to leave.

But Tom Thomasevich, watching from the conductor's window, has to be certain the moving platforms have come to a full stop before turning his key and punching the buttons that open the door.

While this happens, people are poised to exit, impatient, as if this fractional delay—two or three seconds—was not an ordinary part of the 14th Street routine. Now, when they get out, there is more room in Tom's train. Local trains often are held in the station to meet with the expresses that stop there, and Tom's No. 6 is a local. When the downtown express pulls in, a few of its passengers dash across the platform to board the local.

Tom was deliberate in his next moves. Be patient, he said to himself. Be careful. He smiled out the window at his departing passengers. He could only see a couple of feet in each direction because of the curve in the platform, and could therefore only guess whether passengers were clear of the door when he pushed the buttons to close them. A few years before, a man boarding a train out of the conductor's line of sight was trapped in the closing door and dragged to the end of the platform, smashed against the tunnel wall, and killed.

It's a nerve-racking station, that's for sure. People in a hurry trying to get out before the doors open, conductors hoping that the doors don't close too soon and capture and drag someone along the platform. The first second the train moves, it goes 2.5 miles per hour; in second number two, it's up to 5 miles per hour. Anyone stuck in the door of a moving train for three seconds is going to need major repairs.

Tom stuck his head half out the window as the train picked up speed, looking left and right, up and down the platform for about three car lengths, 150 feet. Then he pulled up the window and closed it. When the train entered the tunnel, he had forty-five seconds before the next stop. He smiled to himself, straightened his tie.

A little click announces the opening of his cab door. A tiny noise in a subway car, but one that registers with riders attuned to the slightest change in pitch. They glance up at the sound of the door opening, see the conductor, then go back to nosing their newspapers. Tom stands in the aisle, bouncing one foot up and down in rhythm.

"You ain't nothing but a hound dog!" he sings.

This, too, is not unusual: riders were regularly serenaded by clowns and beggars pitching for money. A man with a trumpet used to announce that he had just landed from Mars, and was playing until he collected enough money for the return flight. His performances were so painful that riders hoping to speed his departure pitched money into his hat as he tramped along the aisle.

Today, when they hear the opening notes of an Elvis routine, they glance up for a second, the nearly involuntary response any human would make in such a situation. Their next move is to immediately put their faces back into the newspaper. These, after all, are subway riders, trained in the First Commandment: Thou Shalt Not Stare.

But as their gazes return to the papers, the thought dawns on twenty people at once.

That's the conductor singing.

Can't be.

They steal a glance: he sure looks like a conductor. Has the hat, the badge, the blue blazer and pants and practical black shoes.

A big toothy smile. Finger snapping. Head rocking.

> *When they said you was high class,*
> *Well, that was just a lie . . .*

9:15 A.M., Beneath the Plaza Hotel, Manhattan: Joyce Bresa

Fifth Avenue is Joyce Bresa's stop for work. Climbing out of the station, before she reaches the street, she passes a metal door with a sign:

PLAZA HOTEL
EMPLOYEES ENTRANCE
THROUGH THESE DOORS WALK
THE WORLD'S GREATEST HOTEL EMPLOYEES

Management's views on the employees changed when the Plaza was bought by ex-billionaire Donald Trump, who made wholesale purges of longtime staff. Nevertheless, the sign was left in place, not because changing it would brew poisonous publicity, but because it had been decades, no doubt, since Trump had gone even half a flight of stairs into that or any other subway station.

On the street, Joyce tacks against midtown at its full morning stride. Here, just outside the station, is parked a line of horses and carriages, available nearly around the clock to anyone interested in the romance of a spin through Central Park—anyone, that is, with

$34 for a half-hour ride, and $10 for additional fifteen-minute segments, and tips for the drivers.

The horses are one of the great preoccupations of the city council. Kids were not learning to read, drugs and AIDS were wiping out a generation, and murders went on at the rate of six a day. These were deplored by the council members in between sessions on the horses. With nearly a total inability to tax or regulate anything or anybody of consequence without the permission of the state legislature, the councillors spent days debating the wisdom of diapers for the horses, rate gouging by the carriage men, and the scandalous conditions under which the horses were stabled. When a horse dropped dead during a crushing heat wave in 1988, there was an unprecedented outcry from the council. Of course, dozens of humans withered as well, but the council immediately launched hearings—*How can we protect these poor creatures?*

All around the poor creatures are the certified splendors of New York. Across from the Plaza is the southern border of Central Park, the apron of 840 acres of hidden knolls and meadows, playing fields and outdoor theater, and around this bend or the next, just past a grove of dogwood whose spring petals carpet every step, a shimmering lake, so unexpected. Joyce sometimes takes her lunch here and strolls with friends from work.

The Plaza itself is the grande dame of New York hotels. From windows two stories high, diners in the Oak Room or the Edwardian Room can gaze out at the horses and carriages, a genteel dressing for the street, and beyond that, to the park.

Across Fifth Avenue is the toy store/fantasy land known as F.A.O. Schwarz. Here Tom Hanks danced across a giant piano in the movie *Big*. Here the doors are locked when Michael Jackson comes to spend thousands on a spree.

As she walks down Fifth Avenue, Joyce passes the arched entry to Bergdorf Goodman, then Van Cleef and Arpels, the stately retail agents of the diamond cartel. Diagonally opposite is Tiffany's.

At 57th Street, she turns right and walks about a quarter of the block until she reaches Henri Bendel's.

Bendel's is right at home in that neighborhood. A department store with the style of a salon, it has a history of launching small designers and making them famous by peddling their wares to the most fashionable women of New York. Shopping at Bendel's is not the nerve-jangling experience of, say, Macy's or Bloomingdale's, where customers fight over the merchandise and figure out for themselves where to find it.

Not at Bendel's. The store works on an old-fashioned service ethic of lavishing attention on its customers, who pay mightily for the privilege. It is a job perfectly suited to Joyce.

She had come to work there just six months ago, having left a job a few blocks away, at the Elizabeth Arden Red Door salon on Fifth Avenue. She'd moved to New York for the job of managing the Arden salon.

"It's world famous," she declared. Behind the Red Door, women were covered for the better part of a day with concoctions of mud, water, and fragrances. All of it was washed, clipped, and sanded away. By the time the women left, they had been pampered and beautified with every cosmetic technique that could be legally applied to living people.

At first, she lived with an aunt in Scarsdale, a suburb north of the city. Then she met Reno at the Hard Rock Café and began to spend weekends in Astoria. One Sunday, he said to her, "This is ridiculous. Why don't you stay here? It's fifteen minutes on the train to Manhattan."

It was, as Joyce saw on the subway map, just five stops to the Red Door, a little bit less than 4 miles. A fifteen-minute train ride, as listed in the transit schedules.

She decided to move in, and quickly learned that her 4-mile trip commanded an allowance of forty-five minutes to make work on time. In the evening, after getting home, she'd need several minutes before she could speak. "I'd walk in the door and Reno would shove the glass of wine in my hand and say, 'Have a bad day on the subways Joyce?' . . . I'd usually grab for my wine before I'd say hello."

In time, subways notwithstanding, they married. And Joyce moved on from the Red Door to Bendel's on 57th Street—one of the most expensive stretches of real estate in the world.

Joyce had a chance to become a Bendel's buyer—the equivalent of running a small store within the store. "You are the merchant. You are the one who takes all the pressure and all the blame and you are the one who has to show all the profit at the end of the year."

The street floor of Bendel's is laid out in a series of miniboutiques, where items are lovingly arranged, an entire display devoted to a single accessory. A belt. No, *the* belt. *The* scarf. High-end retail veneration, with its whiff of refined fetishism.

The largest area of the first floor is devoted to cosmetics, where Joyce works in sales as part of her apprenticeship as a buyer. Here Bendel is very orthodox: virtually all department stores catering to women keep the colors and scents on the ground floor "primarily because it's impulsive," explains Joyce. "It also creates a lot of excitement. There are a lot of things you have to know about to be very good at it. Shoppers rely so much, I find, on the knowledge of the person they're speaking to."

Before she could advise her customers, though, Joyce has to pull herself together: she has, after all, just gotten off a subway train.

9:20 A.M., Jay Street, Brooklyn: David Gunn

David Gunn messes little with power rituals, whether they involve having a car and driver, jostling for position at a mayoral press conference, or having a secretary make his phone calls. He uses his own fingers to dial most calls. He punches in the private number of an office on 64th Street and West End Avenue.

"Sonny."

"Yeah, Dave. How are you? What's up?"

The multinational concern of Morrison Knudsen was on his back. One of the largest engineering and construction companies in the country, Morrison Knudsen was pushing hard for transit work.

"On this R-44 thing, I'm having a hard time. A very hard time. Morrison Knudsen has a lot of political guns on its side. Have you been able to do anything on your end?"

Gunn is speaking with Sonny Hall, a bus driver who'd climbed to the presidency of Local 100 of the Transport Workers Union, which represented 30,000 TA workers. There was a time when Gunn's arrival in any of the transit repair and maintenance facilities would spark a near riot by the members of Hall's union. Bolts would be hurled in his vicinity, raining like hail on the concrete walks. "When they [the Gunn administration] first came aboard, in reality, in many places, the union was running the operation," Hall would say much later. "As [my predecessor] John Lawe was saying for years, 'Management wasn't managing.' "

Gunn, with his boss, Robert Kiley, chairman of the Metropolitan Transportation Authority, had arrived with a view that the union had crippled the greatest mass transit system in the country. The two of them declared war on organized labor and the encrusted bureaucracy of the Transit Authority. "You come into a place that is in chaos, organizationally, physically, morale has gone to hell, shot, the public has no expectations to speak of," Kiley once said. "So you organize yourself as a commando outfit. And you go in, and goddamn it, you know what has to be done, you know how to get there, in your mind at least, and you go for it. And the snipers are sniping and the carpers are carping, and you just basically say, Fuck them, we're going to do it our way or it won't get done."

Their way meant that disciplinary actions increased tenfold; the no-nonsense message was delivered at the expense of hundreds of working people who, neutral arbitrators later found, were unfairly docked pay or wrongly demoted.

Their way meant that people who had hoped to work their way up through the ranks would have little chance of penetrating the Gunn-Kiley circle of managers. Their way meant that a man who had made a career in the system, rising eventually to the chief of the daily subway operations, could come to his office one morning after the Gunn team's arrival and find the lock changed, his personal stuff in a box outside the door—and see in his chair a man whose entire transportation experience consisted of running a tiny bus company in rural Pennsylvania, but who talked a tough antiunion game. That consisted of the man's notice that his thirty-year career in public service was over.

"They came in with the two-by-four but never knew when to put down the two-by-four," said Hall, "when to say, 'Okay, we got your attention, but now we're at that next stage when we got to do this together.' "

The purges were brutal. But the public, by and large, sided with Gunn and Kiley in their war with the union. The public endured trains breaking down, night after night, and had little interest in the nuances of the responsibility for deferred maintenance. The transit workers on the front lines were loathed. In a matter of months, the union ceded work rules that had developed over decades and, indeed, flagrantly limited productivity. Now the same person could, after all, use both a mop and a broom during the same shift.

By this morning, Gunn presides over 2,000 nonunionized managers, as opposed to 300 when he arrived.

By this morning, too, Gunn has "started to realize—yet he would never admit it explicitly—that maybe there was another way" to do labor relations, said Hall. Gunn no longer sees the union as the root of the transportation problem in New York.

And the call from Gunn to Hall is that "other way," Gunn's embrace of a most maligned work force. It is a stunning turnabout. Together, they are plotting against some of the most potent political and business forces in the state to deal transit workers into the last phase of rebuilding the subway cars.

The resurrection of the subway fleet during the 1980s had been accomplished, for the most part, with outside vendors, although most of them never were able to make the cars run as well as promised. More than a billion dollars had been spent to tear out the guts of the cars—engines, door systems, wheels, brakes, air conditioning—and refurbish them. The graffiti were blasted off. Floors were replaced.

This is work that should have been done, in much smaller doses, during the 1970s and early 1980s but was ignored until the cars had to be rebuilt, virtually from scratch. Governors and mayors and legislators had abandoned maintenance of the trains during those years; now that the repair money was in a pot of honey a billion dollars deep, they gathered around to protect favorite contractors.

Most of the vendors had dropped out after a single contract, finding the innards of subway cars too complicated and finicky. The one surviving player was also, by far, the largest: Morrison Knudsen, which had opened a plant in Hornell, New York, some 300 miles from New York City for the overhauls.

In 1989 MK's managers assumed that the overhaul of the last part of the fleet, a line of cars known as the R-44s, also would be done in their factory.

"MK's got bipartisan support—they've got legislators, they've got the executive branch on their side," says Gunn. "This is going to be very tough."

"I know the governor wants the work to go to MK," Hall tells Gunn. "We've been reaching out to him through our people."

The operatives of Mario Cuomo, the basso profundo of Democratic politics, were pushing hard for the contract to be awarded to MK. The people in upstate New York needed the work, they argued loud enough for everyone north of the Bronx to hear. The city's transit workers couldn't do as good a job, they whispered.

Probably more to the point, MK had hired as its lobbyist William Hennessy, a transportation power broker who just happened to be the first state Democratic chairman appointed by Cuomo when he took office in 1983. And Cuomo's campaign team had made a practice of hitting up big engineering and construction firms with state contracts—especially those controlled by Hennessy and other Cuomo appointees—for "contributions" to the governor's reelection fund. Morrison Knudsen, with a billion dollars in contracts from the Cuomo-controlled MTA, had given $9,400 to the Friends of Mario Cuomo, the governor's campaign organization.

Despite this arsenal of influence, the transit workers were not completely outgunned. For one thing, Cuomo owed his political existence to the support of organized labor—including the powerful Transport Workers Union led by Hall.

"We'll keep working it from our end," Hall promised Gunn.

For another, the members of the MTA board had given David Gunn nearly a blank check, free of political influence, to run the Transit Authority. Of course, small political favors and contracts were quietly handled to the satisfaction of all. But for the Cuomo-controlled board to disregard Gunn's and his staff's recommendation and award a huge contract contrary to their advice was a major rupture.

"We're going back to MTA this afternoon," Gunn said. A new pitch for the work would be made by Charles Monheim, a bright young transit executive. Gunn promised to keep Hall up to date.

Then he walked down a short hallway and stuck his head in the door of George Miller's office.

"Ready?"

"Right with you," said Miller.

Miller was the perfect sidekick for Gunn: he was precise, he had the patience and eye for the surgical application of a budget knife, and knew how to make things happen inside the bureaucracy. A slight man, he spent most of his vacations in Chile, and his crisp color photography of the Andes Mountains hung in the office. For a man fastidious of habit and style, it was odd that what looked like a bundle of rags with fuzzy teeth should occupy a place of honor on his conference table.

"They're a reminder," Miller once explained to a visitor. "Don't get too cocky."

This ornament was a journal lubricating pad, a kind of cloth that was used to grease train wheels. In 1985, Miller discovered that the Transit Authority had just placed an order for another dozen cases of the lubricating pads, bringing the inventory to 800 cases—or a forty-year supply for a fleet of 6,000 cars, of which only 6 had the kind of wheels that could be lubricated with the pads. The design of the subway car had changed decades earlier, and the pads no longer were used. Of all the trains in New York City, the journal lubricating pads could be used only on a half dozen old work-train cars—and these were about to be scrapped.

Miller was an expert on the costs of the pathological mismanagement that had beset the transit system for at least thirty years.

For instance, in 1989, every $1 token included about 10 cents for debt service—the interest on loans that the government had taken out, not for any new equipment, the customary reason for debt, but just to do a massive catch-up maintenance program.

Today, Miller and Gunn were heading to the Coney Island repair shop for a look at one of those programs, an overhaul of subway cars whose parts had not been replaced as they were wearing well past the end of their useful life. To get there, they rode an elevator to the station beneath the basement of the TA building. Three subway lines, the A, C, and the F stop there.

Kids from all over Brooklyn use the Jay Street station. Fulton Street, a block from the transit building, was a closed pedestrian mall, and it catered to the appetites and customs of poor young people. On Fulton Street, $100 sneakers were sold. So were four-fingered rings, and bomber jackets, and gold caps for the teeth, puffed rings for the ears, and toy guns.

About ten kids, loud, piled into the F train car with Gunn and Miller. They spread their feet across two and three seats and screamed teen talk across the aisles. The two transit executives held the poles and tried to carry on a conversation about the overhaul plans, but both were keeping an eye on the kids.

When the train leaves Jay Street, it is underground. Two stops later, it begins to climb to the surface, emerging in a sweeping curve from the tunnel just before the Smith-Ninth Streets station. At 89.5 feet above the street, this is the highest point in the subway system, and the platform at the station affords magnificent views of New York harbor and lower Manhattan. During fireworks celebrations, when corporations hire the World Trade Center and South Street Seaport at fabulous prices, the platform at Smith-Ninth is packed with savvy New Yorkers who know that here, for the price of a token, is the best prospect of the city. The TA uses the station for public relations photographs. It also is an important transfer point for a train that travels between Brooklyn and Queens.

As Gunn expected, the kids get out here for the Queens train. As they leave, the tension slides from his shoulders. He glances at the platform and sees one of the kids, a big lug, facing back into the car. The kid, about sixteen, is holding his arms out as if he were keeping a large crowd behind him.

Ding dong.

The chimes sound and the doors close. The kid on the platform rears back and leaps, feet first, into the glass window on the car door. The plate pops from its frame and hits the ground, fracturing into pebbles.

The boy on the platform roars with laughter, then strides off. Gunn swears and works his way toward the middle of the train to alert the conductor, while Miller stations his slight body in front of the broken window. Then he does some arithmetic in his head.

The TA was replacing about 2,500 windows a week. On average, that meant one window on every subway car owned by New York City was broken, badly scratched or kicked out every three weeks. You couldn't send out a new, graffiti-free train with broken windows. Or any kind of train. It was too damn dangerous. The labor and materials were $59.17 apiece to replace them.

That was windows. Then there was the graffiti removal program, and cleaning up after homeless people, some of whom used the trains not only as living quarters but also as toilets, and the cost of running the transit summons program—the tickets issued to fare beaters, litterers, urinaters, rowdy and disorderly people. Most of these fines were ignored, but they served as a slight deterrent, so the TA ran the program at a $2 million net loss.

Not long before this, one transit executive, Charles Monheim, had talked about the car equipment department and how it had responded to changes in the way people behaved:

> We have roughly the same number of employees that we had seven years ago. But the distribution of those people is very different. We in fact have eight hundred fewer mechanics. We have eight hundred or seven hundred more cleaners. What do these people do? They pick up garbage off the trains at the end of the line that doesn't have to be there. They clean off graffiti that doesn't have to be there. The mechanics that we do have could probably be reduced even more if we weren't replacing hundreds of pieces of glass a week and the like. Picking up seats off the roadbeds that have been thrown out the windows of subway cars. In essence, that switch has been in response to the need to essentially fight urban decay and vandalism.

Without it, "there would in fact be not only seven hundred fewer mechanics, there wouldn't be the seven hundred to eight hundred more cleaners. The cost of doing business is higher now that it was five or ten years ago, and that is a dead loss to the Transit Authority, it's a dead loss to the region."

In all, Miller figured, the "social budget" of the TA—the portion allocated to picking up after folks who behaved without any of the ordinary restraints of civilization—was $48 million. Add another $42 million for fare beaters. That was $90 million just for miscreants alone. Seven and a half cents on the fare.

When you threw in another dime for the debt service on the bonds used to clean up the dilapidation of the system caused by bad politics and inept managers, at least 17.5 cents of every dollar fare was going to pay for screwups.

This train will have to be pulled from service at the end of its run to repair the window—and somewhere along the line, people will be delayed, businesses will lose money. The numbers become too high, almost, for one fellow to think about.

9:25 A.M., Brooklyn Bridge, Manhattan: Tom Thomasevich

The instant the No. 6 train pulls into Brooklyn Bridge station, last stop on the Lexington Avenue local, Tom Thomasevich opens the doors.

"All out, please," he says. "It's been great having you. Be very careful getting off the train."

Now, empty of passengers, the train will head for a tunnel and vanish into a most wondrous place: the abandoned City Hall station, "a cool little vaulted city of cream and blue earthenware like a German beer stein," as the *New York World* described it on opening day in 1904.

Once, riders arriving by subway for the seat of government stepped into a station of minor majesty. Chambered ceilings spilled in a gentle curl, one after the other, and daylight purled through a frosted skylight. Glazed green and brown tiles stood in herringbone formation. From great crystal chandeliers poured a waterfall of glass and light. As the centerpiece of the first lines operated by the Interborough Rapid Transit Company—and as the stop directly beneath City Hall—it was lavishly designed.

In addition, the station served as the southern terminal and turning point for the original IRT, so a giant loop of tracks led trains from north to south. Function led to the station's graceful form, the long sweep of curve, and the lovely curling succession of vaulted ceilings. But it also led to its closing on December 31, 1945, when a boom in ridership after the war meant that the IRT trains had to carry more cars. The longer trains meant conductors could see very few of the doors as they were closed. The City Hall station, being only a block or so from the stop at Brooklyn Bridge, was "sealed like King Tut's tomb," as the *AIA Guide* put it.

Today, Lexington Avenue local trains such as Tom Thomasevich's continue to drive through the station to move from the downtown tracks to the uptown. A rider who stays out of the sight of the train crew usually can remain on the train as it turns around, and thus swipe a glance at the station.

During the 1980s, a proposal was advanced by government interests to use part of the station as a parking garage for the limousines and official vehicles of the mayor and city council. Even the thickest city council member could see the lethal symbolism of such an act, and the idea was dropped. The jewel of the system remains shut, its tiles covered with decades of steel dust.

Subway ornamentation is hardly delicate. The original contract for the IRT line declared that the subway was "a great public work" and its design should incorporate "beauty of material as well as efficiency." August Belmont, Jr., the financier who held that first contract, allotted $500,000 for the ornamentation of its forty-nine stations. Some contend that he spent as much, or more, on building and running his private rail car, which was described in a 1956 article in *Railroad* magazine:

> The Mineola emerged [from the manufacturer] as a beautiful vehicle, with an interior trim of natural mahogany, artistically inlaid. Curved plate glass windows to fit the bumper contour extended from roof to floor at each end, providing an unobstructed view of the line ahead and behind.
>
> There was an oval stained-glass window in each side. . . . The steward's galley and the lavatory [were] completely equipped with hot and cold running water. The galley contained an electric grill and an electric oven, as well as a refrigerator, a pantry, and a well-stocked wine locker. A nickel-plated electric coffee urn with a faucet was installed. . . . An upholstered settee [was] placed against the bulkhead, while the other end of the compartment contained Belmont's private roll-top desk. . . . The arched Empire ceiling was tinted a pistachio green, with fine gold trim. . . . Decorative stained-glass panels were installed. Individual chairs stood on broadloom carpet. Portable ta-

bles could be set up by the steward upon request. . . .
There were polished brass gauges and meters arranged
where Belmont could observe the speed, the air pressure,
the voltage and the current. [The exterior] was finished in
glossy maroon, with gold leaf striping and lettering.

Belmont, knowing that the subway he was building would turn
west at 42nd Street, bought up the land, and then sold it to the city,
retaining the right to build on the street. There he put up a hotel
named the Belmont, with a hidden door in the basement. To this door
came his Mineola, where he and his guests—Mayor George Mc-
Clellan, the Astors, the Vanderbilts, Lillian Russell, Diamond Jim
Brady—boarded. Having arranged a special switch in Brooklyn, his
car could run from the basement of the hotel out to a racetrack,
Belmont Park, on the Queens-Nassau counties' border.

"The steward served champagne as they raced downtown along
the express track. As they plunged beneath the East River, the
steward passed the caviar."

The amenities for Belmont's paying customers were famously
modest. Mosaic tiles list station names and, in a few spots, are
accompanied by simple bas-relief sculptures. With the stingy deco-
rating budget, many of the tile craft pieces were executed in terra-
cotta, an economy allowing them to be fired a single time in the clay
ovens, rather than the repeat firings and glazings of other kinds of
tile.

The bas-relief plaques seem to go through alternating eras of neglect and fawning adoration by preservationists. The rider whose eye
picks through the grime can enjoy them, although without the sense
that he or she has somehow wandered into the Louvre.

A sailing ship, the *Pinta*, adorns the wall at Columbus Circle; a
beaver sits at Astor Place, recalling the baron of fur and real estate,
John Jacob Astor. (During an excellent restoration of the station
during the early 1980s, an effort was made to reproduce the beaver
in certain smaller tiles, but was abandoned because many of those
seeing it were reminded not of the century-long-dead Astor, but the
live rats that caper along many tracks.)

A bucolic scene of a farmhouse and burbling waterway are depicted
in relief at the Canal Street station; these are meant to show the

neighborhood home of Aaron Burr, the traitorous vice president, and the sewer that connected the East River to the Hudson and gave the street its name.

Most of the walls, however, are laid with acre after acre of plain white tile. And hunks of this, over the years, have collapsed from the walls of many stations, pushed out by water leaks, gouged out by vandals or just having dropped out from plain exhaustion. These raw wounds in the walls have been an opportunity for the guerrilla crafts of Tim Main, a twenty-seven-year-old artist.

With a canvas satchel of flat-bladed tools, wire clippers, screwdrivers and other gadgets, Main skulks into stations and fills in missing tiles with his own whimsical mosaics.

Along the western wall of the Broadway 86th Street station, Main's tiles were arranged to resemble a window looking out to New Jersey—which is what a waiting passenger would see, if there were a window. A tile map of Long Island, Manhattan, New Jersey, and the Bronx was captioned NEW ENGLAND BEGINS IN THE BRONX. Just before the trial of Bernhard Goetz, the subway gunman, Main installed a giant portrait of Goetz in a gaping space at a station on 34th Street and Seventh Avenue.

He had sought official permission for his work, but was denied. But the same authorities who neglected the collapsed tiles promptly dispatched workers to remove Main's pieces—and restore the cavity to its state of official decay. "You get into arguments over what is graffiti and what isn't," explained a spokesman for the Transit Authority.

Now, as Tom's train pulls around the sealed City Hall station and into position for the uptown trip, he barely glances at the ancient fancy. He has been through the station hundreds of times. The place where trains wait between terminals is called "the pocket," and most crews can hardly wait to get out of it—no matter how elegant or historical. And Tom can't wait, either, to head back uptown. Rush hour crowds will have eased, and there'll be a little more room for the thing he loves best about being a subway conductor: Tom Thomasevich, On Stage.

With Jim Christie in the passenger seat, Tom McGurl steers his Plymouth Fury away from the transit detective headquarters on Gold Street in downtown Brooklyn.

If ever there was a cop made to investigate token booth stickups, Tom McGurl was the one. He came of age in the early 1970s on the streets of Westchester Square in the Bronx, a tough neighborhood of working-class Italians and Irish. When he started looking for work, McGurl had a chance for jobs as a steamfitter or a transit cop. "Work for the city," said his father. "Construction is seasonal. You'll never get laid off by the city."

Two years later, the city fired 100,000 workers. McGurl, new on the force, was out of work and newly married. He took a job as a token clerk. He sat in the booth, handing out change, taking in the abuse, until at last the city began to rehire its police department. He was an aggressive, hyperactive cop, not afraid to put his nose where it didn't belong. On a grim night in 1988, an undercover police officer was murdered by a drug dealer on the Upper West Side. Moments later, another was slain a few miles north. With the city police department in bedlam, McGurl sped to the scene of the first murder and grabbed a key witness off the street. Within a couple of hours, he had a confession from one man, a picture of the triggerman, and his address in Puerto Rico. Of course, he also got bawled out, but good, by one of his transit supervisors, who noted that McGurl was supposed to be arresting subway criminals not chasing street crime.

For all his brilliance in solving cases, McGurl, tall and dark Irish, impetuous, was well matched by his partner, Jim Christie of Brooklyn. A short, silver-haired Irishman, Christie not only knew how to solve a crime, but how to make the case stick. He was deliberate, careful with his paperwork, a twenty-five-year veteran. They were teamed up first when a gang of school-age hoods ran a robbery ring in the Bronx. Every day, the gang would meet at a South Bronx high school and head for the subway, methodically swarming their way north, ripping off gold jewelry. At the end of the day, the loot was pawned in a gold shop on 149th Street.

Prime Minister Divine was the name of the gang's leader, who had half-baked notions about the Koran, the holy book of Islam. White people were the devil and only 5 percent of the blacks were meant to rule the world, the gang members declared. And they took "righteous" names: in addition to the Prime Minister, there was Black Justice, Supreme Allah, and All Knowledge Is Scientific.

They spent their days ripping off other kids, almost all of them African-American or Hispanic-American.

One of their tricks involved a single-edge razor blade—hidden in the mouth, spat into a hand, then drawn quickly across the neck of a victim. Neither detective could believe the informant who told them about it—until one of the kids they busted demonstrated in front of a video camera.

"That's nothing," said the kid as the two amazed cops watched. "I'm just learning. You should see Prime Minister—he can hold two blades in his mouth."

When slick tricks did not make the day, brute force ruled. They tried to throw a girl off the el at Jackson Avenue. They pointed a gun at a baby's head, saying that they would shoot if the mother did not hurry up with her jewelry.

In the end, two dozen of the gang members pleaded guilty and were sent to state prison.

From the institutional perspective, though, the best work McGurl and Christie did was solving robberies of token booths.

One night, a clerk was discovered dead of a massive heart attack, sprawled on the booth floor with his feet tangled in the base of his stool. Someone pried open the door, stepped over the body and grabbed $1,057 in cash. It was a simple crime of opportunity, the press was told—the clerk had collapsed, a passerby had spotted him on the floor, and had forced the door. GHOUL ROBS DEAD TOKEN CLERK, the *New York Post* headlined. With a plague of organized hoodlums battering and threatening their way into a booth somewhere four or five times a week—and with clerks' anxiety rising almost daily—it was a relief for transit officials to attribute one to fate.

McGurl and Christie weren't so sure, but it wasn't their case. One afternoon, several months later, McGurl was looking over the crime scene photographs and noticed what looked like a broomstick lying atop the body of the fallen clerk.

"What's this?" he asked.

No one knew for sure—just some tool that was in the booth, must have fallen over during the robbery. McGurl looked at the list of evidence vouchered from the scene; no broomstick.

From his stint in the booth, McGurl knew that nothing is thrown out. He went back to the station and struck up a conversation with the clerk.

"Broom?" said the clerk. "I don't think so. That would be in the porter's room."

"You're right," said McGurl. "How about checking the locker?"

The stick was in the booth locker, three months later, but it wasn't meant for sweeping: at the end was an ice chopper that had been sharpened into a spear. Clerks didn't use ice choppers—or spears. There were markings on the handle, Indian symbols of some sort. McGurl took the spear and put it in the trunk of his car.

In time, the stick was tied to a Queens gang that, led by a six-foot-four muscle man dressed in Ninja mask, beat in the windows of booths with an ax. One of the gang members wilted under questioning and admitted the robberies—including the "crime of opportunity."

The clerk was alive, said the gang member, when they roared into the station. When the victim saw the fierce masks, and the giant man smashing the ax against the window, "the guy started getting panicky. . . . He started, you know, getting all fidgety. Then he, like, backed up, leaned against the thing and fell down."

In short, they had scared him to death.

The gang had bashed in the windows at eleven token booths and taken $100,000. They all pleaded guilty and received between ten and twenty years in jail.

Tom McGurl knows his way around token booths. So does Jim Christie.

9:45 A.M., East New York, Brooklyn: Kathy Quiles

The doctor has finished checking her eyes and is making notes on his chart when Kathy Quiles mentions her heartburn.

"I feel a little uncomfortable in my stomach," Kathy Quiles says. The long trip from Rockaway to Brooklyn has brought her back to the doctor she trusts for everything from babies to eyesight.

"Let's have a look," he says, commencing the rituals of poking and probing that pregnant women must endure. After a minute, he says, "You're okay. It's all right. The baby's getting into position. We're right on schedule."

Kathy thanks him. She is relieved, but not ready for the long bus ride down Pitkin back to the train station. Very quietly, bus service in parts of Brooklyn had been cut by a third during the most prosperous decade of the twentieth century; citywide, it had been reduced by 10 percent. This was done with just about no public discussion or debate, for the largest public bus operation in the country was a service for those who could not climb flights of stairs in and out of subway stations, the elderly and handicapped, others who could not abide the subway's violation of personal dignity, particularly women, and hundreds of thousands of people who lived out of the range of the subways. In a nutshell, it was for people who were in some way considered out of luck or out of power.

"Honey," she says to Ramiro, "let's take a cab."

They certainly weren't planning on a yellow cab, the only hack service sanctioned by the city of New York. There probably hadn't been a yellow cab in that part of Brooklyn in twenty years.

The availability of legal taxi service in New York is strictly limited by a 1937 law known as the Haas Act, which allows cabs to cruise the streets for fares only if they have city medallions, which are limited to 11,807 for all five boroughs. As a result, these medallions have become a commodity costing ten times the price of the automobile to which they are affixed, and the taxi industry successfully lobbies the city government to permit no increase in the number of medallions (which would water down the value of the franchise), and to strictly enforce laws against poachers—nonmedallion cabs—circulating on their turf.

That turf does not include poor neighborhoods. Official cab service is entirely limited, as a practical matter, to the central business area of Manhattan, the tonier neighborhoods on its perimeter, and the two airports.

In areas such as East New York, gypsy car services—unlicensed, uninsured, often unclean but numbering 32,000, nearly triple the "legal" quotas and gloriously available—are the basic alternative to the city-run buses, which are being reduced by about 10 percent a year, and the city-franchised cabs, a controlled monopoly that for practical purposes does not serve any part of the city beyond its wealthiest corners.

Kathy and Ramiro grab a gypsy cab out to the train station.

"I don't feel too good," says Kathy.

"We'll be home soon. You can lie down then."

"I don't feel like lying down."

Pregnant women are impossible to please.

At the train station, they had to walk through the gate; all the turnstiles had been jammed.

The token suckers are out.

One morning, Dick Oliver, a correspondent for Fox television in New York, was in a Brooklyn subway station, interviewing a woman about a rapist who was stalking the subway system. The broadcast was going out live. Oliver and the woman were standing in front of the turnstiles.

"Are you taking any special precautions because of the rapist?" Oliver asked the woman. Just then, Oliver heard the frantic voice of his producer in his ear.

"What's that guy doing at the turnstiles?"

Oliver tried to ignore the question and pay attention to what the woman was saying.

"Dick," said the voice in the earphone, "we're picking up a guy over your shoulder, on camera, who seems to have his mouth on the turnstile."

Oliver tried to sneak a look over his shoulder while giving every appearance of paying attention to the woman reciting her survival techniques.

"Forget the rapist," said his earpiece. *"Find out what that guy's doing at the turnstile!"*

As Oliver turned around, the camera zoomed in on the turnstile. Lips locked around the coin slot, the man was sucking a token out of it.

Microphone in hand, Oliver walked over to ask the guy what in hell he was doing. At that moment, a transit policeman pushed past and grabbed the sucker. The bust was made on live television.

The golden age of the token sucker dawned in 1986. It was a grim low in eight decades of money-grubbing tactics by private railroad operators, governments, and passengers.

Starting in 1904, riders on August Belmont, Jr.'s IRT all bought tickets, paying Belmont's nickel fare, and then handed them over to a guard who chopped them in half. But by 1920, even with a billion passengers, Belmont was facing a very 1980s sort of problem: he was carrying an enormous debt, as a result of the acquisition of Manhattan's elevated lines, which were competing with the subways for customers. To end the contest, the IRT had bought the els, borrowing heavily. At the same time, postwar inflation began to erode the company's profits. To save labor costs, Belmont installed turnstiles that could be operated with a nickel. This was considered one of the great technological advances of the decade.

It eliminated the ticket choppers—about a thousand jobs—and helped keep the private companies profitable through the 1920s on a fare that had been set up in 1904. The fare held at a nickel until 1948; then a dime was necessary to operate the turnstile. On July 25, 1953, the fare rose to 15 cents.

Two different coins were beyond the competence of the 1920 turnstiles installed by Belmont and his colleagues. The city then went into business selling 15 cent tokens, an event decried by politicians.

"New York City needs more than a token mayor," said a 1953 campaign button for Robert Wagner, who won the election and oversaw an era of frozen fares—and frozen budgets, leading to deferred maintenance.

The token was a brass coin, imprinted with the logo of the Transit Authority, the size and design of which changed with fare increases. In recent years, there have been about 55 million in circulation, since many riders buy bunches to save time on line.

By 1985, with the fare at 90 cents, the minters of the official token had strong competition.

Around the five boroughs, tool and die shops turned out nearly 5 million slugs, selling for a quarter each, that would operate the turnstiles just as well as the 90 cent tokens then sold by the clerks. In fact, transit workers were collecting 13,000 slugs a day in 1985. The city's automatic counting equipment could not weed out the authentic from the counterfeit so tokens and slugs alike were repackaged in plastic ten-packs, then delivered to the token booths and sold by the clerks.

EXAMINE PACK BEFORE OPENING, warned the plastic bag, because the TA didn't give a refund on slugs. So the passengers just stuck them right back into the turnstiles.

When the fare went to a dollar in 1986, transit officials worried their losses would climb.

They returned to an idea that had been developed three years earlier, then shelved. A veteran transit worker named Joseph Spencer had had a brainstorm. He designed a new token, known as the "bull's-eye," because it had a shiny aluminum core surrounded by brass. He also devised a new gadget for the inside of the turnstile that would recognize—and reject—slugs.

Spencer's idea worked. The new tokens, manufactured by the Roger Williams mint of Attleboro, Massachusetts, were much harder to counterfeit. By 1989, the TA's take was a mere 400 slugs a day, a 97 percent decrease since 1985.

In the meantime, the (cynical) principle that all reform results in grotesque, unintended consequences was applied to the newly tooled turnstile. The gadget devised by the mechanic was, in fact, excellent at detecting slugs. But the gadget made the turnstile vulnerable to being jammed, very easily, with a piece of paper.

In a jammed turnstile, the new token, instead of sliding to the coin-return slot, was suspended in the neck of the turnstile. The rider couldn't get in. Invariably, the clerk would end up waving the customer through the gate. And just as soon as the rider was out of sight—sometimes even before—the token sucker would emerge from the shadows to draw out the $1 prize, which could be sold to people waiting on line, or used in many New York stores as currency.

Token sucking was a hustle so low tech and disgusting that even the transit officials found it impossible to believe, much less figure out how to beat.

One clerk filled the slots with hot pepper.

The outraged sucker howled in pain. Then he found a pail of water and doused the slots—and, for good measure, the token booth before he went back to slurping dollar tokens.

The scavengers and bottom feeders sucking tokens from turnstiles were shadows thrown on cave walls by the great bonfire of the New York economy in the 1980s, when hundreds of thousands of new jobs were created in an economic boom driven by Wall Street—and when the last embers of the city's industrial life flickered and died.

In the 1980s, jobs boomed in New York for the office-skilled. Poverty hardened. There were more drug fiends, drunks, mentally ill, and people generally scraping to stay alive than ever before. Young black and Hispanic males were "not simply out of the mainstream—they [were] far from even the eddies," said Samuel Ehrenhalt, a federal labor official based in New York.

The decline of the city's school system has been blamed for some of this; so has the country's most generous welfare menu, in which young people were three or four generations removed from the last working parent.

In that time, the nature of the city's economy had changed utterly, and it had little to do with welfare or education. New York once could absorb a million minimally educated people into its manufacturing enterprises; now those jobs had all but vanished, just as the great movement of southern blacks into the city was taking place.

Now the great open floors of the Ansonia Clock Factory in Park Slope, where hundreds of people had been employed, have been cut into stylish co-operative apartments where, among many, David Gunn lives. The swarming, swaggering Brooklyn docks, where gangsters ruled and thousands toiled, is now an amphitheater of echoes, alive only in occasional screenings of *On the Waterfront*.

A century and a half ago, the city's splendid harbor was its fortune. Maritime trades grew and prospered; bankers followed. Railroads arrived, linking the city to the rest of the country, and immigrants worked cheap and hard, creating the United States' greatest manufacturing center.

Its decline began in the 1950s, starting with Manhattan real estate prices that gnawed at the large spreads of space enjoyed in many businesses. The subway was beginning a slow slide, as its former passengers drove, on newly built roads paid for by the federal government, to newly built suburban homes, bought with low-interest mortgages guaranteed by the government.

Manhattan real estate became more and more valuable. Without a reliable subway to move quickly into the far reaches of the Bronx, Brooklyn, and Queens, land around the business core of the city jumped in price. Manufacturers moved from one loft to another, each time fleeing higher rents, each time settling for less space until finally these livelihoods were whittled out of existence. In the execution of the city's manufacturing base, the subway was a silent conspirator with other large forces.

"Once, the garment industry, teeming with hundreds of hand trucks, and scores of other factories scattered throughout the city employed unskilled teenagers or new entrants to the labor market, who at least got the working experience that enabled them to move up," Saul Friedman wrote in *New York Newsday* in 1986.

Between 1950 and 1989, manufacturing jobs in New York had gone from 1,038,900 to 354,000—a 66 percent decline, as industry moved overseas, to lands where people would work for next to nothing. And even in the booming sector of nonmanufacturing jobs, there was decline in opportunity for the minimally skilled, as Friedman noted:

> Once, young workers were employed by banks to literally clip the coupons on the bonds held by the rich. Others spent their days as file clerks, or stamping checks as they cleared through the bank. Still others were messengers delivering paper work, mail and memos among departments in, say, banks. Now, filing and the transfers of money and records are done almost wholly by computer. A decade ago, a woman fresh out of high school . . . could find a job as one of the telephone company's 14,000 operators in New York, and American Telephone and Telegraph made a special effort to hire and train minority

workers. Now, however, computers have replaced all but about 2,000 operators.

Just about 44 percent of the population of the city was employed in 1989—a sign that most of the people of the city were dependent on someone else for their daily bread.

If the city continued losing jobs at the same rate during the 1980s and '90s as it had for most of the '70s, no one would be working in Manhattan by the end of the century. But New York experienced the greatest job boom in its history between 1978 and 1989, with 453,000 new jobs involved in nebulous but profitable businesses categorized as "financial and business services."

The city continued to stand. But the new jobs seemed to lack the emotional and economic stability of the manufacturing era. As one economist noted: "It's hard to build an economy based on taking in each other's laundry."

Still, the resurgence of Manhattan made the rebuilding of the subways an economic necessity: the cost to business of delayed riders was estimated in 1981 between $166 and $330 million.

"This is almost 40 percent of the size of the city income tax revenues and is borne only by subway riders," reported the Federal Reserve Bank of New York, which noted that that meant the demand for a close-to-the-center home was rising. "Advertisements in the *New York Times* specifying Manhattan residence as a requirement for employment have already begun to appear."

One other development of the second half of the twentieth century changed the city, the subways, and the people occupying both: the GI Bill made college commonplace. White-collar was the career of choice. A "job" working with your hands—is that what you went to college for?

With the increasing transit delays of the late '70s and early '80s grew a seething hostility between many subway riders and subway workers, who were the only government representatives at hand during a crisis. But the anger seemed to go beyond the frustration with the system; what existed was a gulf between the transit workers and their passengers, most of whom had little interest in how things worked, or why they didn't, and who had little empathy for people doing manual labor.

There was a time, David Gunn noted, when

> you had hundreds of thousands of people working in the
> kind of business we're in. . . . In this service economy,
> you have people who are really far removed from the kinds
> of things we do at, say, our 207th Street overhaul shop. In
> my travels around, the guy who looks like he might work
> for us—the guy going to work in his denims with his lunch
> bucket—he tends to be a lot more understanding of the
> system. Then you get the people on the East Side who
> say, "I don't understand how you can put a train in service
> that you *know* is going to break down." Yeah, right. Or
> you have people who think our token clerks ought to treat
> them like they're in Bloomingdale's.

But in the manufacturing economy, "you had jobs that gave people
status," said Gunn. "Tradesmen can develop a real sense of pride in
what they do. A lot of the service industry type of jobs, you can't get
the personal pride in the work. Take people who are good at
welding—they can get a stamp of pride in what they do."

10 A.M.
May 12

A PRIVATE SUBWAY, A MISSING PLAQUE

As the morning rush hour eases, trains are brought into lay-up yards all around the city. On lower Broadway, R trains are parked in a basement area beneath the City Hall station. They sit in a dank solitude where a genius wind once blew.

The first New York subway was built here. It was a spectacular salon, built in secret under the bulbous nose of the city's greatest scoundrel. After the Civil War, New York was settled only as far north as 42nd Street. Jammed into this narrow, four-mile strip of island were 700,000 people. But moving farther away from lower Manhattan was out of the question: it took an hour to journey just from downtown to the suburban rail terminals at 30th Street.

Everyone traveled by omnibus, horse-drawn coaches that choked the cobblestone streets. The only control over this braying, snorting traffic was exercised by William Marcy Tweed, the legendary political boss. He awarded omnibus franchises and counted the bribes. While London and other large cities were opening underground trolleys and railroads, Tweed was killing *off underground competition to his franchisees in New York.*

Not all the opposition to an underground was from crooks. In many quarters there were worries that the subways would be too filthy. Everyone would suffocate. The streets would collapse.

Enter Alfred Ely Beach.

Beach was a nineteenth-century Leonardo da Vinci: he devised the first useful typewriter, then a Braille typewriter, and held dozens of other patents. He was a lawyer who counseled other inventors—and often backed them financially. Thomas Edison brought his talking machine to Beach's office. In his spare time, Beach edited the daily New York Sun *and founded* Scientific American.

From his office in downtown Manhattan, Beach watched the wretched congestion and dreamed of pneumatic tubes. He envisioned passengers riding in a little pellet of a car that would be shot through tubes by the wind of giant fans. When the train reached the tube's end, the fans would be reversed and suck the pellet back.

Rather than pay off Tweed, Beach decided to build his line without telling City Hall. In 1868, he rented the basement of Devlin's Clothing Store at the corner of Broadway and Murray Street, and sent gangs of men to dig in its basement. His twenty-one-year-old son, Fred Beach, was the foreman.

Worried about cave-ins, Beach invented a tunnel shield that became an industry standard. By day, they dug and burrowed, using a tunnel gouger also invented by Beach. At night, they wheeled the dirt out of the store and hauled it away. They worked directly across Broadway from City Hall and the infamous Tweed Courthouse. But for two years, as the Tweed gang went about its daily plunder, its horses clattering over the moles, no one discovered them.

When the 312-foot tunnel was finished, Beach outfitted nearly a third of it as the waiting room. This would not be the much-feared tunnel of dankness: Beach wanted a public relations blaze that would kindle enthusiasm for expanding his tubes all over town, as far north as Central Park. Frescoes were painted onto the walls of the waiting room. A fountain was delivered one night. So were a fish tank, zircon lamps, Greek statuary, even a baby grand piano. The car itself was a cylindrical tube, 9 feet in diameter, finely upholstered and seating 22 passengers. The tunnel opened in February 1870.

It was the wonder of New York. In the first year, 400,000 people hurried to pay 25 cents to sit on this train that rode the wind. The revenue was turned over to charities by Beach, who was acclaimed as a genius

He lived to see Tweed die in prison. But his beloved pneumatic tube scheme was becalmed by other political forces and a national financial crash. After he surrendered his dreams, Beach rented the tube as a wine cellar, then as a target shooting gallery, and finally sealed it. He retired from the inventing game and set up an institute in Savannah to educate freed slaves. He died in obscurity in 1896.

In 1912, forty years after the Beach tunnel closed, workers digging a stop near City Hall for the new BMT lines broke through a brick wall. They gazed at the statuary, the frescoes, the ruined remains of an Aladdin's Cave.

Today, the scene of Beach's triumph has been subsumed into the lower level of the City Hall station of the BMT line. Most of it is now a lay-up area for trains with nowhere else to go, and as such, was the leading studio for graffiti writers in the 1970s—people once again thumbing their noses at the government just upstairs.

A plaque once marked the site of Beach's tunnel, but it is long gone.

10:05 A.M., East New York, Brooklyn: Joe Caracciolo

For some reason, this idea of a manhole cover was bothering Joe Caracciolo. In all his years working for transit, he had never heard of manhole covers on a platform—not until someone called one in as missing. Of course, he'd sent a crew out right away. His guys, the ornamental ironworkers crew, he regarded as the best. They would find the hole and they'd cover it, whatever it took, cut a plate right there with the tools on the truck. You couldn't have people falling down a manhole.

But what manhole? He tried to picture the station—Beach and 90th Street in the Rockaways. A regular elevated station. Why a manhole?

By ten o'clock, things had gotten quiet in the locker room, and Joe felt a little itchy. Let me go see what this manhole is about, he decided. Down the block, he grabbed the A train. That took him out to the Broad Channel station, right on Jamaica Bay, and he stood on the platform waiting for the C to arrive. A little peninsula, a quarter mile wide, and two trains—one to the south, one to the north. Nothing easy about getting to Rockaway.

Funny how a little thing like a manhole could get under his skin. That's how life had worked out for him.

In the late 1960s, the Western Electric Company, which had put bread on the Caracciolo table for several decades, announced that it was closing a plant on Houston Street in Manhattan and moving to Tucson, Arizona. For the same money out west, the company would get a plant three times the size, with parking for all its workers.

In the Bensonhurst neighborhood of Brooklyn, this was discussed earnestly. Mama Caracciolo decided the family would stay in New York, so Joe's father took a civil service test to qualify as a subway car mechanic at the Transit Authority and passed.

Just home from the navy was Joe, whose idea of being busy was to grow a ponytail. One day, Papa handed him a transit job application and told him to go take the test or don't come home.

The next morning, Joe stood in the BMT station, waiting for the buzzer that would sound to show the arriving train:

NEXT TRAIN CONEY ISLAND.

If I go that way, he thought, I'll go to the beach and have a dynamite time.

NEXT TRAIN MANHATTAN.

But if I don't go to the city, my father will break my neck.

Joe chose the straight line in his neck and took the train to Manhattan. The test had five parts: plumbing, carpentry, masonry, tinsmith, and ironwork. He knew plumbing, a little anyway, from his father, who fixed their old house. He passed all five parts of the test and was assigned to a job as an ironworker helper.

"What ironworker?" he asked. "I'm a plumber."

"You're a helper," he was told. "You're supposed to be able to do all the trades. Besides, we're doing you a favor."

He could be a plumber if he wanted to travel to 125th Street and Broadway, a long ride from Bensonhurst. Or he could be an ironworker a couple of miles away in Brooklyn.

Caracciolo learned fast. An ironworker was the Atlas of the subway. He held aloft the tracks and the trains and all the millions of lives standing on them. He patched and rebraced the hundred-year-old elevated bridges that carried the trains above the streets of the Bronx, Brooklyn, and Queens. He learned how to carry the welder's torch, where to point and how to fire it, at just the right distance, to keep the sparks from popping off the metal.

"Go ask people how to do a job in transit," says Joe, "and the first words out of their mouths—well, we get the ironworkers to hang a scaffold. Any trade, carpenters, masons. First, get the ironworkers."

He learned all this at the feet of men who had spent twenty and thirty years prowling through the transit system. In private industry, Joe reckoned, there would never be this kind of training. No way is a guy fifty-five years old going to hand his job over to a kid out of the navy. In civil service, the old guys were protected by their seniority. The helper was No. 350 on a list, the ironworker was maybe No. 10. "He'll show you anything you want to learn," said Joe. "You can't hurt him."

After the old guys gave him his trade, he took the exam for foreman and became their boss.

Ironworkers could do anything. One day, an old water main broke out in Brooklyn. The torrents swirled down Jamaica Avenue around the columns of the el, ripping through the asphalt, tearing deeper and deeper. Overhead, a train rolled along and the motorman felt his stomach bumping around his throat. "It's like a roller coaster out here," he radioed to the Command Center.

A column had been undermined, and part of the el had sunk 18 inches. The ironworkers were called.

"First thing, we put shoring up," Joe remembered. "Twelve-by-twelve timbers.

> And we fixed all the cracks that happened while we were putting the shoring up. A couple of gangs fixing the cracks, changing their connecting angles. One gang with the shoring. As we shored it up, we got underneath the column with hydraulic jacks.
>
> Jacked it up, shored it up. Jacked it up, shored it up. Jacked it up to the right height. We had an engineer looking through the surveyor—whatever that is called. He said, it's perfect, shore it up. We had the masons pour the concrete foundation. We jacked it up higher to bring it back down onto the bolts. Brought the column back down on the bolts, put the nuts on, bolted it up, closed up the street, put the fender on, it was perfect. It's still like that now, three years later.

Less than twenty-four hours after the hundred-year-old el had sunk a foot and a half, trains were running on top of it again.

His seniority rights let Joe pick another job besides the heavy ironwork. He chose ornamental gang—fixing staircases, garage doors, the gates in the station. Jobs large and small, with a lot of variety. A manhole cover, it was kind of mundane. But Joe had never seen one on a platform. You couldn't pick up an el every day of the week.

Now, where is the C train?

10:15 A.M., East New York, Brooklyn: Two Teenagers

Also wondering about that C train are two young women, Muria Acevedo and Marisol Velez, who have just finished a successful expedition to a Brooklyn shopping mall. The girls are due to graduate from high school in a few days and have gone out for new clothes. Muria found a very hot pair of white slacks. There was going to be a party, and she had to have new pants. When the C arrived, they get on the next to last car and find seats. Mission accomplished.

10:18 A.M., Aboard the No. 6, Approaching 14th Street: Tom Thomasevich

"Thank you very much, ladies and gentlemen," says conductor Tom Thomasevich, in the No. 6 train's version of lounge lizard pitter-patter. "When the King died, a large percentage of rock and roll died with him."

The train is now swinging back for the uptown run. There had been a brief stop at Brooklyn Bridge, barely time to make the crew room and relieve himself. (The company was paying him good money today to skip lunch, a practice universally condemned by physiologists specializing in human performance, who say a full shift without a break cuts alertness and causes mistakes. But "no lunches" was embraced by the TA's efficiency experts. It's much cheaper to pay 100 train crews a half hour overtime to skip lunch, at 1.5 times the normal salary, than to hire additional workers and pay them salary plus benefits, which approximately doubles the hourly cost.)

In any event, Tom is now about to land at 14th Street again, this time bound for midtown, the Upper East Side, Harlem, and then the Bronx.

As the train screeches into the station, he pushes back into his cab to watch the platform and make the announcements. He smiles and waves as the riders give him big grins. "You have a nice day now, and a good weekend," he advises.

An express arrives across the platform, but instead of the hasty exodus to catch the speedier ride, most of the passengers in Tom's car stay put.

"I'm gonna stay on the local," Gary Geller announces to no one in particular, eyeing the express. "This guy's great. He's the next Elvis."

Now the train is leaving the station, and once it has entered the tunnel, the conductor's door opens with its gentle *click*. Those who have just boarded glance at the conductor, then go back to their papers or daydreams. The people who rode from downtown lean forward, smiling, waiting for his next move.

Tom stands sideways at the head of the aisle, one foot forward, his head bobbing back and forth to the beat of a drum on a jukebox back in Bensonhurst, where he was a kid when the King reigned.

> *You ain't nothing but a hound dog,*
> *Crying all the time!*

The newcomers are startled, then seeing the pure joy on the face of people who know the routine, giggle along.

"I wouldn't have bought the newspaper if I'd known he was on the train," says Peter Marti.

"Right? Save twenty-five cents," says Rosie Morales. "At least he don't walk around with a can."

"It's nice to see someone entertain without their hand out," agrees Geller.

Here are three strangers, all having dropped their newspapers— the approximate equivalent of a woman in a Muslim country peeling naked on Main Street. The newspaper is the chador of the subway car, the perfect psychic veil, armor against unwanted intimacy. No one is fully dressed in the subway without something to read. The *New York Daily News*, the city's first tabloid, was founded in 1919, a year after the subways first carried more than a billion riders. It was a newspaper that could be handled down under without the fuss of the full-sized broadsheets. (By 1991, three of the city's four surviving daily papers were tabloids.) Paperbacks, which can be held in one hand, are far and away more popular in the subways than hardbacks. And the invention in 1979 of the Walkman tape player by Sony was a major advance in fortification of the soul, which is ever in danger of being rubbed raw on the train. How can anyone push an unwanted stare on a person whose head is full of music and whose face is buried in a newspaper?

But five seconds of live music from Tom Thomasevich had stripped them bare.

> *. . . And you ain't no friend of mine.*
> *When they said you was high class,*
> *Well, that was just a lie . . .*

"I think I'm going to have my family come down just to see him perform," says Hilda Rivera.

Twenty-third Street has come, and people leave reluctantly, smiling. "Takes me home with a good attitude," says Marti.

Tom leans through the window, waving people off, with little of the caution exercised by most conductors. Over the years, the conductor has become a fulcrum where the neglect of subway upkeep by the city's governors met the anxieties of the riders who had to suffer with the breakdowns and grotesque conditions created by the official indifference.

The only representative of the state within reach was the conductor, who could look forward to snarls and gobs of spit. Slaps from teenagers who thought it was a goof to whack the dude with his head out the window as the train pulled out. From the occasional psychotic, the slash of a razor. Tom faced these risks, too, but he tamed at least one car full of riders and made it a point to look the other people in the eye as they passed him. *Human being here*, he was saying. *Human being here.*

Inside the tunnel, he steps out of his cab.

Again, the fingers snap a moment, finding a beat:

> *The warden threw a party in the county jail.*
> *The prison band was there and they began to wail.*
> *The band was jumpin' and the joint began to swing.*
> *You should of heard those knocked-out jailbirds sing.*
> *Let's rock! Let's rock!*

And everybody in the whole cell block is a-dancin' to "The 6 Train Rock."

10:19 A.M., Aboard the C Train: Kathy Quiles

"I am getting pains," Kathy says.

"Let's get off at Euclid," says Ramiro.

"I don't want to go to Euclid. I don't want to go to Woodhull."

Woodhull Hospital, where their son Jonathan had been born, was an unpleasant memory to Kathy. She'd liked the hospital in Rockaway, St. John's, where their last baby, Sabrina, had been born.

"Have it your way, honey, whatever you say. We'll go back to Queens."

"They're not too bad."

They sit in the last car of a train with approximately 2,700,000 miles on it, after twenty-seven years of running night and day, 100,000 miles a year. It has a recent coat of paint on it, a kind of deep red.

10:20 A.M., 181st Street, Manhattan: Anna Lans

"What do we have?" said Christie as they drove uptown.

"A gun and knife caper," said McGurl.

"Gun *and* knife?" Christie said. Why bother with a knife when you had a gun?

In the station, they surveyed the massing of transit workers and picked out the lieutenant who had called them. They wanted to know about this cop who was supposed to be in the station.

"I kinda believe the kid," said the lieutenant.

"All right, we'll try talking to him," said Christie.

Callahan has little to say. "Everyone is trying to railroad me on this thing," he says disgustedly.

"Listen," says McGurl, "I'm not here to hurt you. If you weren't here, I won't hurt you—but if you were, we'll help you. This kind of thing follows you for the rest of your career unless we get it cleared up right now. Think about it."

With that, McGurl walks over to the booth and goes inside with Christie. Anna repeats her story: the male black, male Hispanic. Medium height, medium build. While Christie speaks with her, McGurl looks over the booth sign-in sheet. The porter had logged his name in at 6:10—the same moment the robbery was underway.

They step outside. "She's describing half the city," says Christie.

"Not even a token on the floor," says McGurl. "The cleanest booth I was ever in."

"We gotta bring her down to the district," says Christie. "Let me talk to the supervisor."

This is a very delicate matter. Transit workers who are robbed almost invariably are sent to a clinic, and then home sick for a period to recuperate from the shock. Instead, Christie wants to bring her to the district police station. He motions to the supervisor and steps away from the workers in the booth.

"These clerks are getting knocked over left and right," Christie says sympathetically. "This is getting terrible. You know, we need to get a little more from her, so we're going to bring her down to District Three"—a police station a few stops down the line.

"No, she's going to the clinic—she needs medical attention," says the supervisor.

"We'll take her to the hospital ourselves, we just want to get her settled down and thinking a little clearer—get a better description," says Christie.

"The procedure calls for the clerk to go to the clinic, if she is in need of medical attention," says the supervisor.

"We don't want anyone getting hurt by these guys," says Christie. "Just ten or fifteen minutes more. We'll get her settled down, get her something to eat."

While this chat was underway, McGurl had wandered to the solar can, which is the subway system's name for a trash receptacle. He didn't have to root around: on top of the heap were stacks of white boxes, ripped apart. He snorted. Empty token boxes. This supposed robber had taken the time to tear open the boxes *and* throw them in the trash?

"McGurl."

Tom turns around. The kid, Callahan, is standing behind him.

"I been here since four-thirty, like I was supposed to be," he says.

"I believe you," says McGurl. "I think she took the money. But how can we prove you were here the whole time?"

Callahan reaches into his shirt pocket and fishes out a telephone number.

"Call this girl, she'll tell you," says the rookie. "I was sitting up the ramp, my ass up against the railing to take the weight off my feet. This girl came by and we got talking. She gave me her number. Go ahead and call her up. That's her office number, she's there now. She saw me right here."

McGurl's gut told him the young cop was telling the truth. But how could anyone hit a token booth with a cop in the station?

"I'm not calling her," says McGurl. "I know what she's gonna tell me. Show me where you were standing."

There are two ways out of the station: one is by the elevator up to Fort Washington Avenue. The other is along a ramp, which slants up toward an exit on Bennett Avenue. This, Callahan says, is where he parked himself before dawn.

"Stand here a minute," says McGurl. "Don't move."

He walks back to the booth and stares up the Bennett Avenue ramp. He can't see Callahan. That means whoever had robbed the booth didn't know the cop was there, either.

10:45 A.M., Over Jamaica Bay: Kathy Quiles

Joe Caracciolo heard the whoosh of air. Sounded like the train had "dumped"—lost air pressure in the brake line. The train, of course, had stopped. That was the genius of a fail-safe system. He looked down at the water of Jamaica Bay for a couple of minutes, then decided to make himself known to the crew. For what, he didn't know. He didn't carry tools—that was for the guys in the truck to worry about. Hell, he didn't even carry a safety vest. But he knew how to handle himself on a structure.

He was in the middle of the train and worked his way toward the front car. It was a long freaking walk. The motorman was standing outside the cab.

"What happened?"

"I think we hit something in the back—leastways, it sounded like it came from the back," said the motorman, Robert Jermolowitz. "I think we dumped all the air out of the lines."

Then Jermolowitz headed toward the rear end of the train. Joe trailed him. A train is two city blocks long.

A short blast of compressed air, like a punch to an ungirded stomach that knocks out the wind, is the sound of a train losing its brake pressure.

It is immediately followed by another sound of air escaping, from the lips of passengers savvy to the sounds of an ill train.

"Tsssk," Marisol Velez says disgustedly.

"Pssssss," sighs Muria Acevedo.

"This is the 10:09 C out of One Four Five to Command Center."

"This is Command Center."

"None of the brake valves were pulled, but I have a blow of air coming out of the south motor."

"All right, we'll get an RCI on the road."

The RCIs were Road Car Inspectors, roving mechanical trouble-shooters who could perform on-the-spot repairs to stuck trains. In the spring of 1989, they were hard to come by: their ranks had been depleted, and the savings in salaries used to pay for more graffiti cleaners. It took longer to get one when he was needed.

"I don't know about that RCI. We have a sick passenger on the train. She's pregnant. Looks like she is in labor."

"What is she in?"

"Labor. I mean, that's how it looks. We need medical help."

"What car is she in?"

"She's in the last car."

"And you're getting the blow of air from the south motor?"

"That's right."

"Stand by."

In the Command Center, the dispatcher put down his headphones and spoke to the desk superintendent.

The damaged part of the train was keeping the rest of the train from moving. Just as a single subway car could move the entire train, so a single brake could stop it.

They could have uncoupled Kathy's car and driven it to the next station—except it was the last car and the only direction it could go was backward, against traffic. That was extremely dangerous and had to be done very slowly.

The other choice was to electronically disengage the damaged area of the train and use the other cars to push it into the next station. This also was a risky maneuver, since the motorman would not be in the front car—where the damage was—but in one of the middle cars. He couldn't see the traffic ahead. The conductor would have to ride in the front car as the lookout.

"Command Center to 10:09 C."

"This is the 10:09 C."

"We want you to sectionalize the train and operate from the good section. Have the conductor establish communications and flag for you. We'll have EMS respond to Beach 90th Street."

"Thank you."

"Good luck."

10:50 A.M., Coney Island Yard, Brooklyn: David Gunn

The backstage and wing areas of the Metropolitan Opera House are three times larger than the stage itself, and at least as interesting as most of the productions.

Backstage for the New York subways is located at the Coney Island yard in Brooklyn. Here, the visitor discovers that subway cars actually come apart in two pieces—the wagon, the compartment where the passengers sit, lifted as if it were a toy by huge cranes moving on tracks across the ceiling, and the truck, consisting of engine and wheels, that sits beneath the wagon and generally never leaves the ground.

In the yard, the trucks are moved along tracks into special chemical baths, where the grime is blasted away, down to the bare metal. Then a liquid of metal particles is applied so that a huge magnet can search for hairline cracks.

In the wheel shop, the flanges are inspected when they are worn to 2.5 inches. The flange is the groove on the wheel that sits on the track. Wheels start out with 4-inch flanges; after 320,000 miles, roughly eight years in the subway, 1.5 inches of the flange has been eaten away. If the flange wears too low, the wheel won't stay on the track when the load shifts as a train crosses a switch or goes around a curve.

All this requires that the wheels be popped off their axles, trued in a milling machine, and then pushed back onto the axles—with 85 tons of pressure.

Even though this giant garage is well backstage and far from the public eye, its floors are grease free. The stage manager, David Gunn, insists on it.

Today, Gunn is sizing up his Coney Island operation the way a bettor anxiously eyes a horse in the paddock after he's put down a big bet.

In 1926, with the subway system entering adolescence, New York City opened the world's largest maintenance and storage yards for trains atop 70 acres of swamp near Coney Island. The place has been sinking ever since.

Through all the years, half the city's subway cars have been repaired in this wobbling facility. Everything on a subway car, from the wires in the air-conditioning thermostat, to the flanges that keep the wheels on the tracks, can be taken care of here—at least in theory. No matter how many things are broken, most subway cars can be patched together—at least so they can get out of the shop and back onto the road.

The place not only sat on a swamp, its day-to-day business was carried out in tropical torpor. In 1984, when Gunn arrived in New York to run the subways, there were 1,100 people working in the Coney Island yard; of them, exactly one reported to a nonunion boss.

The TA was taking twice the time of outside vendors to perform an overhaul.

"What about the cars we are rebuilding?" asked MTA chairman Robert Kiley in a speech he gave in February 1984. "Dave and I saw trucks—which are the undercarriages of the subway cars—that had been laboriously stripped down and were being rebuilt with the same old nuts and bolts and component parts that had just been taken out. Which is about the same as subjecting yourself to the trauma and expense of a heart transplant only to wake up and discover that the doctor put your old, damaged heart back in place."

Even as the city and state had come to realize that it was time to spend money on the subways, little had been done to build a management that could be held accountable for how it did anything. The billions acquired in 1981 for rebuilding the system stood every chance of being sucked into a bureaucratic wind tunnel and never seen again: a replay of the previous generation's efforts to build new lines.

But Gunn had a reform blueprint, and Kiley was able to sell it to the legislature. By 1985, they had laws in their pockets that exempted 1,200 new positions from union jurisdiction. Each of those people was responsible to the senior management of the subway, up the chain of command to Gunn. In time, the TA grew to 2,500 managers, 10 to 15 percent higher than private sector companies, and 7 percent greater than transit systems in Chicago, Los Angeles, and Philadelphia, a TA consultant found.

And though the public still lacked any way of demanding genuine accountability for subway operations—short of the governor tossing out Kiley, which was unlikely without full-scale riots in the tunnels— there was some internal control over the bureaucracy with the creation of the new managers. This was muted by the layers of people— for some positions, ten deep—that separated the man at the top from his executives.

Today, Gunn has twenty-five managers running the Coney Island shop. He often cited it as a great success, but within the bureaucracy, it was well known that the shop remained a disaster. A class of people known as professional managers had come to Coney Island—most of them from Pan American, the airline company—to run the operation. That meant they knew nothing about trains, and they proved it. The subway cars repaired under their supervision were the worst performing in the system. They had trouble putting enough cars on the road to meet the service requirements for the morning and evening rush hours. And on a major overhaul project they had just completed, they were a year behind schedule and nearly 40 percent over budget. Eventually, and reluctantly, the Pan Am group were rousted from their management jobs and told to hide somewhere else in the transit system.

Coney Island remains for David Gunn ground zero of his plans to overhaul the subway system—both physically and spiritually. Kiley had publicly—and mistakenly—boasted of the overhaul work done there since he and Gunn had taken over. Here, Gunn wanted to overhaul 280 lemons, a line of cars known as the R-44. Their purchase in the early 1970s was the single worst thing ever done to the subway system.

The car was famed as the Corvair of the New York subways. More than a few people thought Gunn was crazy to even consider rebuilding them—and especially to have transit workers do the job. The R-44 was the misbegotten birth of another era.

In 1970, the aerospace industry was in one of its periodic crises. Designers and engineers were fleeing the business. Many of them moved into a young federal agency called the Urban Mass Transit Administration (UMTA).

The country was just then awakening to the reality that over four decades the rail networks had crumbled for lack of investment. (During those years, federal subsidies had nurtured the automobile age, including the construction of the interstate highway system at a cost of $140 billion.) In this smog-filled environment, the Clean Air Act was passed. To provide some balance to the highway system subsidies, UMTA was given money to distribute as grants for mass transit projects in crowded old cities that had nowhere to put interstates—and had watched their middle-class citizens pack up and move to the easy-driving suburbs.

UMTA had money—big money, it seemed—for a new generation of subway cars. And its experts from the aerospace industry had plenty of ideas on how they would be built. Not surprisingly, key design concepts for the new cars were strikingly similar to the advances made in aviation. Many of the systems then being built, or on the drawing boards—in Atlanta, Washington, San Francisco—were using technological advances to reduce the need for manpower, which is by far the biggest day-to-day expense of mass transit. In New York, close to 80 percent of the budget goes to labor. That was the first important element of the design: automation.

The second had to do with age. The New York subway system and others like it, such as Chicago's and Boston's, were getting older. The weight of the car, especially on the creaking, elevated structures, was a worry; the els just weren't as predictable, from an engineering perspective, as they had been when they were built in the nineteenth and early twentieth centuries.

One of the great advances in aviation came when aircraft were strengthened but not made proportionally any heavier than they were in the days of the Curtis Jenny, when an airplane's skin consisted of shellacked Irish linen stretched over a skeleton.

The modern jet plane applies a property familiar to anyone who has ever noticed the strength of a soda can: one literally can stand on it. But the same mass of aluminum, flattened into a sheet of foil, is unable to support its own weight. Rolled into a cylinder, that sheet of aluminum develops enormous strength. Thus, the skin of the jet is an important structural member of its body. Why not apply this idea in designing a subway car? The lighter cars would reduce the stress on the old els, and could run on less electricity.

Despite its allure, the design theory was not sound, even on paper. It did not take into account the different natures of the stresses on aircraft and subway cars. About 90 percent of the structural load carried by a jet occurs during the massive thrust and braking of takeoff and landing. The rest of a jet's life is spent in the air.

A subway car, on the other hand, is subject to more or less continuous stresses of a lower order. The new, thinner metal was not stiff enough to resist the constant flexing a subway car endures, as its passenger load rises and falls, and the train moves up and down hills. This causes constant fatigue, which shows itself as spidery veins in the structural supports.

Yet there was hunger for newer, better cars to prove that the city could save its subways. The rest of the world-class cities were installing shiny new trains. New York's were drab and old; the basic train technology had changed little over the years, with most advances being made incrementally and in areas that had scant impact on the rider's comfort.

On a hot July day in 1969, a dramatic change was announced at City Hall, when a prototype of the R-44 was presented. A sleek, shiny car was posed for pictures. "We believe," MTA chairman William Ronan said, "that the new design developed at the instigation of the Metropolitan Transportation Authority is the greatest advance made in subway cars for New York City in more than sixty years."

Ever since, the people of New York have stood on the shards of great promises made that day. It was a jet built for a place with no sky and it never flew.

Fully automated, the R-44s would require no train crew. "Speeds of 70 miles an hour are expected to be possible on sections of the rapid transit system that are to be built within the next ten years," the MTA announced. "These will include the new Second Avenue subway and other additions to the system in the Bronx, Queens, and Brooklyn."

The best insulation known to man—Teflon—would protect the wires. An ingenious brake system would be the safest ever installed. Longer than the standard 60-foot car by one quarter, the 75-foot cars could carry 25 percent more passengers but would require less maintenance, because now eight cars could carry the same load as ten. Thus, they would be more reliable and cost less to maintain. Best of all, they would be lighter, which meant that they needed less energy to move, and they'd be easier loads on the tired old els that carried many of them. Then reality set in.

The Second Avenue subway wasn't built, so neither was the automated track needed for an automated train. The automation didn't exist in New York in 1970, doesn't exist now, and won't until at least the twenty-first century—long after the car's life expectancy has passed. This was "like buying automobiles for a community without roads," warned a special report from the city council.

Most of the early alarms about the new cars were raised by Stephen Dobrow, president of the Committee for Better Transit, who orchestrated the city council outcry. Dobrow, a professor of electrical engineering, did a simple calculation and predicted, correctly, that the longer trains would slow down the commute. Not when they were moving, but when they were standing in the station.

Yes, each car was 25 percent longer and held more people, Dobrow noted—but the new trains had fewer doors than the old, and so created delays at the stations as throngs pressed to get in and then out. Fifth-grade arithmetic showed the problem:

OLD CARS
10 cars × 60 feet = 600 feet

10 cars × 4 doors = 40 doors

NEW R-44S
8 cars × 75 feet = 600 feet

8 cars × 4 doors = 32 doors

There were 20 percent fewer doors for the same number of commuters. When citizens' advocates such as Dobrow complained, they were ignored by Chairman Ronan. (The advocates then dubbed the MTA the Holy Ronan Empire; the chairman retaliated by initiating a criminal prosecution against the group for using, without permission, an MTA logo in a spoof publication. The case was dismissed.)

Meanwhile, the automation that would have sent the trains whistling along without a motorman was, of course, never used in the cars because of the lack of tracks. However, the automatic brake system was kept active. And it did prove to be the safest ever used on a New York subway car; the slightest fluctuation in the signal system—the routine rattles to which the older trains were oblivious—would trigger the automated brake, known as the P-wire. Of course it was safe. What could go wrong with a car that couldn't budge?

The Teflon insulation on the wires melted, constantly, shorting out the car. (Teflon is a semiliquid that flows at relatively cool temperatures.) With so many systems automated (though not working), there were about 50 miles of wire in every 75-foot car. Finding a troublesome wire required a full-scale surgical team.

The cars were introduced during an exodus of the Authority's most experienced employees, who were taking advantage of a twenty-year pension won by their union and put into effect as of 1968. By one estimate, some 70 percent of the skilled mechanics left the Authority between 1968 and 1971, when the first of the new cars were delivered.

Not only did the extra length of the new cars not reduce maintenance, but with all the design problems, the R-44s drained every mechanical resource the TA could muster during the city's fiscal crisis in the 1970s. "The overtime working on those cars put more steak on our plates than anything," said one mechanic who has spent most of his career at the TA undoing the errors of the designers and manufacturers. "Steak? That subway car bought houses for people. It was a state-of-the-art farce."

Worse, it led to the neglect of the rest of the fleet because so much attention was demanded by the R-44s and their successors, the R-46s. By one industry measure, the R-44s were virtually dead from the moment they arrived in New York City: their "mean distance between failures"—the number of miles a car traveled without breaking down—was under 10,000 miles between 1972 and 1976. By contrast, during that same period, another line of cars, which were then more than ten years old, ran 45,000 to 55,000 miles between failures.

Perhaps the worst moment in the modern history of the subways came when a TA executive called up a junk dealer who had recently bought a batch of retired subway cars. The conversation, as recounted by an insider, went like this:

"You can't pick up those scrapped cars yet," said the official.

"Why not?" asked the junkman.

"We're pulling the R-44s off the road; we need to run those old ones a little longer."

"They're my cars now," retorted the junkman. "If you want to use them, you got to pay me."

The city ended up paying more to rent its junked cars than it had received for them as scrap, while the greatest subway cars ever were parked on a siding for two years until the city could scrape the resources together for more tender loving care. "You were concentrating all your resources on a very small part of the fleet," says Charles Kalkhoff, a senior TA manager during the period. Naturally, neglect of the older, more reliable cars eroded their ability to run thousands of miles a month.

One hidden consequence of the R-44 disaster was the TA's flight from new technologies when money became available in the 1980s to buy cars. Although there had been major advances in how trains work and use power, the TA decided to return to a type of subway car that had not changed in any important way since the 1950s. These old-style cars, purchased from Japanese and Canadian suppliers, turned out to be very reliable. But they had none of the ease of computer diagnostic techniques that were in use elsewhere around the country, which would reduce labor costs. They also lacked the ability to capture any of the friction forces as the train was halted, a process known as regenerative braking, which also would save money on electricity. They were 45 percent heavier than cars then being put into service in Chicago. Jerrold Nadler, a New York assemblyman who studied this, went to the MTA and urged them to reconsider their orders. "They didn't laugh me out of the building," Nadler recalled. "They ignored me."

So as the MTA set out to make the largest purchase of new cars in its history, it stuck with thirty- and forty-year-old-models. Transit brainpower had been spent on fixing lemons, not keeping up with the field. "That was the real productivity loss," says TA executive Charles Monheim. He estimates that the new technology in trains could save 25 percent in labor and energy expenses.

And then there was Coney Island.

Like the older cars that did not get the attention they needed because of the R-44 lemons, the old Coney Island yard also suffered in the lust for new things during the early 1970s. When the R-44s were bought, the repair bays in Coney Island were too short for the new 75-foot cars. To remedy this, and to renovate other worn-out shops, $8.7 million had been allocated in the bond issue of 1967. But the projects were deleted from the 1972-73 budget. Once again, it was over the protests of citizen transit advocates.

"8.7 million dollars was withdrawn from T-63 and T-66, which would provide for modernizations of the Coney Island shop and yards, and other yards and inspection shops on the IRT and BMT," testified Marc Roddin of the Committee for Better Transit on December 21, 1971 during a hearing on the 1972–73 capital budget. "If we are to provide safe and efficient service to the public, we must rehabilitate the shops and yards. Coney Island may be the largest subway car yard in the world, but it is also the world's most antiquated."

The public has been blamed over the years for keeping the fares unreasonably low and for having little appreciation of the nuts and bolts of infrastructure. Here, as in a hundred other cases, members of the public dedicated to the cause of efficient mass transit spoke against idiotic folly. Here, as in a hundred other cases, they were ignored. Now, despite warnings from the public and its elected representatives, not only did the city not have a railroad where it could run these automated trains, it did not even have a place to repair and inspect them.

Coney Island returned to the budget in the mid-1980s. By then, the cost of rebuilding it had climbed from $8.7 million to $70 million. Among the jobs was sinking 5,000 piles to stabilize the workshops. With the yard adequate at last, Gunn had to see that the people who worked in it were skilled and able to manage ongoing repairs.

Now David Gunn was intent on rebuilding these cars. Why?

"I just had a gut feeling that we could make them work," said Gunn.

10:55 A.M., Transit Police Office: Anna Lans

The big Louis Vuitton bag is cradled across her lap. She never takes her arms off it. As Anna sits in the district office, she offers no further details on the criminal or his escape.

"He went up the ramp," she says. "The two of them."

"There was a cop stationed up there half the night," says Christie.

"Oh, I don't know, maybe they went the other way," she says. "I thought they ran that way. Listen, I gotta go to the clinic."

"They got, what, 4,500 tokens?" asks Christie, ignoring her. "Do you remember what they put them in?"

"They had, like, a brown bag," says Anna.

"You've been robbed before?"

"Two times," said Anna.

Christie and McGurl know this; twice in the previous six months, Anna has reported robberies. By coincidence, the stickup men were the same nondescript medium-build Hispanics with gun and knife, accompanied by a male black of medium build.

There is a knock on the door.

"Excuse us a minute, would you?" asks McGurl.

Outside, a sergeant wants to know how much longer. This woman is entitled to a clinic visit. They are keeping her here altogether too long.

"We'll be done in a few minutes," says Christie. "Get off our backs."

The sergeant turns away, muttering threats.

"She's holding that bag like it's got her life savings in there," says McGurl.

"How are we going to get into it?" asks Christie.

It's a delicate question. At any moment, she can demand a lawyer. Questioning would cease, the attorney would arrive, and that would be the end of the game.

"I'll knock it off her lap if I have to," says McGurl.

"Let's talk it off her first."

11 A.M.
MAY 12

THE
COSMIC
SUBWAY

How low does the subway go?

In search of sites for his research on cosmic rays, the Nobel Prize–winning physicist Victor Hess set up a temporary laboratory in the 190th Street station on the A line, one of the deepest stations in the city.

There, in the summer of 1947, Hess made a startling geophysical discovery.

Hess had taken a 300-pound piece of Quincy granite to the platform of the station, 160 feet below the street, so that he could measure its radiation without interference from cosmic rays.

Hess, a professor of physics at Fordham University, had won the Nobel Prize in 1936 for his work in Europe on cosmic rays. Hess had discovered that from somewhere out in the cosmos—no one really knows where, even now—small atomic particles come and smash into the earth. Hess sent balloons into the atmosphere with instruments he designed to detect the cosmic rays.

By 1947, Hess had changed his focus. Dropping into the earth, via the 190th Street subway, he avoided distortions from the rays he had discovered. At the level of the subway platform, 95 percent of these cosmic particles would be screened out.

With all the other sources of radiation accounted for, Professor Hess discovered that the granite still gave off detectable rays and predicted that most rocks on earth would give off some penetrating radiation.

As far from the sun as he could get in New York City, the mysteries of the universe unfolded, just a little, next to the arriving A trains for six weeks in the summer of 1947.

11:02 A.M., Times Square: Scene

Even in the evergloom of the subways, there are signs that spring has caught on.

Here, for instance, at the crossroads of the world—well, technically, just underneath them, in the Times Square subway station—is Mattie Fulks, on her way to a shopping excursion for a warm-weather wardrobe.

Earlier in the day, Mattie had pronounced herself sick with high blood pressure and played hooky from work. Now she is walking briskly toward the Broadway train, without even a sideward glance at the *Dianetics* table, the Muslim perfume table, or the cardboard box staffed by a man of no discernible creed who has a display of yellow-and-brown wiggling wind-up dogs—"No batteries needed! It goes on its hind legs, too!"—when she spots two young men in lab coats.

"Hypertension screening," says one of the men.

"Contribution only two dollars," says the other. "Get yourself in the pink for springtime."

Mattie decides she felt woozy and ought to be able to cite actual numbers should anyone from work ask how her blood pressure is feeling. No matter what kind of scam these guys are running.

She sits at the table and pulls an arm out of her raincoat. One of the men wraps what looks like a blood pressure cuff around her and listens, through the roar of nine different train lines, to the flow of blood in her arteries. A passerby asks what hospital or medical group they are affiliated with.

"We're with Heart Health and Breath," the man says in a tone suggesting that anyone conversant with the medical racket, who had heard perhaps of the Mayo Clinic or the Cornell Burn Unit, also would know of Heart Health and Breath.

Another commuter sits down at the table and wants to know how much.

"Two dollars," says the man.

"I think I'm feeling in pretty excellent health," says the commuter, rising from the chair.

"Just do the best you can," says the HHB man, but the mark has left.

Mattie, meanwhile, stands up, having paid in full. The Breath portion of the Heart Health and Breath program consists of the blood pressure man not wasting any of his: he simply writes her score on an official-looking piece of red paper and hands it over to her without a word.

How did she do, a companion asked.

"One twenty over seventy, it says," says Mattie. "I guess they're legit, I don't know. That's our train," and she rushes down the stairs.

11:05 A.M., Above Jamaica Bay: Kathy Quiles

Most subway trains are fitted with a kind of love seat that is next to the end doors. Suitable for two people who are at least friends. Miserable for anyone else.

As Joe Caracciolo strides into the last car, he sees a couple of people hovering over that seat.

Someone must have gotten hurt when the train came to the sudden stop, he decides. He keeps moving toward the rear, behind the motorman, who is climbing out the back door of the train to inspect the undercarriage and to see if something on the roadbed has halted the train.

"Oh my Go-o-o-o-d," comes a voice from behind Joe. "Somebody help me, I'm dying."

Joe stops short. He looks back at the cluster of people near the love seat.

"What's the matter?"

"She's having a baby," someone tells him.

"Oh shit," says Joe. "Oh God."

11:07 A.M., Below 42nd Street, Manhattan: The System

In a corridor beneath the grand edifice of the New York Public Library, Ewa Konopka sits on a folding chair. At her feet is a small metal attaché case, flipped open. The corridor is very busy: it connects two subway lines, the Flushing and the Sixth Avenue, and thousands of people walk from one to the other. Ewa sits quietly, as if she were by herself, reading a paperback. By now, she has been there for a week.

"You're here every day," says a passerby to Konopka. "How come you don't ask for money?"

She laughs. The passerby did not expect an answer. Ewa is a geologist, being paid by a construction company blowing dynamite charges to expand the underground storage for the library. And in the suitcase at her feet is a seismograph, to measure the strength of the blasts and provide a warning if they get too close to the subway.

New York is never quite finished. Each decade brings new real estate developers, bombing through the rocky and tunneled earth of Manhattan Island for their building foundations. "We try to keep them from blowing up the subways," says Bob Kopera, director of civil and architectural engineering for the Transit Authority's track and structures department.

To keep the subways safe for anarchy, builders must notify the TA before they begin digging. If a blast site comes within 50 feet of a tunnel, the TA requires that a geologist be stationed nearby with a seismograph to measure the strength of the explosion.

"We're not always successful," notes Kopera.

Not long ago, a contractor needed just one more charge to finish excavation for an office tower in Long Island City, Queens. The pit was about 20 feet below the street, next to the Court House Square stop on the G line.

Three . . . two . . . one . . .

"It actually blew a hole through the tunnel wall, and went all the way across the platform to the opposite wall," said Kopera. "Knocked a couple of columns out of plumb, and a lot of tiles off the wall. We were very lucky that no passenger got hurt—our inspector had just ordered a train out of the station."

Then there was the building of the giant pseudonautical yuppie shopping mall known as the South Street Seaport. A few years back, the city drove piles into the East River, the better to hold the barrels of beer and baby bankers on the pier above. Right downstairs, lying quietly in the mud of the East River since 1932, was a pair of cast-iron tunnels that bring the A train to and from Brooklyn. The piles from the Seaport were aimed into the mud around the tunnels, but the contractor sucked up so much river sediment in the process that the Brooklyn-bound tube sank an eighth of an inch before the TA screamed, rather loudly. The project was redesigned.

Once upon a time, the bomb was on the other foot: a century ago, when New York was choking on horse-drawn traffic and the need for rapid transit was universally agreed upon, the construction of the subways was held up for the entire 1890s—in great part because property owners along lower Broadway, then the commercial heart of town, feared for their buildings if the city were to dig up the avenue.

In fact, the lower Broadway real estate interests prevailed. With the backing of the state courts, they forced the original IRT line to go up the East Side of Manhattan to 42nd Street, where it crossed to the West Side.

Their worries were not unfounded. On January 27, 1902, subway workman Moses Epps walked into a construction shed at 41st Street and Park Avenue to warm his hands. He lit a candle, then stepped outside. He returned to find that his lunch bag had caught fire. This was going to be a problem, because the shed also held 500 pounds of dynamite. Moses threw a bucket of water on the fire, but it wasn't enough. The explosion blew out the tower clock in Grand Central Station, knocked diners off their chairs in the Murray Hill Hotel, and killed five people. Moses lived.

These days, folks on 42nd Street are a little more cautious when it comes to dynamite, and it is this legacy of exploding New York that brings Ewa Konopka to the corridor below the library, with her seismograph gadget, there to protect the subway.

A man sits down next to her in a spare folding chair, unrolls his sleeve and extends his arm.

Ewa looks at him for a moment and says nothing.

"What's the matter?" says the man. "Aren't you going to take my blood pressure?"

11:09 A.M., Transit Police Office: Anna Lans

"Can I go now?" asks Anna. "You know, I'm here wasting my time, you're asking me all these questions. I got one. Why wasn't you there when I was getting robbed?"

"We don't like your answers," says McGurl, "and we have some more questions. It's important to me that we all feel comfortable with each other. Isn't that right?"

She says nothing.

"Please, have some coffee," says Christie.

"It's standard procedure that people we question open their bags. Security protocol," says McGurl. "Now I'd feel a lot more comfortable if you could open that bag up. Wouldn't you, Jimmy?"

"I think it's up to Miss Lans—do you mind if I call you Anna?—it's up to Anna here. I think we've tried to be nice, Anna. Is there anything we could do for you that we haven't done? Let's just finish this up and we'll get down to the clinic."

"It's a question of personal safety," says McGurl. "Would you mind opening up your bag now?"

A calculated risk. She can say no and leave, or ask for a lawyer, and they have no basis to hold her. Christie winks at Anna, then smiles indulgently at McGurl. Isn't he being a pain?

"Look," Anna sighs, still clutching the bag, "it happened before the cop got there." That meant the young cop Callahan was in the clear.

"Tell us," says Christie.

"I went out to pull the wheel a little bit earlier than I was supposed to," says Anna, referring to the turnstile counts. "If I'da called it in then, they woulda had my butt for being outside the booth too early. I'm sorry, I didn't want to get that kid cop in trouble."

"Please open the bag for us, would you?"

She unzips the bag, reaches into it, and pulls out a handful of tokens.

"They took, like five thousand—I got a couple for myself. I figured I was entitled for all the trauma, like," she said. Opening her fingers, a score of tokens clatter onto the table.

"Put the bag on the table," Christie orders.

She sighs and hoists it as if it were loaded with barbells. The table jolts when she drops it. Inside are 2,000 tokens, most of them packed in little plastic bags of ten.

"Okay, I took more than a couple," she says. "But we're getting stuck up all the time down there. Nobody cares about the clerk."

11:10 A.M., Over Jamaica Bay: Kathy Quiles

Kathy Quiles had leaned heavily into Ramiro when the train stopped short.

"Due to mechanical difficulties, the train will be held here shortly," conductor Julio Hernandez announced.

At that instant, an electrical impulse moved at the speed of light from Kathy's brain to her uterus, forcing the sheath of muscles to contract. She screamed.

"What's the matter, honey?" asked Ramiro.

"The baby is—arrruhhhhhhhh—coming," Kathy groaned.

"Now? What are we gonna do? They gotta move this train."

"Oh honey, what am I gonna do?" Just then, she felt the wave of another contraction beginning to break over her.

"Oh my God," she said. "Somebody help me."

"No problem, honey, you be okay," said Ramiro.

"Who are you?" asked Joe.

"I am Ramiro Casiano. That's my wife."

Joe leaned over the love seat.

"What's the matter, sweetheart?"

"I'm dying," said Kathy.

"You look okay to me."

"Arrghhh," said Kathy. "I'm gonna die, I'm gonna die."

"You're not gonna die," soothed Joe. "There's nothing to having a baby. What's this, your first?"

"No," said Ramiro. "We got six kids at home already."

Joe turned to him. "You have six kids and you're putting me through this? You can do this without me."

Kathy giggled. Ramiro chuckled nervously.

In the next car, people began to press their noses against the glass, hungry for a morsel of information about the commotion, which now, it seemed clear, was not the sort that ended in knives or guns.

The motorman had climbed back into the car. A brake pipe had ruptured. That meant no one was going anywhere. The conductor made an announcement. "Due to mechanical difficulties, we are unable to move the train at this time. We expect this condition to continue for approximately twenty-five minutes."

Kathy looked out the window, and through the girders of the bridge, and down at the tiny peaks of waves in the bay. Why here?

"Ramiro," said Joe. "Would you get these people out of here? This is getting to be a circus."

Ramiro turned around and asked everyone to leave the car. "Please," he said. "A little privacy for my wife."

"I think you gonna need some women," said Marisol.

"Let us stay and help," said Muria. "We're women."

"Thank you, I appreciate that," said Ramiro.

"All right, you wipe the forehead," said Joe, pointing to Muria, "and you, you got a watch?"

Marisol nodded.

"Then you time the pains, the next time she gets one."

Joe hunched over the seat and ran a finger along Kathy's cheek and spoke softly. "You know you have very beautiful dimples, I could lose my finger in there. You're very pretty, you know that?"

Kathy smiled, then screamed. "Ooooooohhh God! God! God! Oooohh!"

"How long was it?"

"A minute. And a minute since the last one."

"Let's try the breathing," Joe said. "You know how to do that? Let's do it." He tried to remember the famous Lamaze concentration exercise, that silly breathing sound.

"Ffff ffff ffff ffff fffff."

"PhPhPhPhPhPh," puffed Kathy.

"Very good," said Joe. "Again, ffff ffff ffff fffff."

If I have bad breath, I'll kill this girl, Joe thought.

Through the steel girders of the Broad Channel bridge, Kathy could see the pleasure boats skimming across the water. Their sails caught the air and the boats fairly flew. So free. Kathy Quiles is not much for self-pity, but now, she could see in the Mastic fire and the Brooklyn Arms junkies and the squalling chaos of their hotel room, a life sentence, served everywhere she went. Even on a stalled subway train, between the punishing contractions of birth, she could watch, from beyond the bridge girders—beyond another set of the bars behind which she seemed to live—the sailboats riding lightly over the waves with an ease she would never know.

She could have cried, but this guy, this Joe guy, he was too sweet.

"Why don't you get a little more comfortable, I mean, you know, lie down on the floor?" asked Joe.

"No, no," said Kathy. She was half sitting, half lying in the love seat. "This is best for me."

"You want to do a little more breathing?"

"Just hold my hand."

Joe laid his hands in hers. As the contraction swelled, she squeezed his wrist and moaned. "I'm dying." Tears came to Joe's eyes.

"I'm sorry," gasped Kathy. "Am I hurting you?"

"No sweetheart," said Joe, smiling. "You go ahead and squeeze as hard as you want." His wrist, the one attached to the arm that had nearly become a permanent part of a staircase, was killing him . . .

Two years earlier, Joe and his ornamental-iron gang had been replacing a staircase at Broadway Junction on the Canarsie line. They had built three tiers of scaffold underneath the stairs and were welding connections and braces onto the underside, enough to make the stairs last another hundred years.

There was a piece on the very top that Joe wanted to check. He scampered up the scaffold, moving in quick, short steps because his guys were a half level below the top and he had to pass them. Just then one of the men had brought the torch too close to the metal, and the metal fought back, popping embers in a sputtering cascade. A few went down the welder's shirt, so he beat at his chest with one hand.

The other hand was the torch hand, and he swung it back, still lit, just as Joe put his arm onto that level. How long was the welder's torch on Joe's arm? A second, maybe two. One more second and it would have been riveted to the scaffold.

Water! hollered every cell in his brain. Joe turned and in three giant steps was down to the bottom level. Then he jumped into the air, onto a 4-inch iron angle that was on a wall. Next to the angle was a broken pipe from which water was pouring. He held his arm under it as the flesh washed from the bone.

"I'm standing on that little angle, thinking, how did I get out here? It was like I had Krazy Glue on my shoes."

11:15 A.M., Over Jamaica Bay: Kathy Quiles

Two years later, as Kathy squeezed his wrist, he felt the torch again. He could barely speak to her. She was lost in pain, and so was he.

"I'm gonna have the baby here," said Kathy. "It's coming very soon. Arrggghhhhhhhh."

She started pounding on his chest, but Joe didn't mind. At least she had let go of his wrist.

"Wait a minute—what are you hitting me for? He's the guy that did it to you," said Joe, pointing to Ramiro. "I didn't even get to watch. So don't kill me."

Kathy laughed. Then she sobbed. "I can't believe I'm gonna have the baby on the train."

"You're not gonna have it here."

"You don't think so?"

"Nahh."

A strange look came into her eyes.

"It's coming now. Take my pants off."

"No, no."

"Take them off."

Out of nowhere, a Jamaican woman has appeared. "You have something to catch the baby in?"

"What?" said Joe.

"You got to have something clean to catch the baby. Take off your shirt, mon."

Joe peels off his sweatshirt and hands it to her. Ramiro, watching, takes off his shirt and hangs it over the window on the door to block prying eyes. Kathy swings her legs over the metal bar at the end of the seat, a makeshift stirrup.

"Uhhh," says Kathy. The head of the baby appears.

"Uhhh." Before the head hits the sweatshirt, the feet are out.

The Jamaican woman, identity unknown, hands the baby over to Joe.

11:15 A.M., Transit Police Office:
Anna Lans

Anna stayed with the robbery story for a few minutes. In her bag was a credit card receipt from the Howard Johnson Motor Lodge on the West Side of Manhattan.

She was divorced, on the heavy side, and Darrell was the best thing on the horizon. She was living with her mother, so the hotel room was their love nest. Between that and his crack habit, he'd gotten expensive. Last week, she had been out sick. She'd come up with the scheme then. She was supposed to meet Darrell down at the Howard Johnson's after work.

"What about the job at 215th Street?" asks McGurl, referring to the last time she had reported a robbery of a booth she was working in.

Before she can answer, there is a knock on the door. The cranky sergeant walks in.

"Downtown wants to know, are you ready to go to the clinic?"

"Miss Lans will be staying with us for a while," says Christie.

11:16 A.M., Above Jamaica Bay: Kathy Quiles

In the car, no one moved. The train motors were quiet as the dawn. The seagulls had ceased their wailing. The little waves of the bay paused in their lap-lap-lapping at the piles of the bridge.

I gotta make the baby cry, Joe thought. He gently slapped the rear end. Nothing. He slapped again, a little harder. Still no noise. Then he reached under and lightly slapped the feet.

"Wa—"

There must have been a breeze over the bay, and on it riding the soft sunshine of late spring, and perhaps a taste of brine, the vagrant pleasures of a fair day in New York, while on the C train they prayed as one for life to squall.

"Wa——aa," coughs the newborn.

"A healthy baby," says Joe.

Marisol and Muria hug Ramiro. It is raining tears. The Jamaican lady pulls open the door into the next car. Every eye is on her.

"It's a boy."

Thirty minutes into the delay on the Broad Channel bridge, the riders of the C train, the tiredest train in the weary old city of New York, begin to cheer. Strangers fall into strangers' arms. A music of enchantment, sobs and laughs and exclamations, rises and to its giddy beat step a whirl of blacks and whites and browns.

"It's like the United Nations in here," says Joe, laying the baby on Kathy's stomach. "You're going to have to name this baby Charles for the C train."

"You go by Joe or Joseph?" asks Kathy.

"Me? Joseph."

"He's Joseph Ramiro Casiano," says Kathy. "I'm calling him for you."

Turning away, Joe feels his knees buckle. Marisol puts her arm under his elbow. Muria has opened the bag from the shopping center. She unwraps the white pants of soft cotton that she had picked out for the graduation party, and in them gently swaddles Joseph Ramiro Casiano.

"No, no," says Kathy. "Those are brand new."

"So is he," says Muria.

11:25 A.M.: The System

The birthplace of Joseph Ramiro Casiano was painted a deep dark red, just a shade lighter than brown.

"Deep red. Tuscan red. Well, box car red. It's actually Fox red. Railroad red," says David Gunn.

Call it Gunn red.

In 1984, when he came to New York to run the subways, Gunn assumed that everything had gone to hell because it all looked as though it had been decorated there.

In fact, a year before Gunn set foot on Jay Street, some 200 cars had been completely rebuilt—new engines, air conditioning, new tiles, better lights. And the graffiti had been sandblasted off. What a shame it would be, one of the members of the MTA board had said, if these overhauled trains were just sent out and immediately scrawled on. In a moment of inspiration, she suggested that they be painted white.

The notion was so utterly wrong, so contrary to all dictates of common sense, so close to being the definition of preposterous, that the board was enchanted. Yes, they said, paint them white. It will be a challenge to the graffiti writers.

By the time Gunn arrived, there was no sign of any of the overhauled cars. They had been mixed in with the remainder of the fleet and had vanished in the graffiti haze.

"Fifty million dollars and you couldn't tell anything had been done to the cars," Gunn said. He convened his top staff. They would pick a color for the rebuilt cars, distinguishing them from the rest of the trains. And they would protect them.

"I want a simple color," Gunn announced. "And I don't want lines in the car—they have a fake paint scheme with a painted blue stripe, trying to make it look like a modern stainless steel car. Well, it doesn't work. Also, if you've got a stripe on the car, when you're trying to get rid of graffiti, you've got a masking problem."

A few days later the group returned. "The board room was filled with people," Gunn recalled, "with all these buckets of paint. There must have been twenty people there. They had these swatches. And people were going, look at this, look at that, how about this.

"Everybody was an expert. This was better than that color. This looks dark here, but it'll look better when you get it on."

Gunn walked out of the meeting and back to his office. He dialed a number in Philadelphia, where he had been working until just a few weeks before and reached a man named Joe Loughlin, the superintendent of one of the city's trolley lines.

"Joe," said Gunn. "Would you get me a gallon of Broad Street red?"

"Sure," said Loughlin.

"Can you get it to me right away?"

"I'll have somebody deliver it to you."

Early the next day, a messenger from Philadelphia arrived at Gunn's home with the bucket of paint. "I brought it in, and we reassembled the group with their swatches. I said, 'Clear the space.' I opened the can of paint. And I said, 'That's the color.'

"They're all saying, 'But—but—'

"I said, '*That* is the color.' There was a little mumbling, grumbling. '*That's* the color That's *it*. Paint a train.' That was probably the most obvious decision I made."

And that was how Gunn red came to replace the wallpapered madness that had amused, annoyed, and provoked New Yorkers for most of two decades.

The day before JA and REAS blew out of Los Angeles, they'd driven to the U-Haul place and rented a container for the car roof.

As he packed up, getting ready to leave town, JA figured he had racked 700 cans of spray paint. Actually, he had 700 left—having gone through 3,000 cans during his eight-month stay in Los Angeles. "I was getting a hundred and fifty cans a day," JA told REAS. "The paint is beautiful out here. The racks are incredibly easy."

Which meant it was no trouble for him to swipe cans, a dozen at a time, from the shelves and racks. In New York, they were locked away by ordinance. Not so in L.A., which in its innocence, had never been invaded by the likes of JA on "racking" binges. Some kids called it "inventing" their paint. The penal code calls it theft.

By whatever means, JA and REAS would be returning home with an arsenal of unprecedented proportions by New York graffiti standards, all of it packed in the U-Haul roof container.

JA had left his mark behind on the West Coast. Of course, there were no subways out there—it was, after all, L.A., the expressway capital of the world. So JA bombed highway walls. Buses. All through Venice. He warred with KSN—Kings Stop at Nothing—a major graffiti crew on the West Coast.

"Within a week or two, I just wiped them out, everything they had, for no real reason," JA said.

JA had been in Los Angeles to try an acting career. As the movie director who'd filmed *Joe, Rocky,* and *The Karate Kid,* his father, John Avildsen, had found JA a part in *Karate Kid III* as a henchman of the evil guy terrorizing Ralph Macchio. When that wrapped up, the young Avildsen found little work acting, and spent his time picking tag fights with the local graffiti writers. "They were making millions of public threats that I was going to be shot," said JA, "that they had the Bloods and the Crips looking for me. Which they swore to be true."

REAS—Todd James—had arrived in town a week before, to keep him company on the trip back to New York.

JA and REAS were part of a small crew of upper-middle-class white boys in Manhattan who had taken to graffiti writing. Most of the kids in graffiti were poor Hispanics and African-Americans. But there were folks like JA, the son of a major movie director; REAS, a gifted artist from Manhattan's SoHo; and the Smith brothers, known as SANE—David Smith—and SMITH—Roger, whose father was a professor at New York University.

The Smiths' most famous tag was executed on the Brooklyn

Bridge, the haunting, romantic nineteenth-century engineering poem that straddles lower Manhattan and Brooklyn. One night, they struck near the top of the giant stone parapets of the bridge. The next morning, a few hundred thousand people riding trains on the Manhattan Bridge, just to the north, could see the SANE SMITH tag. "A million writers will tell you that they thought of doing it," said JA admiringly, "but only the Smiths went and did it."

The audacity of these boys—and their status as privileged children—made them choice targets of the police and government authorities. Law cases involving white graffiti writers made the papers. And the white boys were prolific. The Smiths and JA were sued by the city—with their parents also named because the vandalism had occurred while they were minors.

Then there was the handwriting analysis case brought against Todd James by the Manhattan district attorney, who tried to prove that the REAS tag discovered on a row of trains one night was his. Of course it was; the prosecutors just couldn't establish it as a matter of law.

For all these kids, seeing their name on the news was just another way of getting up—writing their tags, their graffiti names. So was getting arrested.

One week, Roger Smith was busted. In a rare twin success, the cops nabbed JA the following weekend. He was taken to the transit police vandal squad office in the East New York section of Brooklyn, where he was booked. "I went into the bathroom to wash the fingerprint paint off my hands," JA recalled, "and I looked in the mirror and saw something on the wall behind me. Nah. Couldn't be. I turned around, and sure enough, there was SMITH, in that squiggled handwriting, above the urinal. He'd tagged the vandal squad's own bathroom. In their own fingerprint paint."

As they drove cross the country on the interstates, JA and REAS got up in the California desert. In Oklahoma. In Texas. No hassle. The stakes were bigger, though, because a slow-moving court in the Southwest had the time and appetite to sink its judicial teeth into a juicy graffiti case—unlike the judges in New York, who could barely find time and space to try violent psychopaths, much less a kid with a spray can. Also, REAS's mom was getting married and he had to get back for the ceremony. So on their road trip, they threw up a few tags here and there, but didn't stop for any major attacks. "That's for the next time," said JA.

Back in New York, JA was generous with the L.A. paint, among his friends, anyway. But he kept racking, whenever someone left a shelf unlocked. His goal, he said, was "trying to have seven hundred or so at any one time—so I could go out and use twenty in a night, if I felt the need."

11:30 A.M., Aboard the No. 6, Northeast Bronx: Tom Thomasevich

The stops of the northeast Bronx, St. Lawrence and Parkchester, Castle Hill and Zerega, roll past, and now Peter Marti is getting off Tom Thomasevich's No. 6 train.

A woman boarding at the next to last stop sees the happy faces and stops Marti.

"This was a nice train ride?"

"Yeah," says Marti.

"Ohhh," she says, like a kid who just missed the last ration of candy. "I wasn't on it."

"You gotta know the right people," says Tom.

Michelle Colomer, seven, is sitting in the lap of her mother, Ethel, who ties a blue ribbon in her hair. "He sings nice," says Michelle. So Tom serenades her:

> *For who knows when*
> *We'll meet again*
> *This way?*

11:45 A.M., Bushwick, Brooklyn: SONI

You could have a car, maybe, if you lived in Bushwick and you had enough money. SONI's father had a car. He got up at five in the morning to drive to the bodega he ran, and he stayed there until midnight. This wasn't a nice suburban town where there were arguments about borrowing the car. The old man had the car eighteen, nineteen hours a day, that was it.

But New York kids don't need a car to get around. Even when their arms are too short to straphang, long before they can apply for a driver's license, Bushwick kids have the L train—the Canarsie line. The L train could take you anywhere. You could ride it all the way into Manhattan, but even on shorter journeys, a new world rose above every local stop: Myrtle, DeKalb, Jefferson, Morgan, Montrose, Grand, Graham, Lorimer, Bedford. Or you could, as SONI did, ride it to the G train, which would take you back and forth to Queens.

Around the same time JA went to work in Hollywood, SONI started a job at Pergament, a discount hardware chain in the Middle Village area of Queens. It was a long commute, but he had to get some money. He was thinking about college.

Today, though, SONI was off from work, and with SLICK and AUDIE was heading into the city on the only car they'd ever known, the L. They were going to take care of JA once and for all. This was it. A few cans of gray spray paint had been procured, and there was more with SONI's cousin downtown.

The truth was, they were all getting a little tired of graffiti, but JA wouldn't let it lie. The pride of U5—their graffiti posse—was at stake.

The beef with him had started a year before, when they had done some big pieces out in the train lay-up at 121st Street in Queens. A very sweet lay-up it was, too, because the trains would be parked on some elevated tracks between rush hours, from ten in the morning until three in the afternoon. You could go there and take off your shirt, catch some sun, and work in the leisure of daylight, rather than in the shadows of the tunnels.

The boys from U5 had hit the yard with green house paint. Using rollers, they had tinctured three cars, from top to bottom, windows included. That was the base; then they launched the colors. They'd started several pieces—masterpieces, or "burners"—when the police arrived.

After the members of the Bushwick crowd had either escaped or gotten handcuffed and led away, JA arrived with SMITH, and they proceeded to write all over the cars that the U5 crew had begun.

"You use white, yellow, baby blue, pastel aqua, a hot pink, plum, and you blend with the colors to make a vibrant piece against your background," explained JA. "They didn't get halfway through that stage when they were raided. I didn't know what it said, or even who wrote it. If it was done by someone I knew, I would have tried to finish it for them."

Instead, he launched a rocket attack of his own tags.

This was the start of the hostilities, the Fort Sumter of the late graffiti period. U5, with SONI leading the retaliation, began to write over JA's tags. He buffed back. And so on, for weeks on end, and no one was running any productive pieces on the train.

One day, there was a call to JA from SONI.

"We want to squash beef with you," said SONI. Call off the quarrel.

"Fuck that. You dissed me, man. That's that. Time for war."

"Let's meet up."

"Nah."

"Yo, why don't you want to squash beef?"

"Yo, you set if off, you know. Face the music."

"Yo man, c'mon, let's meet at 121 lay-up," said SONI, picking the same train yard where it had all started.

JA considered for a moment. "Yeah, I'll meet you there at twelve tonight. Dress warmly."

"Bet."

That night, the U5 crew waited for JA. They had brought a bucket of yellow house paint, and began to tag the cars with handprints. SONI and AUDI did burners. As the hours stretched on, no JA. Someone kicked in a few windows on the cars, frustrated by his arrogance. Around 2:30, the last of U5 had left the yard, through the hole in the fence, next to the Long Island Rail Road tracks.

A few minutes later, JA and two pals strolled in through the same hole. They pulled out spray cans and slashed the U5 burners with paint, and laid their own tags on top. Then the coup de grace:

VICTORY IS MINE—AGAIN!
EAT SHIT!

Gratified by his labors, JA drove back to Manhattan. The next morning, his phone rang early.

"Yo," said SONI. "You didn't show up."

JA laughed. He could roll out of bed, still half asleep, and spit a rival square in the eye.

"I just waited till you guys left so I could stamp all your shit," said JA.

SONI realized then what JA had done, that the train would parade his humiliation across the city. He scrambled for a retaliatory tactic:

"Yeah, well, one can is going to dog all that shit you did," said SONI.

"Too late," cackled JA. "It already pulled out."

SONI knew the time, knew that JA was right: the train already was in service.

"Just something to make them feel stupid when they saw the train go by," JA later explained.

This was the last attempt at a truce between U5 and JA, although for a while, the war went into an extended cease-fire—when JA moved to L.A. for his work in *Karate Kid III*.

After a couple of months, the guys in U5 were getting restless. Their lives were going on. Married. Kids. Jobs. Graffiti writing was getting old. The trains were beat. The trains were clean. A train with a big piece on it, something you'd worked on all night, wasn't going out of the yard. Hell, a train with a *tag* wasn't going out. It was getting to be a waste of paint.

AUDI called a meeting and made an announcement:

"This is the deal. We're going to close down U5 for 'ninety. Before then, we're going to king the city. The streets. Write everywhere we can. After we reach our goals, like a writer wants to, we're going to break up U5, because we don't want U5 to fade away, like a crew that was tough, and the new writers come up and they go over us. We don't want to go out like that. We want niggers to know that when U5 was strong, nobody would take us down.

"Even if they buff us after we stop writing, they know that if we was together, they couldn't handle us. That's the point."

Later, AUDI explained, "It went beyond trains. Streets, mainly. What we hit now is trucks, the streets, things that still move. Like the train used to be. Garbage trucks."

AUDI could talk tough. He could talk about kinging the city. But his boys were growing out of it.

Then one day, JA returned, and he seemed to have more paint than God.

11:50 A.M., Far Rockaway: Kathy Quiles

The C pulled into Beach 90th Street in much the same fashion that troop trains arrived home in war movies: to hooting and hat waving.

A squad of police and EMS converged on the trains. Something went wrong with the doors and the conductor could not open them. Ramiro stepped between cars and lifted chains, waving to get help. Baby Joseph was turning a strange color of blue. The paramedic began puffing through a tiny breathing tube and ran the baby to a squad car. Along the way, his color returned to pink and never failed. Joe Caracciolo ran part of the way with the medics, then walked to the train. Kathy and Ramiro already had left in an ambulance with Muria and Marisol. The train was taken out of service.

Now Joe stands on the platform by himself and wonders where to go.

Might as well see about that manhole cover, he decides. Now that I'm out here.

12:05 P.M., Howard Johnson Motor Lodge, Manhattan: The Detectives

The security man at Howard Johnson's was an ex-cop. He brought Christie and McGurl to the room listed on Anna's hotel receipt. They knocked on the door.

"Yo," says the voice inside.

Half dressed, Darrell opens the door.

"Yo, Officer," he says.

"We're here for the tokens from 181st Street," says McGurl.

Darrell reluctantly opens a closet where 4,000 tokens, still pack-aged, are neatly stacked.

"Is this all of them?"

There are more under the bed, and a few hundred loose ones on the spread. Earlier, on Tenth Avenue, Darrell had bought a couple of vials of crack, paying in tokens, and hired a hooker. Then, like some Eastern potentate, he had wallowed in his fortune, a harlot by his side, paid for in the world's most secure currency, a New York subway token.

"I was going to dump the bitch anyway," says Darrell.

From a sign on the 111th Street stop of the Flushing line:

**TIMES SQUARE
UPTOWN DOWNTOWN
MANHATTAN
VIA SECOND AVENUE
ELEVATED**

NOON MAY 12

SIGNS OF THE TIMES

Finding your way around the New York subway is easy, the humorist Dave Barry once wrote, since the train lines are named "after many famous letters and numbers." There are ten thousand signs in the naked subway, few of them accurate. Where is the Second Avenue el promised by the sign in Queens? An excellent question. It is certain that it was torn down and sold for scrap between 1939 and 1941. Once, city folklore held that the metal was bought by Japanese concerns, which melted it, recast it as ammunition, and shot it back at New Yorkers and other Allied soldiers during World War II. However, hardly anyone in New York remembers that war anymore, and on May 12, 1989, all that is left of the Second Avenue el is this sign in Queens, directing the unwary into a time warp.

12:10 P.M., Aboard the No. 6, East Harlem: Tom Thomasevich

"Since my baby left me, found a new place to dwell," Tom sang. Downtown, the next to last run of the day. Every stop, new people boarded who had yet to hear his shtick. All day long, people were amazed by Tom Thomasevich.

He was thirty-eight years old. Subway conductor was the best job he'd ever held. Some famous people were subway conductors—the guy with the toothpick on "Hill Street Blues," Washington, who intoned in that rich baritone, " 'Hill Street Blues' will be right back." Look how well it worked out for him. Maybe things wouldn't be that good for Tom, but at least the transit job had let him buy the house out in Ronkonkoma, a real house, where he could raise the kids. He didn't exactly practice his singing. He fooled around on the electric organ, but not enough to be able to key in more than a few songs. Working around the house, I don't get the time to do things, he told himself.

When he had been in high school in Bensonhurst, he could move around pretty good on a baseball field. Good enough to get a tryout for the Mets. That was something to talk about for a while. Maybe he should have started when he was a kid, playing every day. When he first came to work for the transit, he was assigned to platform duty. He hated it. Boring, walking along the platform, no one to talk to. So he'd started humming. Then he started singing. Then he was assigned to the trains.

Down at the end of Lonely Street,
At Heartbreak Hotel, I get so lonely, baby, I get so lonely,
I get so lonely, baby, get so lonely,
I could die.

Singing is against the rules of being a conductor, although no one in the Transit Authority was exactly sure which regulation, so some official fool declared it to be "bad conduct" and gave Tom a ten-day suspension. Why, they wanted to know? Why do it at work?

"I do it on the train, I guess, 'cause I don't know anybody. I do it for the kicks. It makes my work easier, I'm more relaxed. I do my job. I make the announcements. I don't hurt anybody with the doors."

Ten days in the street, they gave him.

When he came back, he kept singing—if it seemed that the beakies, the Transit Authority official spies, were not around. But you never knew.

Although it's always crowded,
Still can find some room,
Where those broken-hearted lovers
Cry away their gloom.
Oh I get so lonely, I get so lonely,
Get so lonely I could die.

At times, the riders applauded him. They loved him.

Of course, Tom's act plays to just one car at a time. Elsewhere on the No. 6 train, the passengers are lost in subway glaze, armed with the wariness of the long-distance rider.

The woman is fifty-six years old and this day is wrapped in a shawl against the air-conditioned chill of the car, perched on a seat in the downtown local, where every slit-shut eye looks at nothing and sees it all.

The boy is a big six. He stands by the door, sweetly unknowing of wariness or hooded glances: He stares at strangers and the dark tunnel rushing past the windows, the ordinary plenty of daily life.

At 28th Street, the woman wonders aloud about him. Why does he seem to be so unattached to anyone else in the car? No one pulls him away when the doors open at stations. No one pays proprietary attention. Who does he belong to?

She breaks the code of silence and risks insulting someone whose eye may have strayed from the child.

"Is this boy with you? Is this kid alone?"

He is wearing white Nike sneakers, royal blue pants with a white stripe down the side, and a purple striped polo shirt. "Is your mother here?" she asks him.

He grunts.

"Is your daddy here?"

A blank look. She asks him the same questions, this time in Spanish. He does not answer. He has brown curly hair and big brown eyes. His ability to hear and speak is an open question.

The woman finds a pencil and paper.

He is delighted. He scribbles some lines. She looks at the paper and wonders if there is sense buried in the scrawl. You could put any kind of symbolic meaning to it, she decides.

Brooklyn Bridge. Last stop. Still a mystery. The throng moves on.

In the station, there is a spot on the platform where the street vents somehow gather whatever wind the day holds and funnels it into the subway. On the platform, the boy stands in his purple polo shirt.

She wraps her shawl around him. They walk to the dispatcher's tower at the end of the platform. The transit police are summoned. She gives them the boy and goes on about her day. The boy rides with the police to a district office, where he is fed candy and cop love. In the South Bronx, a mother walks into the 40th Precinct station and says her mute son has run off again.

Later, the lady from the No. 6 train talks on the phone to a public information man named Al O'Leary of the transit police and tells him about the ride. No, she says, she wants nothing to do with the press. No names. No interviews. "I only did what any Christian should do," she says.

A startling move in New York, where publicists preen and millionaires elbow for page one. In the subways, the great public commons of the city, the heroes hustle along anonymously until they are called to break stride. They share their shawls, then keep moving.

12:55 P.M., Aboard the A Train: Scene

Comes a time when a family rides the A train and the baby is howling in the hungry way babies have and the mom is burrowing in her bag for a milk bottle that she finds and then drops onto the floor.

The dad stares at the bottle, which has landed nipple-side down on a layer of leavings from a thousand shoes, and then he scoops it up, brushing away bits of lint and dust with his fingers and stashes it back in the bag.

But Baby, eighteen months, has spotted the bottle moving from bag to floor and vice versa and is certain that is what he was crying for. The feed-me alarm rises louder in the train and the mom lifts the baby to her shoulder and their little boy is covering his ears in exasperation at his baby brother and the dad is sitting there as this goes on with no sign of abatement.

Dad pulls the bottle out of the bag. He swipes at the dirt on the nipple. Not good enough. Lifts it to his very own mouth. Swirls his very own tongue around the rubber. Puts it all the way into his mouth. The bottle thus cleansed of subway car crud, he presents it to the nearly hysterical baby.

It is to be hoped that they all lived happily ever after.

The official statistics for May 12, 1989, report the following:

Full fares:	*3,487,881*
Half fares:	*131,000*
Students:	*243,000*
Total:	*3,861,881*

1 P.M.
MAY 12

GETTING
ON

What brings people into the subway? It's probably easier to figure out what drives them away. Between 1956 and 1969, the number of people getting on a subway didn't change much: about 1.3 billion a year. Then the city went into an economic free-fall, and so did the subways. The number of trips declined by 300 million annually, a 23 percent decrease—just as Manhattan was losing 20 percent of its jobs. Of those still going to work, more were taking cars. A transit strike in 1966 taught many people they could drive into Manhattan, avoiding the crime, which was growing underground, and the service, which was shrinking. When the city recovered—and the subways with them—the riders didn't come back as fast as hoped. Studies found these factors affecting ridership:

■ ***Jobs,*** *first and foremost. For every 1 percent increase in*

Manhattan employment figures, there's a .56 percent increase in subway riding.

- *■ **Availability of cars.** A 1 percent increase in car registrations in the city is associated with a .22 percent decrease in subway riders.*
- *■ **The fare.** For every 1 percent increase in the fare, there's about a .20 percent drop in ridership—a hugely powerful factor. The fare has increased seven times since 1970—on average, 20 percent each time.*

In the early 1970s, the MTA flirted, briefly, with an experiment: it offered half-fare service on weekends. Ridership went up 30 percent. But income dropped 19 percent and seemed to kill any appetite for more tinkering with fares. Today, the elderly and disabled are allowed to travel for half price. Students get in free with a pass.

About 169,000 people a day jump the turnstiles and pay nothing.

1:10 P.M., Crossing the East River: Scene

The day seemed to hold little promise for subway riding, but at least there was something to look at as the D train chugged across the Manhattan Bridge toward Brooklyn.

The walkway next to the tracks had been stripped to girders, and you could see straight down to the mad currents of the East River. Men in hard hats walked along the beams. If they misstepped, they would land in a net that was strung a few feet below the length of the bridge, and maybe the net would hold.

Beyond the girders, the Brooklyn Bridge and lower Manhattan loomed beneath a sullen and squat sky. Here was the promise of a city summer, when no pleas were taken by the dull, bossy weather, when there was nothing to say but this: Get to the shore.

On this Coney Island–bound D train, the internal scenery consisted of one advertising poster. This meant there was no colored paper to filter the tubes of fluorescent light behind the ad frames. The hazy blue light was cold, but the car was hot with warm breaths pushed through it by a lazy fan. Even the beach didn't seem worth the train ride—except for the company.

On board are Marisa Brimley and her son Christopher, age five months, lying back in his carriage, chewing on his bib. Marisa and Christopher had started the journey about two hours earlier from 149th Street in the Bronx and are going to the Aquarium with nine others, all young mothers with their children in short pants and white socks and baseball caps. The trip is one of many social service programs organized by the borough's New York Foundling Hospital.

Marisa is talking strategy with Christine, a mother of three children.

"My money was tight," says Christine. "So I got two packs of Kool-Aid, and I made them up. That's what he's got," pointing to her son, Titus, who is carrying a green plastic jug. "Then I heard they wouldn't be getting sandwiches on this trip. I had the chicken, so I made that up. So I didn't buy the mayonnaise. That was a dollar."

"That's right," says Marisa.

"I didn't buy the meat, that's another dollar saved," says Christine. "And no sliced cheese, and that's a dollar. So you're talking three or four dollars right there."

Marisa, who lives on Stratford Avenue in the East Bronx, changes the subject. "I get sick of that apartment, and the street. Those drug dealers, you know, the crack dealers."

"You got those crack dealers, too?" says Christine. "One day the kids were outside the house, we didn't go to the beach. I had to grab 'em and run. [They] were shooting. It was like dodging bullets. I said, 'Okay, kids, that's it. You going to the beach every day till you're sick of the beach, then you gonna keep on going. Them drug dealers, they making their money. They don't care."

"They don't care what child is in the way," agrees Marisa.

Sandra Pabon, who had organized the trip, says, "These folks have to get out of the Bronx, even for the day. Just with the train, they feel good, like they're going somewhere. It also teaches them how to travel with the carriages, the bags, the babies."

"I tell you, they taught me how to travel," says Christine. "I was out at the beach every day last summer—Brighton or Coney on the train, or Orchard on the bus."

"The main objective is to take the kids away at low cost," says Pabon. "It's to show these young mothers that you can go places beside the city parks and the pumps on the street. The welfare checks run out quick, but you still get the beach, the Aquarium, for a dollar. Instead of having to pay five dollars apiece for you and your child in the movies, you can go out, just like all those people. You can get your bag, you pack up and you go."

It is now just after one o'clock, and the mothers who had left the Bronx two and a half hours before are models of patience. A few of the older kids are kneeling on the seats, looking down from the elevated tracks as though they were in a crow's nest, sailing above tenements and parking lots and a barbed-wire train yard.

Suddenly, around a curve, the wooden tracks of the Cyclone dance across the sky. The Wonder Wheel paddles the clouds.

"This is Coney Island," shouts Titus.

"Coney Island," screeches his brother, Kwane. Everyone old enough to know what that means smiles in relief. Everyone too young to know just smiles.

The subway map calls the station Eighth Avenue, but the Chinese of Brooklyn call it "Blue Sky." Wait. These stray notes find a melody.

In the Times Square stop, the players in an Ecuadoran band wear hats atop the hair they have braided to ward off evil spirits. Between roars from arriving trains, they race through panpipe music of the mountains of home: a drum made of calfskin called a *bombo*, bamboo pipes known as *zamponas*, guitars, ukuleles. The music—fresh-sounding, frantic—and the musicians, exotic even in the subway, seem to have been blown across the world by a stiff Andean breeze.

In the morning, young Mexicans meet a man in Washington Heights who drives a station wagon full of cut flowers. They buy armloads from him, sort them into bouquets and pack them into shopping carts. Then they lug the carts and flowers down into the subway, and catch rides around town, baby breath and roses and carnations peddled for three dollars a bunch.

The city of New York, a mite in a huge land, every year absorbs 15 percent of the immigrants to the nation. By the numbers, it is preposterous. Of the 3,625,122 square miles in the United States, 322 are in New York City, nine one-thousandths of a single percent of the country's land mass.

An arithmetical iota, but one, as E. B. White wrote, that "is to the nation what the white church spire is to the village—the visible symbol of aspiration and faith, the white plume saying that the way is up . . . this vigorous spear that presses heaven hard."

"In my country, they call the whole United States New York," said Jose Ramon Gomez, brother of graffiti writer SONI, two of a family that came whole from the Dominican Republic to Brooklyn.

"They say, Oh, you're going to New York—doesn't matter whether you're going to Boston or wherever."

Through all its years, the city has ridden on the appetites of those who disembarked at Ellis Island and Kennedy Airport, climbed off Greyhound at the bus terminal, blinked into the muted lights of Penn Station and Grand Central, all those breaking short tethers and stunted opportunities.

Today, a cousin or someone from the village says welcome. Then the newcomers are shown to the subway.

In the last two decades of the twentieth century, New York is being reborn on the quiver of immigrant hopes. Aboard a train bound for the North Bronx you hear the brogues of southern Ireland. One may tell of the young man from Cork, who, arriving at Kennedy Airport, spots a $20 bill on the floor just outside customs. "Ah," says he, not bothering to stoop over, "I'll wait for the big ones in the Bronx."

Come to Queens and hear the Flushing line called by its too-glib nickname, the "Orient Express." Truth be told, the name derives, fairly enough, from the Chinese community that overflowed from Manhattan's Chinatown and landed in Flushing.

But the Flushing line starts at Times Square and ends 9.5 miles later near Shea Stadium in Queens. Along the way, it's navigated by the woman from Honduras, who rode in an automobile perhaps two or three times in her life before coming to the United States. The No. 7 train carries more than her and more than Chinese: Koreans, Colombians, Indians, Guyanese, Irish, Peruvians, Brazilians, Argentinians, Ecuadorans, Filipinos, all have settled in the shadows of the el. This is not a *New York Times* crowd. *La Prensa* and the *Irish Voice* are more like it.

By the end of 1990, a third of the population of the city will be foreign born, the City Planning Commission reckons, and there never has been a time like it—at least since the last time, at the turn of the century, the dawn of the age of the subway, when the borders of the developed city were pushed farther and farther every day, and the population of New York just about doubled every two decades. It was a European city, then in the political control of the Irish who had fled colonial poverty and famine around the time of the American Civil War. During the first years of the twentieth century, Italians and

Eastern and Central Europeans crowded the city. In 1910, the city was 41 percent foreign born. A decade later, the ladder was pulled up. Restrictive immigration measures went into effect. War, Depression, and new laws against people of color caused the number of immigrants to drop in New York. All the migration was internal, from the South, as blacks moved north looking for jobs, and Puerto Ricans shuttled between their island and the islands of New York. Then a barely noticed law took effect in 1968. That year, immigration quotas, with historical bias against non-Europeans, were lifted. Even Latin Americans, who hadn't been held back by the earlier constraints, suddenly started arriving, when a boom of babies made things crowded at home. In the Dominican Republic, the death of Trujillo eased departure rules and allowed people to leave. Dominicans swept into the city and are now the number-one immigrant group. Nearly half of the city's black population is foreign born, Caribbean people who are thriving in the city. Koreans opened green groceries on nearly every corner. Between the new races of the city, squalls rose and raged, then vanished into the necessity of accommodation. Whites were largely left out of it: they had gone to the suburbs, where their legislators in Albany organized raids on the immigrant city treasury to support suburban roads and commuters and schools.

Nowhere else in the world does life rise and dance in such colors. But New York is a city bereft of memory, without aged wisdom. Who is left to remember the spent promises of an earlier generation? No one stayed to see anything through. Most of those who had been lied to about the Second Avenue subway in 1954 were gone. By 1989, so were most of those who had been promised it once again in 1967. The costs of these failures are indemnified even today by the sweat of the glad-for-work immigrants, who pay subway fares larded by interest payments for tunnels that went nowhere. For the hungry newcomers, the old debts were just levies on a new life.

The subways have replaced Ellis Island as the port of entry for immigrants: they are a dipstick for reading social shifts. In the period of restrictive immigration, when the factories were vanishing, and all roads led away from the city in the 1950s and 1960s, riders dwindled. The subways sank, and then slowly rose again, on the backs of some 3 million foreigners who became New Yorkers after 1970.

In 1977—even as the trains were in mechanical meltdown—the ridership decline halted. Over the next ten years, ridership rose 8 percent, due to an additional 75 million rides a year, most of them by immigrants on the Flushing line. On the eve of the January 1990 fare increase, Asians queued at the end of the line, Main Street in Flushing, for a half hour and longer—there to buy tokens that would be worth 15 percent more the next morning. More tokens were sold at Main Street than anywhere else; people went into mattresses for cash and asked the clerks if they could buy boxes of 1,000.

The No. 7 is more than the route of a train. It reveals a brilliant swath of humanity that rekindled a fading city. Its nickname, the Orient Express, is wrong not only because of all the other peoples on the No. 7 line, but because it implies that it is *the* Orient Express, when in fact New York has a minimum of two.

Listen again for the name "Blue Sky."

The Chinese have come in such numbers that they not only completely filled two Chinatowns—one in Flushing, one in Manhattan—but also launched a new settlement in the Sunset Park district of Brooklyn, which reaches directly into the Manhattan Chinatown via the N train to Canal Street. In the evening, the immigrants head back to Sunset Park, the stop officially known as Eighth Avenue. But even for native English speakers, the signs in the subway are almost incomprehensible. For the Chinese, mastering English was enough challenge. Subway signs are another dialect altogether.

So to reach their new homes in Sunset Park, down the hill from the Eighth Avenue station, the first point on the N line where trains emerge from the underground tunnel and into daylight, the Chinese, ever practical poets, tell newcomers to ride until the N train comes out of the tunnel—"Ride until you see Blue Sky."

2 P.M.
MAY 12

A RIVER OF JEWELS

═══
═══

These days, the black coats worn by many of the Hasidim in the Diamond District are bulletproof. Beneath them are vests and secret pockets where fortunes are carried. Of all the thousands of people who work in the diamond trade on 47th Street in Manhattan—Indians, Venezuelans, Italians, and Asians—the Hasidim are the most recognizable.

The street swarms with runners and loan sharks, cops on horseback and millionaires in rags, all of them rushing from Fifth to Sixth Avenues and back again, as though they were riding the waves in an aquarium tank.

In a swirling, bobbing mass is a few hundred million dollars in diamonds and gems, walked and subway'ed around Manhattan six days a week: "You can't believe the extent to which people are going up that street with hundreds of thousands in gems—in nothing but white envelopes," said Michael Berne, of a security company called Fairfax Consultants.

"Something happens on the street, we shut it down," said Jeffrey Staub, who runs a business at the corner of 47th and Sixth. "The person will just start shouting for help, and

someone will trip the guy making trouble and the rest of us will bury him."

Some years back, when there was a particularly vicious and public robbery, then-Brooklyn District Attorney Eugene Gold explained how diamonds get to 47th Street. They arrived at a customs building on Varick Street in lower Manhattan, said Gold, and the practice called for up to $100,000 in goods to be transported on the subway; above that, a taxi was hailed, very casually.

For those who work 47th Street, it is a safe, comfortable sleeve of the city where people can scratch off a piece of the treasures buried inside their clothes. The block is protected by its own earnest chaos.

"To the outside, it just looks like a bunch of people running wild in a one-block area," said a manager for one of the biggest stone dealers in the world. "Guys may be walking down the block with several hundred thousand dollars of merchandise in their pockets."

So how do they stay alive?

"They may look like they are alone as they go from building to building. They're not. They take a different person, they vary the route. They make the deposits one day, not another. It is a compulsively paranoid business."

Today is a Friday, and by 2:00 P.M., the block begins to lose a few volts of its vigor; the Jewish Sabbath begins at sundown, and the Hasidic dealers are now dropping their diamonds in vaults for the weekend, if they are big-timers, or slipping them deeper into their clothing if they are not.

Then they will board the subway at the Sixth Avenue end of 47th Street and ride home to Crown Heights, in time for the chores that must be done before the candles are lit.

3 P.M., On the Road and in the Subway: Tom Thomasevich

Tom is spinning along the highway to Long Island and glances at the clock. He's away, and not a moment too soon.

The three o'clock school bell is a call to arms, a trumpet sounding the armies of the afternoon into the clash.

Time to get paid.

Onto the Broadway subway swarms one group, seventeen in number, not quite evenly divided among boys and girls, kicking out windows, punching on passengers for their jewelry or their feebleness.

One young man has neither feebleness nor money nor chains worth having. Teenagers at each limb, he is dragged to the end of the car, where the struggle is to throw him out the door and onto the tracks.

"Hey, let him go," hollers a man who has seen quite enough.

The victim is dropped to the floor, forgotten, and attention turns to this Subway Samaritan.

From the pocket of one of the schoolboys comes a knife, a dazzling, awesome, nine-inch blade of a knife found only in the pockets of crazed murderers and occult freaks. The young scholar carrying it hands it off to a companion with these instructions:

"Yo, man. That guy seen you. Do him."

The Samaritan is stalked, in a sputtering frenzy of teen hormones and mob terror, until one of the kids grabs the knife wielder and orders the Samaritan off the train.

Payday, the kids called the afternoon hours when they prowled the trains. In 1987, the number of kids aged fifteen and under arrested in the subway system was 498. The final tally for 1989 was 1,054.

Toward the end of the decade, the subways saw more and more robberies, and they were being done by kids: arrests in 1989 for robberies by juveniles nearly tripled over 1987. And kids were being charged with a greater share of the robberies: in 1987, youngsters accounted for 266 of the 2,051 arrests for robbery, or 12.9 percent. By 1989, juveniles were a quarter of all robbery arrests—784 of 3,146.

Twice a year, transit workers pick the shift and jobs they will take. For Tom Thomasevich, who had risen from bed hours before dawn, this means that now, just before school lets out, he will be calling it a day.

Not only adults were terrorized: kids, the primary targets of the gangs, transfer out of desirable Manhattan schools to avoid train rides from outer boroughs.

Recreational crime, says a transit police official. Nearly half the cases brought to juvenile justice courts aren't prosecuted—just lost and forgotten.

For all that, as the ranks of the city's police departments swelled during the last half of the 1980s, New York saw and felt crime rise off its statistical charts, to the point where the press could pick from among five or six murders for the outrage *du jour*. More cops and more jails and more judges had not stopped the growth of crime. Getting tough, by itself, wasn't working. And the fear of crime had crawled under everyone's skin.

And by 2:30, Tom Thomasevich wants nothing else but to get the hell home to Ronkonkoma.

A young man has an empty car to himself. He is dressed to a prosperous turn in a soft, determinedly shapeless jacket. Good shoes. Across his pleated lap lies a big, fat fashion magazine. He has a sharp eye, and not only for his own threads: he warily inspects the two people who walk into his car. One man sits next to the conductor's booth; another plants himself across the aisle and opens a newspaper. They have no interest in him.

As the No. 6 train sits at Brooklyn Bridge, idling until its push up Lexington Avenue, the young man seems to be waiting, not only with a watchful eye, but with a careful ear.

Ding dong.

Ahh, the chimes of the closing doors.

He immediately opens a yellow envelope and pours the white powder onto the back of the fashion magazine, which is propped on his tightly clasped knees. He taps the pointed corner of the envelope, and a few more powdery wisps run onto the back of the magazine.

With the side of a credit card, he chops and sifts the powder, exploding tiny lumps into little white smithereens.

In a meticulous hand, he draws three keen lines in the powder. A $5 bill is rolled into a tight tube. The entire operation takes less than a minute. He bends his head so an end of the tube is at his nostril and in three short snuffles makes a single line vanish. By now, the train has reached Canal Street, and the personnel composition of the car does not change. The man with the newspaper is peeking over the top of the sports pages at the man across the aisle.

Ding dong.

The doors close, and now the train gallops along toward Spring Street. Into the other nostril goes the $5-bill tube, like the hose on a vacuum cleaner. *Sniff-ifff—ifff-ifff.* Another line gone.

In a violent breach of subway etiquette, the man with the newspaper is staring, frankly, but the magazine man is too involved with the white geometry to gouge out the intruding eyeballs.

At Spring Street, again, no one interrupts by getting on or off. *Ding dong.* On the way to Bleecker Street, the train rocks and shakes a bit. The third and final powder line breaks apart into spidery little veins. The magazine man makes a noise of disgust with his mouth, as if he is going to write a letter to the MTA about these trains.

He straightens out the line, but by now, the train is pulling into Bleecker, and he must wait, impatiently, to inspect the entering passengers.

Only one. Another man who cares about clothes: he is wearing three or four jackets and two or three pairs of pants and has something to say: "Excuse me ladies and gentlemen," he begins. "My full time job is . . ."

Ding dong, chime the doors. The magazine man bends over and snorts the last line. ". . . being homeless," says the man in three coats. "I work at it twenty-four hours a day, seven days a week. Any help you could give me would be gratefully appreciated."

The magazine man unrolls the $5 bill and tries to smooth it out. It keeps curling back. "Help me out, sir?" asks the man with the three jackets.

The magazine man reaches into his jacket and coins jingle as he fishes through his pockets for a quarter. "Fuck the change!" hollers the man with the three jackets. "Gimme the five. You just gonna blow it up your nose anyway." The train now has arrived at Astor Place and opened up. The man with the newspaper steps out toward the stairs. He can hear the doors on the No. 6 train closing, and the theme music of the subways being played yet again:

Ding dong!

3:25 P.M., 125th Street: Rene Ruiz

The train is called the No. 1 because it incorporated the first line in the city, starting way down at the foot of Manhattan Island, and reaching all the way into the northern reaches of the Bronx, past a village then called Kingsbridge. It's the Broadway local: a lurching journey along the spine of the city.

For most of its trip, it runs underground. But just after passing Columbia University at 116th Street, the No. 1 breaks outside. A fault in the Manhattan rock base runs across the city at 125th Street, sneaking out of the Hudson River. The subway does not climb here; the land along the geological fault is nearly at sea level. To have stayed underground after 116th Street would have required the tracks to have plunged down nearly 100 feet, into the uncertain soil of the fault, and then climb back ten stories into the 137th Street station. No thank you. The engineers chose caution and hung a bridge across 125th Street.

The daylight is a landmark for Rene. Since 1970, the city has given travel training to six thousand young retarded people, "who have no conception of 'alone,' or 'danger,' or even what an intersection is," Carol Polsky once wrote. It "is rather like teaching reality as a second language." Wicked New York. Where nothing works. Where no one works anything—except miracles of chance-taking.

The train slips back into a tunnel for the 137th Street station, the stop for another great landmark, City College of New York. Its buildings are hewn from Manhattan schist that was excavated when the Broadway line was dug.

Seven more stops. 145th, 157th. At 168th Street, Rene looks out the window. Men are lying on unfolded cardboard boxes. 181st Street, 191st. Here the subway tunnels through Fort George Hill, the most difficult digging of that first line. Deep mining techniques were required, and workers discovered mastodon bones buried in the earth. The cost of running underground forever, or to the end of the line, was daunting for the people in charge. Put it on an elevated once you get out of Fort George, they ordered the IRT company. Dyckman Street, named for the old family that had farmland hereabouts before the Revolution. Their old fieldstone homestead is a few blocks away, the only eighteenth-century farmhouse still standing in Manhattan.

One more. 207th Street. No token clerk here. Not enough people. Rene is people enough. He is waiting when the conductor pushes the buttons, opens the doors. He steps out, onto the platform, into the fresh air. From the window at 130 Post Avenue, Grismelda Ruiz is leaning to see if he has gotten off, but the view is obstructed.

She watches the street for the trickle of riders, held for the moment of their journey by the No. 1 train, then slipping back into their neighborhood. She sees the men and the women and the normal kids streaming every which way.

She sees them all and then she sees her own.

He looks up at Mama leaning in the windowsill, Mama with the sparkling eyes.

Wave.

He waves.

4 P.M.
MAY 12

POWER TO THE PEOPLE

As usual, traffic creeps along the FDR Drive. All those rush-hour car czars, 3,000 an hour, could fit in just 1.5 subway trains. Each driver leaving the road for the subway would reduce noxious emissions by 78 pounds annually.

Subways have made New Yorkers the most energy-efficient people in the country. The mass transit network saves 250 trillion BTUs—over 2 billion gallons of gasoline a year.

But Manhattan's ozone pollution is second only to that of Los Angeles. Its traffic congestion is outsnarled only in Houston and New Orleans. Regional car ownership skyrocketed in the 1980s. National subsidies for automobiles are $300 billion a year, $2,000 per car. Between 1981 and 1989, one piece of those subsidies, federal highway funding, increased 19 percent; mass transit funds were cut in half.

In 1986, Detroit spent $5 billion on car advertisements, more than all capital spending on mass transit that year.

Since 1970, trains have become less efficient, using about 44 percent more electricity, while energy used to move a person one mile in a car has decreased by a third. Trains are *less crowded and more air conditioned, increasing per-capita energy consumption.*

Money helps, but not without brains. In 1970, New York subway bosses bought lighter cars to be run on robot-controlled track. The robots never arrived. A decade later, New York officials planned the largest purchase of rapid transit cars in the nation's history—$1.8 billion for 1,775 new cars to carry riders long into the twenty-first century. That time, they chose thirty-year-old models that wasted energy and were 44 percent fat.

Still, nothing beats subway efficiency. On May 12, 1989, 3,861,881 New Yorkers rode them.

Electricity tab: 413,000 kilowatt hours.

Translated: less than one half an ounce of gas per rider.

4:15 P.M., Lexington Avenue and 53rd Street: Scene

In a mad rush to get home, Nathan Jackson finds himself trapped in unwelcome conversation about Darryl Strawberry, stuck with a traveling companion who has no subway tokens and must wait in line ten minutes to buy one, and shuffling down an escalator that is, once again, out of service.

He tramps down the eighty-seven stairs at Lexington Avenue and 53rd Street, wondering why people don't pick it up when a train is coming. He hears his F arrive. He moves roughly a dozen steps in the middle of the eighty-seven down. Then he listens to the trail of taunting noise a train leaves behind for those who missed it.

At the bottom of the crippled escalator is a woman in a wheelchair, her head spasmodically thrown to one side, her left eye seeming to stray in aimless orbit. Crowds part around her.

I am going to make the most of my time here, decides Nathan. We all have sporting consciences, do we not, as we dodge the latest pitch from the latest subway beggar. Shift the magazine. Stare into space. Into his pocket went Nathan Jackson, fingering through dimes and pennies until he captured a single quarter and fed it into the woman's coffee cup. At least he felt decent. Tranquil. A quarter well spent.

He moved down the platform, in search of an opening, finding a pocket of space that would carry him onto the next train.

Back at the escalator, a transit cop is shaking the wheelchair, to the point where he seems ready to spill its twisted cock-eyed cargo onto the platform.

"You got to move," hollers the cop.

"Why can't I stay?"

"I say so, that's why. You can't obstruct the people coming off the stairs."

Hearing the ruckus, Nathan strolls back, along with a large group. White cop shaking black woman in wheelchair. This is getting interesting.

"Move it. Now."

"Leave her alone," says a voice in the crowd.

"What's the matter, she's not bothering anyone."

"That's right, I'm not bothering no one."

The cop is fed up. He is not interested in taking a vote. The wheelchair woman has got to go. Grabbing the handles, he rolls her to the foot of the up escalator. Unlike the down staircase, this one is running.

"Leave."

Muttering, the woman begins to wheel herself onto the bottom step.

"Oh no," says the cop.

"What?"

"You can't go on the escalator in that chair."

"Why?"

"It's too dangerous and I'm not letting you. Get out."

"Fuck you," she says, her eyes suddenly level.

With that, she rises from the chair, cursing. She folds it in half, and boards the escalator that will carry her up and away from the subway, away from the place where the lame walk and the savvy are hustled.

"I make my fucking money anyway," she hollers over her shoulder to the cop, shaking the cup with the change she has collected. She seems to have the last word, but Nathan Jackson is standing there, his tranquillity in shreds, adrenaline rising with his laughter. He has been taken. He wants a refund.

"Yo, bitch," hollers Nathan. "Gimme back my quarter!"

The front door of 347 Madison Avenue is protected around the clock by two armed guards. The security at the headquarters of the Metropolitan Transportation Authority dates from the arrival, one afternoon, of an unhappy subway rider with a knife who was looking for the person in charge.

Today, as David Gunn walks into the faceless office building, he and his entourage flash their passes to the guards and board the express elevator to the executive suites.

Almost every modern subway catastrophe can be traced to this building. MTA headquarters is a twenty-story holding pen for a bureaucracy that had not existed until twenty-one years earlier and had done little since its creation except make wrong and expensive decisions. It was the MTA that dreamed up the colossal route expansion program—without anyone figuring out where the stations would go or even making a ballpark guess on how much any of it would cost. And it was the MTA that decided that basic maintenance should be deferred in the early 1970s. And it was people there who had bought a fully automated train for a railroad with fully *un*automated tracks.

But it was there, too, that the locus of the political power of the subway system could be found. Gunn was the president of the Transit Authority, but that was just a subsidiary operation of the MTA, which also ran the commuter lines from the suburbs around the city and a group of toll bridges and tunnels. He has had to come here from his office in Brooklyn to plead the case for rebuilding the R-44 subway cars in-house.

At bottom, his reasons are simple.

"He wanted to go with his heart, and his heart said people have worked very hard here for five years to restore a measure of credibility," explained one friend, Charles Monheim, a young executive who was in charge of car overhauls. "And his feeling was, by God, if they can compete fairly, they should get the work. And I think in some measure he viewed winning part of this work as a vindication of stuff he had been working toward since he came here."

Sentimental reasons would not stand by themselves. For one thing, state politicians had been working the phones on behalf of the Morrison Knudsen firm—and against the transit workers.

As Gunn had told the transit union, the company was backed by both the legislative and executive branches.

But the biggest clout was from the executive chamber of the state, government and people whose power rose from their proximity to Mario M. Cuomo. Morrison Knudsen had picked William Hennessy as their lobbyist—after he had served Cuomo as the state Democratic chairman. Even a close ally of Cuomo's, Sonny Hall, the president of the Transit Workers Union, said he was getting explicit messages from the governor's staff that this contract would be given to Morrison Knudsen—and not to Hall's workers in the TWU.

The governor himself did not take a stand on the question, his aides say. People around him, however, were not bashful about sending the word to the MTA, which would have the final say: "I got phone calls from a lot of people talking about the Knudsen firm, that they had made a commitment to New York," recalled Barry Feinstein, president of a Teamsters Local who was appointed to the MTA board by the governor. "I got calls from people in government, whose names I will not discuss with you, who asked about it, and I told those two people to go fuck themselves and not to call me about this stuff. . . . We got phone calls from guys who have no business making phone calls. That makes me nervous."

And though it worked to insulate politicians from accountability for the subways, the MTA was a creature of the governor and the mayor's office—and mostly, the governor's, who appointed the chairman and a controlling bloc of its seventeen members.

So when the governor's political agents called for a contract with Morrison Knudsen, Gunn had to do better than cite his loyalty to his workers. His gut views had to be dressed with technical and financial arguments, for in the end, the decision would be made by a man who nearly defined the term "technocrat."

Robert Raymond Kiley grew up in Minnesota and aspired to be a fighter pilot, but he flunked the eye test. As a student at Notre Dame, he joined an organization funded by the CIA, the National Student Association, which he worked for full time after graduating summa cum laude. In 1963, he joined the CIA directly, achieving the title of manager of intelligence operations, with responsibility for domestic spying. In 1968, he became the executive assistant to the director, then Richard Helms.

Long before Kiley joined the CIA, in 1952 and 1953, the Central Intelligence Agency had launched a program with a branch of the U.S. Army to investigate biological weapons. The project eventually was dubbed MkNaomi and included among its objectives the testing and stockpiling of "severely incapacitating and lethal materials." Poison dart guns and killer fluorescent light bulbs were developed by the scientists in this program. It would continue for twenty-eight years with results comical and disastrous. One of these was the subway experiment involving light bulbs filled with gas. "I never heard of that one," said Kiley, "but there were some real cowboys back in those days."

In 1970, Kiley left the CIA and went to work in Washington with the Police Foundation. Two years later, he landed a spot in the administration of Boston mayor Kevin White. He worked as a deputy mayor during the city's grim fight to carry out court-ordered school desegregation in the early 1970s. One day, he received a call from New York: his wife and two children had been killed in a car crash in the Bronx.

"Keep the agenda short," Kiley later urged his staff. "Life is short."

He cut a strong figure in Boston politics and was appointed in 1975 by Governor Michael Dukakis to be chairman of the Massachusetts Bay Transportation Authority. He hired David Gunn to be the chief operating officer. With strong support of the *Boston Globe*, Kiley and Gunn warred with the transit system unions. But Kiley lost the job in 1979 when a governor backed by the unions replaced Dukakis. He found work in think tanks and as a part-time professor at Boston University.

Kevin White left the mayor's office in 1983, and Kiley was one of six who ran to succeed him. He finished sixth. A few months later, he got a call from New York: Mario Cuomo wanted him to chair the Metropolitan Transportation Authority and oversee a rebuilding program.

Kiley resisted.

On a Sunday afternoon in late autumn 1983, the governor sent the state plane to Logan Airport in Boston and flew Kiley and his new family to New York. They were whisked by state car from the airport to Cuomo's offices in the World Trade Center, overlooking the glorious New York harbor.

During the courtship, Cuomo "was letter perfect in how he handled himself," Kiley would recall.

> He gave me a ten- or fifteen-minute history. The MTA was a very central part of his campaign as a symbol of independent authorities that were beyond the control of elected officials. He came up with proposals and conditions to assume control. All the proposals died in the legislature, except one, and that was the creation of the inspector general (an independent auditor reporting to the governor). He said, "We went through a real fight and I lost. I'm going to do what the legislature wants."
>
> I think he was sending me a message that he would keep his distance.

Until the struggle over the Morrison Knudsen contract, Cuomo had kept his word.

Kiley came with a team and a set of assumptions. The team was led by David Gunn. Among the assumptions, as Kiley stated them during a spat with the transit union during the summer of 1986, was that labor had been nothing but a force for decay.

"They want business as usual, with no changes, and it's business as usual that brought this system to its knees," Kiley had said. "They are resistant to change, any change, all change."

In fact, the transit unions had been vital lobbyists of the legislature for the rebuilding of the system—another important part of the Kiley agenda. The transit workers had screamed loud and long when they were forced to put trains on the road with worn-out parts. They issued regular warnings that the innards of the cars were badly worn, and just as regularly, their warnings were ignored. Of course, those cautions often were larded with defenses of indefensible work quotas and rules that made productivity a joke.

As a result of jockeying by, among others, the transit unions, the citizen transit activists, and the business community, the Kiley team arrived with full sway over the largest local public works program in the country, and perhaps in history: a $16.3 billion capital program to rebuild the region's network of subways, buses, and commuter railroads.

Kiley rarely ventured into the train yards and shops. In his circle of friends and acquaintances, he showed a rich black humor, and a deft analytical mind. But the reach of his social and professional circle was narrow, and certainly, transit workers were well beyond it. He rode to work in a chauffeured MTA car, though he was only a ten- or fifteen-minute subway ride from his office.

Both he and Cuomo were viewed by their aides and the press as brooders. They had little use for each other. Cuomo rarely spoke to Kiley, and privately, Kiley marveled at the governor's hermetic habits and cocoon political style. "Nearly complete disinterest," was how Kiley had characterized Cuomo's involvement in transportation affairs. Cuomo himself had insisted that he let Kiley run the transit system without interference. "When I talked him into taking the job, which he didn't want to do, I made it very clear to him," said Cuomo.

> I said, Bob, I'll tell you exactly how this will work: You will take this job. I am very serious about your calling the shots. I'll advise you if I can, I'll tell you what I think can be done, what should be done, what I'd like done, and I hope you won't make it harder on me than you need to make it—I'd like to believe you'll try to protect me, consistent with your own obligations—but you'll call the shots.
>
> You ask (Kiley) about his first term, and now his second: the guy has never once picked up a phone or had anyone pick up a phone and say, Kiley, you better do it this way.

A few months after Cuomo made those comments in a newspaper interview, his operatives suddenly broke away from the customary lack of interest. The word had come from the governor's mansion in Albany that this contract ought to go to Morrison Knudsen.

Added to that political weight was Kiley's recognition that although the MTA long ago had stopped persuading the public of the sincerity of any of its promises, the organization still ate self-deception for breakfast, lunch, and dinner. It told itself lies about on-time performance, customer satisfaction, the frequency of service, the causes of accidents, among others. So when the Transit Authority—even Kiley's trusted ally and friend, Gunn—claimed that the agency could work as capably and cheaply as Morrison Knudsen, Kiley was skeptical.

"It would be typical in the Transit Authority to do a fairly sort of cursory look at the costs and underbid the job," TA executive Charles Monheim explains.

> And then when the real costs come up, you ended up being ten, twenty, thirty percent higher than the outside vendor. . . . It's important that people have an opportunity to make a real decision, not a phantom decision based on fantasy numbers. But also, that we push our people to really think about things as if this were their money, and not just public funds, and if we need an extra ten or twenty million dollars, well, of course it would be there.

That meant the TA's bid price had to include not only labor and material, but also the expense of moving trains to shops where they could be worked on, design engineers, draftsmen, and warranty outlays for redoing work that went wrong. "These costs are not insignificant and would typically be ignored," Monheim explains. For once, the TA was playing on a level field. He thought that the people in charge didn't want to accept the fact that the TA could be competitive. It went against the grain of the views held by the agency's technocrats and political operatives alike.

"In some respects the easiest thing to do, both in terms of managing risk and in terms of insuring a job of certain quality at a certain price, is to go outside," Monheim concedes. "If you give it to MK, you know what price you're getting . . . and you have a reason to believe that you're going to get a product of a certain quality because they're contractually obligated to deliver it. In-house, if something goes wrong, what do you do? You've assumed all the risk and you don't save a lot in insurance money by doing it."

In fact, the insiders realized that an overhaul program just winding down, performed by the TA itself on another line of subway cars called the R-42s, had turned into a colossal fiasco. The Gunn team's image as crackerjack managers had been tarnished, and badly, by the R-42 project. The work had been done at the Coney Island shop and the cost overruns had been about 40 percent, raising the price per car from $500,000 to over $700,000. The main snag was that the Coney Island facility was in the midst of a heavy reconstruction while workers were trying to strip down cars. The design had been so fouled up that when the doors were reset, they didn't fit. While the work was underway, Gunn had discovered that the cars had more severe structural flaws than expected. No one had stopped the project before it got out of hand: through all the delays, the funds kept rolling, siphoned from other projects. Eventually, the TA spent almost as much to rebuild the twenty-year-old R-42s as it would have cost to scrap them and buy brand-new cars.

The specter of that effort is one more hurdle to overcome. Now, as Gunn and company are settling into seats in Kiley's conference room on the seventh floor of the MTA building, Monheim is designated the lawyer for the defense—the one who will make the pitch.

Without a doubt, there was a tension, unspoken, between the two old friends, Gunn and Kiley, who had contrary gut positions on the decision. "Remarkably, not in an overt way but in a sort of psychological way, they were at each other," one participant would say later. "I would say that Kiley seemed somewhat detached."

Kiley could say that the TA's management had bungled the previous overhaul on the R-42, and ultimately, satisfy the political pressures by giving the next one to the favored contractor.

Just a few days earlier, Kiley had received a call from William Agee, head of Morrison Knudsen. Agee and Kiley had known each other in Boston, and Agee wanted to know why this contract had been held up. MK had put in its bid, it was the lowest and best bid of any of the outside companies, so what was the delay? Agee suspected that a transit executive with whom he'd had an argument was stalling the contract.

Kiley had invited Agee to his office for an audience, a nearly unheard of privilege for an MTA vendor, and there he pleaded his case.

By the time Kiley met with his staff, he was strongly inclined to give the work to MK. On the surface, it seemed a tag team of arguments, influence, and political clout that would be impossible to overcome. Gunn could say that the transit workers didn't botch up the overhaul of the R42 cars, but he'd have to concede that his own managers had. The best to be said was that if the mistakes had been expensive, they had at least been educational. As Monheim watched Gunn's moves during the meeting, he thought something else had taken hold of his boss. He seemed to enjoy making this decision as difficult as possible for Kiley, Monheim thought.

Kiley was accompanied by his counsel, Steve Polan; the executive director of the agency, Mortimer Downey; and Thomas Goldstein, the budget director. It was a sharp crew that Monheim faced as he laid out the factors in recommending that the work be kept inside the Transit Authority.

The key elements were, in short, reliability, cost, and risk.

On reliability, MK came out ahead, but only slightly. Its work on earlier overhauls had been just adequate. Vendors other than MK had been substandard—at times, sending cars back into the subways in worse condition after a half-million-dollar overhaul than before a single screw had been changed. So MK was, by far, the most reliable outside contractor the MTA could turn to. The TA's best in-house work had been equal to MK's. But only its best—the worst had been well below what the private company could do.

On cost, the two proposals were very close. After the private meeting between Kiley and Agee, MK had cut its price by $20,000 a car, leaving the bid on the table at $474,246 per car. There had been intermediate price reductions, as they say in the retail department store trade—the first figure submitted by MK had been $528,899, some 12 percent higher than when all the dickering was done with. The transit workers were a few thousand dollars higher, but in a $140 million project, no one thought that the decision should turn on a difference in price of less than 1 percent.

Then Monheim turned to risk. "Cost and risk are very related," he would explain. "But presumably, you'd be willing to pay a little more to, let's say, an MK for having a fixed price and, change orders (overruns) notwithstanding, very little possibility of seeing the price rage out of control.

"The real sort of wild card is that we have excess employees."

A large chunk of labor—nearly 150 people—had been hired for

another overhaul project that was due to start in the fall of 1989. Instead, *that* venture had been shifted to an outside vendor. And the result was workers who would soon be idle. Layoffs were a very difficult pill, politically and administratively. In fact, before the MTA meeting, Tom Cassano of the union had mentioned casually to the transit executives that if the workers were laid off because the R-44 contract had gone to an outside concern, he'd have to see about stopping all federal aid. The mass transit law protects public employees by making the money unavailable if aid will result in government workers losing their job to those in the private sector.

The TA was effectively stuck with 150 people.

"And so, if we don't do the R-44 overhaul in-house, we in essence have a dead loss," Monheim told Kiley and his staff. "Yeah, they can do something, but we don't need them. Basically, those doing the R-44 in-house would absorb a fixed cost. And so while strictly in dollars and cents, things look relatively comparable, even if we don't do the job, we are going to incur some of the costs of doing the job. Namely, the people who are here who don't have work."

When Monheim finished his presentation, there was a silence. A technical question was raised about the financing costs of each side's proposal—one that the transit workers came out ahead on. The meeting ended with no decision. A few of the staff people from each of the executive staffs paused outside the office while Gunn went on ahead with George Miller and Monheim.

In the elevator, Gunn and Miller may not have been euphoric, but at least they are very pleased.

"Good job," Gunn tells Monheim.

Upstairs, someone in the staff huddle makes a suggestion. "What do you say we split it, half to MK, half in-house?"

"Sounds good."

And they begin to work out the details to lobby their respective— and finally, receptive—bosses. In the finest New York tradition, the competitors split the difference—rather than slitting their throats.

You could travel New York for days without seeing a nun dressed in the old-fashioned habits of Sister Eva and Sister Helen and Sister Terra. In their long black habits and the veils draping the hair and forehead, with just their hands and faces exposed, they are throwbacks, serene and pious fixtures in the evening subway tumult.

"Have a blessed evening," they say, smiling ever so gently, when someone breaks out of the surge of humanity to drop a coin or a bill in their bowls.

They call themselves the Sisters of Saint Joseph. Most folks think of them as the Sisters of the Subway. Going on three decades now that they've parked themselves, their folding chairs and little brown bowls and smiling faces around the great hubs of the New York subway system, Grand Central and Bloomingdale's and Times Square.

Time was, back in the 1950s, a Sister of the Subway didn't have to take the train all the way home to Brooklyn. After a long day bestowing blessings and gently shaking her bowl, Bishop DeVernon LeGrand would drive up in the beige Cadillac and drive her home to a brownstone in Crown Heights.

The house is four stories high, on the corner lot at 222 Brooklyn Avenue. Things went on there, they say, in the old days. Bishop DeVernon LeGrand had nineteen children by various followers. The government said he was running a "charity racket" with a "harem of fund-raising sisters."

One night in 1965, the cops came and dug up the backyard. Seems that three of the sisters had disappeared. None was found. But the police said fifty children were caged at night in the basement of the church, and Bishop LeGrand did a spell in jail for it.

After his release, he invited a twenty-year-old girl to the church. Then he raped her. So did one of his sons, Noconda LeGrand. Two of the nuns were angry about this and ratted on them. They were murdered by the bishop and another son, Steven. The bishop also knocked off a wife and a girlfriend.

Two other sons chopped up folks and were sent to prison.

Noconda came home from prison after doing time on the rape case in 1984—he wasn't convicted of murdering the witnesses—and he assumed command of the church. Today, the nuns wait at the bottom of the stairs, averting their eyes, telling anyone who asks that the money is for orphans in Brooklyn, mentioning the old LeGrand house in Brooklyn.

"We also have Camp Liberty in upstate New York," they say. "Have a blessed evening."

The LeGrand family owns a farm in Liberty, New York. There the bodies of the bishop's victims were diced into little pieces, burned, and buried on a piece of land bought with money collected in little brown bowls on the laps of women in black robes at the bottom of the staircases in the subways of New York.

5 P.M.
MAY 12

DUMB BLONDS

At 5:01 P.M., a conductor on the R line closed the doors on the train. A red light in his cabin stayed on, indicating that a door had not closed properly. He opened and shut all the doors again. Still the light would not go out.

"Yeah, motorman," he radioed to the first cab. "I'm not getting indication."

"Indication" is train lingo for a signal that all the doors were closed. Without it, the train couldn't leave the station. Passengers have been dragged in doors left ajar. But this time, the problem wasn't the doors: it was the train, eight R-68 cars that are the most expensive ever purchased for the New York subways.

With gleaming aluminum skins, air conditioning, comfortable seats, the R-68 cars were the subway equivalent of the dumb blond. Handsome in the extreme, mechanically scatterbrained. They were prone to starting without anyone in the driver's seat. Inspectors found broken screwheads glued onto the train, and faulty welds covered with putty and painted over. One time, a train of R-68s pulled out of a station with a babystroller—and baby —jammed between the doors *because all the alert systems for the train crew had failed. Metal filings were found in the door pocket.*

The subway car fleet appeared to have been reborn in the 1980s: nearly 2,000 new cars were bought, and 4,000 rebuilt from head to toe. David Gunn kept the graffiti away. Nearly all were air conditioned. The cars were cleaner and more comfortable than at any time since the subways opened. People who had been away from the subways for years, or even those who had seen only movies in which they were death traps, were shocked by the improvement. The new trains more than quadrupled the distance between mechanical failures, reaching 30,000 miles.

But beneath bright and shining armor were cars that fell far short of the reliability of two decades earlier, when a much older fleet ran 50,000 miles between failures. Despite the billions spent on new and overhauled cars, little effort was made to force the contractors to supply what they had been paid for. The R-68 is a prime case: although each of the 425 cars is supposed to travel more than 30,000 miles between mechanical failures, a modest standard in the industry, few of them have ever achieved that figure. It was built in France by a consortium known as Westinghouse-Amrail. Compared to Japanese and Canadian cars that were bought during the same period—and which ran two or three times as far between breakdowns—the French trains were near-lemons.

On May 12, of the 6,318 cars owned by the TA, 19 percent are not available: some 1,200 cars, $1.2 billion in rolling stock, are sitting in maintenance yards.

5:15 P.M., Jay Street, Brooklyn: David Gunn

David Gunn gives every appearance of being an adult—he is well over six feet tall, has beaten cancer, and has run three major rapid transit systems—but he is possessed of a child's energy. After a big meeting, he'd bounce in and out of his office every five or ten minutes, replaying winning arguments and turns of phrase with Peter Barrett, an aide who was particularly low key. Gunn would sit down in his chair, return a phone call or two, and try to read a memo, but some fugitive thought would come to mind, and he'd spring to his feet and stride across an alcove to Barrett's cigarette-hazed office. Gunn is a bubbler, a kid, people say, explaining why they find it impossible not to like him.

Today, when he gets back to the thirteenth floor at Jay Street, the MTA meeting just past is still on his mind. At his office, his secretary, Monica Santanelli, hands him a batch of messages and reminds him of an appointment that would delay any postmortem of the meeting just past.

A gang of Parisians awaits him in the office. Gunn is well practiced at the hearty greeting, though his hospitality tends to run no further than coffee and bowls of unsalted and butter-free popcorn. Which means that people frequently get right down to business when they come to see him.

"How did you do it?" asks the head of the delegation.

The question was kind of funny. Everybody was always wondering why the New York subways couldn't be like the French—or the British, or the Swedish—and yet, all those systems had come to New York this year for advice on cleaning trains.

"New York," Ed Koch once said, "is where the future comes to audition." An arrogant remark, in some respects; accurate, too. At the end of the 1980s, graffiti was reaching the status of pestilence in many of the world's other major subway systems, just as it was being eradicated from New York's.

Gunn wastes no time gloating. He cannot forgive New York's failure to stop graffiti at the very beginning. "You better deal with it now or it will become a massive problem for you," he warns the Paris delegation. "I mean, there was, in my opinion, no excuse for that ever getting out of control here the way it did."

It began, in a burst of innocence and excitement, around 1970 and captured a certain kind of imagination outside the borders of the middle class: for the art crowd, it was the great spirited voice of the ghetto rising. For Europeans, it was as exciting as jazz.

That year a Greek-American kid from Washington Heights named Demetrius went to work as a messenger. He rode the subways from one end of the city to the other, delivering packages and envelopes. Soon, people noticed cryptic words scrawled on the walls of stations, in cars, everywhere, it seemed. TAKI 183. As his name rolled across the city on subway cars, he became an underground mystery.

Maybe these were surveyors' marks for the new subway line that was always being built. Or a coded message for terrorists. Then the *New York Times* discovered that TAKI was a person. It was a diminutive for Demetrius. On the condition that they not reveal his last name, he explained why he wrote:

"I didn't have a job then, and you pass the time, you know," he said. "I just did it everywhere I went. You don't do it for the girls, they don't seem to care. You do it for yourself. You don't go after it to be elected president. . . . I don't feel like a celebrity normally. But the guys make me feel like one when they introduce me to someone. 'This is him,' they say. The guys know who the first one was."

Demetrius of 183rd Street between Audubon and Amsterdam Avenues, known evermore as TAKI 183, caught fame.

For New York kids, the subways always have been a nearly perfect form of mobility: no driver's test required. Not much cost. Available around the clock. No parental hassle. But also, no status—no way to whitewall the tires, no flashy equalized stereo systems, no five-speed transmissions to gun up and down the avenues.

Graffiti changed all that. Tags, spray-painted on a car that moved past millions of people, evolved before their bleary eyes into a typography of flourishes and stars, clouds and crowns, the ornamentation so thick and rich that the names were recognizable only to other kids. Even the names were code: FLASH. SCENE. CRASH. DAZE. LEE. DONDI. They reigned in a dark empire unknown to the authorities of the street world. The kids could find emergency hatches in the sidewalks that led directly into tunnels, or pad along catwalks to areas where trains were laid up. The third rail, carrying 640 volts of electricity, was instant, fried death in the eyes of the adult police officer; young graffiti writers danced over it, knowing where to put their feet. The more juice, the bigger the thrill.

Official notice of the graffiti phenomenon came on a summer day in 1973 when Mayor John V. Lindsay went to Brooklyn to cut the ribbon on a new municipal swimming pool. The new pool was a typical Lindsay-era project: an amenity in a poor neighborhood that, symbolically and practically, might cool people off during the deranging heat of New York summers. Lindsay was beyond his hour of hope then, his campaign for the presidency having died a quick and public death, and his energies for running New York City having waned after seven and a half years. The press no longer cared where he went or what he did. Still, the pool was a Lindsay win. It had survived in the city's capital budgeting, a brutal process often dictated by powerful construction interests more concerned with roads and giant edifices.

As he walked in, Lindsay looked around. Before a single drop of water had been stirred by swimming kids, graffiti had been splashed over the walls of the pool, on the benches and the walkways.

A group of neighborhood boys, outfitted for the ceremony in bathing suits, crowded around the mayor.

"You gotta see the locker rooms," one of them said. There, it was the same story: marker scrawls across the new cabinets, on the floor, the walls.

"It's stupid," said the boy. "Brand new and it's messed up already."

Steaming, Lindsay returned to City Hall and walked into the office of his chief of staff, Steve Isenberg.

"Get the fucking place cleaned up," Lindsay ordered. "I want you to get on top of the graffiti." Isenberg launched a press war against the manufacturers of spray paint, and pushed shopkeepers to shelve cans and markers out of reach. Laws were passed making it a crime to carry an open spray can. Vandals were sentenced to clean up their own messes. Lindsay sniped at the MTA about its ineffective measures against graffiti. More than half the fleet had to be stored outside secure areas and there was no stopping the tireless writers.

By the end of his final term in 1973, the city was spending $10 million a year on graffiti removal. The announcement raised goose bumps among teenagers around the city. Ten million! And they, the kids, with spray paint they had "invented," grabbed for free in hardware stores, were winning: by then, 63 percent of the subway cars were covered with it. The number grew daily.

To catch the graffiti writers, transit police spent long nights hunkered down in the weeds of Bronx cemeteries, positioned on tombstones with infrared binoculars that allowed them to peer into the adjacent train yards. The few kids who were caught laughed at the cops. They walked in and out of courts crowded with violent criminals. In the police vandal squad, Roger Smith had tagged the men's room with the paint that had just been used to fingerprint him.

And if any mayor had stuck his head out the window of City Hall, he risked having his nose tagged with Day-Glo pink or gringo gold: not 100 yards from City Hall was a major production center for subway graffiti.

In the very hole in the earth occupied, a century earlier, by the magical wind subway train tunnel of the inventor Alfred Ely Beach was the perfect studio for graffiti.

Behind a locked, unmarked door in the City Hall BMT station is a flight of stairs down to an unused platform and level of tracks.

Here in this lay-up area for the N and the R lines were prime spaces for the graffiti writers of the 1970s and 1980s. The city had built two stations on top of each other. The lower one was part of an expansion plan that was dropped. The facility was unused, except for storage of trains between rush hours. The Rolling Thunder Writers— the RTW crew—took over the lower level and executed "burners"— colossal murals—that are still spoken of with awe among graffiti alumni.

The simple tags of TAKI 183, once mistaken for the dry musings of an engineer laying out a tunnel, had given way to great dancing murals. Love letters, and political messages, girls with improbable breasts, soared atop the old trains. Cartoons moved across the city eye.

The City Hall lay-up, old Beach's tunnel, was perfect for such detailed work "because it has a platform, and (we) could do top to bottom writing. There were lights there," said REAS.

"In the yards, a lot of times, you have just a foot and a half to work in, and the trains are way taller than you can reach," said JA. "City Hall was perfect."

It aroused the imagination and the indignation. "The thing that depressed me most about the subway, and everyone else, was the graffiti," said Felix Cuervo, a federal worker who grew up in the city and did not learn to drive until he was over fifty. (And gave it up when he turned seventy, in favor of the subways.) "When the city was on the verge of bankruptcy in the early seventies, each time I saw a graffiti-covered subway car, I felt like crying—the graffiti seemed to me a realistic symbol that my hometown, if New York City can be called a hometown, was really going down the drain."

No doubt millions felt just like Cuervo. But graffiti chic also arose. "I've always wanted to put a steel band with dancing girls on a flat car down in the subways and send it all over the city. It would slide into a station without your expecting it. It's almost like that now," Claes Oldenberg, pop artist, told *New York* magazine in 1974. "You're standing there in the station, everything is gray and gloomy, and all of a sudden one of those graffiti trains slides in and brightens the place like a big bouquet from Latin America. At first, it seems anarchical—makes you wonder if the subways are working properly. Then you get used to it. The city is like a newspaper anyway, so it's natural to see writing all over the place."

Norman Mailer wrote "The Faith of Graffiti," an extended, meditative essay on subway pictures. "At night, the walls of cars sit there like the mechanical beast of omnibus possessed of soul—you are not just writing your name but trafficking with the iron spirit of the vehicle now resting. What a presence."

He was loudly denounced, essentially for thinking the graffiti had any value. The only correct value was to curse graffiti from the pulpit of public office and the editorial page. Not a word of these homilies could reach the ears of the boys and young men who labored in the graffiti world; in fact, Mailer had captured the wild noise of their hearts. Painting on walls was a game for "toys," the apprentices of the graffiti world. Subways were the peak.

"The main thing was to hit the trains," said SMITH.

"It's more of a rush—you're communicating with the trains," said JA.

"Things that move," said AUDI.

"Writing is like an addiction," adds REAS. "You get a Ban deodorant roll-on and take the top off. You buy the ink, put it inside the roll-on bottle, then get a chalkboard eraser and tear a strip. If you had drippy tags, it showed you had a lot of ink and you were taking over the entire space. It was—"

"Vandalism," says SMITH, laughing.

"It was good," says REAS. "You were like, yo, check out my drips."

The tirades that greeted Mailer were unlikely to persuade REAS, or, if they did, would only encourage the black spirit that lifted his gifted hand to draw, on a station wall, a startling lifelike pile of steaming turds with a balloon message: EAT IT.

Guard dogs were assigned to the yards, briefly, at the behest of Mayor Koch, despite worries that they would cause more trouble by being hit with trains than they would solve.

"I would prefer wolves," Koch announced. He had sworn off the subways, but the graffiti issue was a nightly blight on television news—not only because people were talking about it, but because the decline of the subway system had become the number-one problem of average New Yorkers during the 1970s. Every night, breakdowns and fires stranded thousands. This demon, graffiti, was the most visible icon of a failing, dying subway system, collapsing from government ineptitude, ignorance, helplessness, not from Magic Markers.

If Koch or any other senior public official had been a regular user of the city subway system, they would have known that graffiti were no more than a signature on a plaster cast on a leg: what kept the patient from walking wasn't the cast or the scrawled names on it, but the fractured bone beneath it, unable to carry any weight. The graffiti were a symptom, yet on the lips of scores of politicians and newscasters, they reigned as both substance and style.

But graffiti were an empire tottering of its own weight. The quality and energy of the writing dwindled in its birthplace with the rise of its cachet. "The top names were pulled into the mainstream art world," notes SMITH. Gallery exhibitions were organized, and tourists, especially Europeans, would come to view subway-style murals. The writers began to earn good money—money unheard of in the scrape-by streets of the Bronx and Brooklyn where the greatest talents had bloomed. Money that lifted the best of the writers and artists out of the subways.

"After 1982, that was when you started to see a lot of throw-ups," said SMITH. "A throw-up? That's when you just throw a tag up on a wall. You'd start getting whole trains, just tags, people tagging over other tags." The writers started wars that consisted of little more than illegible scrawls over someone else's throw-up, like dogs waiting to lift a leg at a cherished fire hydrant.

The age of graffiti was coming to an end. Not only were the galleries pulling out the most inspired talents, but the arrival of Gunn and his boss, Robert Kiley, at the Transit Authority, had signaled a whole new approach to the war with the tottering cast of writers.

David Gunn started his first year by hiring hundreds of new car cleaners. To pay for them, he did not replace mechanics as they retired or quit. A few voices protested that this substituted cosmetic improvements for the meat and potato work of maintenance, but even with fewer mechanics the reliability of the trains nearly tripled during Gunn's tenure. This was due, primarily, to replacing 70 percent of the battered old fleet with new or overhauled cars. The old fleet remained terrible.

As part of his emphasis on the appearance of the trains, Gunn appointed A. Richardson Goodlatte as the chief mechanical officer. Goodlatte, despite his title, was mechanically illiterate: once, he testified before the legislature that he was unable to read blueprints. He said that he didn't know which end of a wrench was up—not surprising, since his academic training was in accounting and political science, which gave him little preparation for the upkeep of $6 billion worth of cars and their associated pneumatic, electrical, and mechanical systems.

But Goodlatte was meticulously organized. And he was devotedly loyal to Gunn. He launched a Clean Car program with missionary fervor. Every week, he chaired a graffiti task force at the Transit Authority—with high-ranking executives from every department within the 50,000-person bureaucracy. With Gunn's backing, Goodlatte worked line by line.

Once a car was declared graffiti-free, it was not allowed to leave a terminal with new writing on it. Instead, the train was removed from service. The edict was enforced with suspensions and penalties for train dispatchers who violated it.

It was a profound insight: writers felt greatest pleasure seeing a fresh tag or piece moving through the city, a supreme achievement, equal to a suburban kid's Simonized car. With that thrill gone, so was the drive to write. "The trains are dead, a waste of paint," AUDI had said in 1989.

The Gunn administration was relentless. It accumulated scores of Labor Department violations by operating unsafe car-wash facilities where workers often were drenched in mists of toxic chemicals. When the governor finally applied pressure, Gunn and company instituted a worker safety program. By then, two hundred people had been treated for central nervous system damage brought on by exposure to the harsh chemicals. Acid washes were applied that stripped graffiti—but also ate through the floor boards, corroded electrical parts, and undermined structural elements of the cars. A transit manager who pointed out that the acid also had lethal effects on the workers handling them was banished to bureaucratic Siberia.

Even during a drought alert in 1988, the subway car washes continued to operate, as if these somehow were exempt from the strictures imposed on every other government agency and business in the city.

Bull strength knocked out graffiti. But it wasn't just a group of transit managers.

"For some unexplained reason this summer is proving to be an exception to the historic rule that summer is the worst season for graffiti," a member of the TA graffiti task force reported in August 1985. "Except for the Number Seven line, which is still hit regularly, hits have been minimal—about one a day per line on the average."

The graffiti writer Roger Smith had a theory. "Look at the kids from my block," says SMITH, who grew up in what is acclaimed as the city's toughest drug neighborhood, where a middle-aged United States senator and federal prosecutor arrived in preposterous biker gear and still were able to score crack in a few minutes.

"Any kid in Washington Heights, they stole chains, they wrote graffiti—when they were nine. When they were thirteen, they started holding drug money. Now they don't write graffiti, they have incredible cars. Around 1985 was the last burst of creativity. Mass amounts of people were dropping out to gangs, crack. The arrests for graffiti are way down."

Hard as it was for adult society to admit, graffiti writers had been basically nonviolent, and creative impulses attended at least the ambitious projects.

In 1986, when SONI and SLICK came downtown from Bushwick with AUDI, they'd unlock a gate and sneak into the City Hall lay-up. But the lay-up had been taken over by the Hot Crew, with the Rolling Thunder Writers having vanished for more profitable pursuits.

The Hot Crew had guns, ran drugs, and used the lay-up as little more than a hideout during police crackdowns on crack trade in the street. The gang, from a Lower East Side housing project, consisted of "the most scheming people. You wouldn't want to write when they were there," said JA. "They cut this one guy from ear to ear with a razor. That's why you wanted to go in bulk—if not for the company and the comradery, then for the protection."

"We never let no other people push us around," said AUDI. "We fought for what we believed. In this neighborhood, you were fighting since you were a little kid."

U5 was made of tough kids, but they were hardly criminal class. They were interested in splashing a few tags around, and toyed with ideas of becoming graphic artists. Those who stayed with graffiti generally stayed away from drugs.

Those who didn't, the "generation of stupid slaves," as SMITH described them, had no patience for the bloodless vandalism of painting a train.

Gunn beat them. Galleries took the talent. Crack killed the rest. By late 1989, the kids had just about given up on the subway system: from the peak of eighty a day, the hits were down to four or five, an easily manageable number. And it was this success that brought people from around the world to see David Gunn.

As the Parisians leave, Gunn shakes his head. He doesn't think they're taking it seriously enough.

"They come over here now and ask us how you get rid of it. They're making the same goddamn mistake made here. They're not treating it as an absolute priority. Right now. If they did, they could deal with it before it becomes a big mess. In the last year, I guess, British Rail was over here, Paris, and Stockholm."

5:50 P.M., 57th Street, Manhattan: Joyce Bresa

Reno was home from his trip to the South. He had been gone a few days, and now all that stood between him and Joyce was the R train. As Joyce pushes open the doors of the employees' entrance at Bendel's, she feels a clammy puff of air at her face. It's hot, all right, not quite the sonic heat of the worst summer days in New York, when the asphalt, like deep-piled carpet, swallows the heels of shoes, but it's hot enough to work up a sweat just crossing 57th Street toward the subway. I hope the train is air conditioned, she thinks.

5:55 P.M., City Hall Lay-up: The System

As Joyce Bresa walks along 57th Street, Mark Vales is in the City Hall lay-up, checking out the 6:05 "extra" R that would be put into service at Canal Street. Vales doesn't bother with the radio test; the motorman who relayed the train from the yard to him should have done that already. Some forty of the electrical shoes on the train were out of alignment; this meant that they were not gripping the third rail properly. He could not have noticed all of them because it required a gauge to detect the misalignment.

Moreover, Vales met most people's definition of overextended. Today was his fifteenth straight day on the job. In the last two weeks, he had worked 160 hours, averaging more than 11 hours per day; on some nights, he was on duty for 18 hours. If he were a horse trotting Central Park, the brains in the city council would be working on a law to protect him. Or his trainer would shoot him.

But he was just one of the thousands of men and women who run trains in New York while working longer hours than would be permitted on any railroad in the country. It costs more to put a fresh crew on the road, when benefits are counted, than to pay overtime. As a result, each year TA president Gunn—and his schedule makers—were hailed as model managers for increasing the "productivity" of the transit workers. Train operators were running more miles per worker than they ever had.

The overtime worked by employees in "safety sensitive" positions was up by some 94 percent. Ignored in this were the safety implications of people working tired. One train operator fell asleep and crashed a locomotive. Another, who had worked twelve consecutive days, threw a switch at the wrong moment—and sent two trains onto a head-on collision course. (The trains stopped in time.)

Experts say fatigue works as a depressant on the central nervous system—just like alcohol or narcotic drugs. Because of this, federal law requires most railroads in the United States to strictly limit the number of hours someone can operate a train or route it from a switch tower. The idea is that alertness counts. The ability to detect a signal decreases after four hours, studies by consultants to the National Transportation Safety Board have found.

But the subways don't cross state lines, so most federal laws don't apply. A major exception is the federal drug testing rule. The TA was spending $5 million a year to screen the blood and urine of its employees, although drugs or alcohol were rarely factors in accidents: only 1 of 121 collisions and derailments from 1986 through 1988 involved the use of alcohol. This, of course, makes perfect sense when the cultural values of the transit workers are considered: most of the employees are lower-middle-class people, struggling to get by in a very expensive city. Life is hard enough without chaining their legs to an addiction—outside work.

They were hard-working employees, glad for the chance to make $24.63 an hour in overtime. And their supervisors were delighted to have them put in the hours—and keep "head count" down.

A study done by *New York Newsday* in 1989 examined twenty

accidents blamed on human error. Of those twenty, seven of the culpable employees had worked longer hours or had shorter rests between shifts than would be permitted on a federally regulated railroad. Some had worked 18 or 19 hours.

And 25 percent of the transit workers in important safety jobs were working more hours than would be permitted by the federal law, a sampling by John Pritchard III, the system's inspector general, found.

So train operator Mark Vales's long hours are not unusual. Today, in fact, is his regular day off. He'd volunteered to come in and was assigned to do "extras"—a job with no fixed schedule or route.

His dispatcher sent him to wait in the City Hall lay-up. From there, he could go in either direction on the R line, a route that ran to Brooklyn, out to the very southern edge of the city, up to the Verrazano Narrows and the great entrance of the New York harbor. Or he could take it the other direction, toward midtown, swinging east beneath the East River.

Things might have worked out that he wouldn't have to go in either direction. If the trains ran close to schedule, with no breakdowns, he'd just put in his time in the crew room and go home at the end of the shift.

But that night, there had been a switch fouled up in lower Manhattan. No R trains had been able to run for nearly an hour, and the crowds were mounting on the hot platforms. As soon as they were able to get a train out of the yard, it was brought to City Hall lay-up. And Mark Vales was going to drive it.

6 P.M.
MAY 12

FANNING
THE
FLAMES

At 5:40 P.M. on May 12, a track worker reported a track fire near Franklin Avenue in Brooklyn. It is one of ten fires to be reported that day. Most are in trash cans on the platforms. The rest are litter on the tracks, or cables that suffered an electrical arc. Three times, they are serious enough to require evacuation of a train. Getting burned is much less a worry than the smoke.

Air in the subways has worried people since the Civil War. Nineteenth-century political bosses protecting their street car franchises said riders would suffocate in underground trains. The steam engines of the London underground petrified everyone. A black inventor named Granville T. Woods devised the third-rail system for running trains on electricity, eliminating the noxious by-products of steam locomotives. Most tracks were built close to the surface with gratings on the street for fresh air.

Trains moving through the tunnels have a piston effect, forcing great billows of air ahead. Artificial respiration is performed by three hundred giant fans, although with 25 percent out of order, that sys-

tem has fallen into disrepair. The TA is loath to turn on the fans to remove heat during the summer because of the high electricity requirements, and few of the people who are supposed to run them—dispatchers in the Command Center—even know how to turn them on.

During a smoky fire in the early 1970s, a passenger died and the city resolved to replace fans then six decades old. A staggering bureaucratic snarl developed. On May 12, 1989, eight huge fans are sitting in a warehouse in New Philadelphia, Ohio—exactly where they have been since the TA ordered them eleven years earlier.

6:15 P.M., Beneath the Plaza Hotel:
Joyce Bresa

As she came down the stairs, Bendel's switchboard operator Renee Guttierez spotted Bendel assistant cosmetics buyer-in-training Joyce Bresa on the platform and walked toward her. Then she thought better of it. What if we're stuck here waiting a long time, Renee wondered. What am I going to say to her? Renee pretended that she didn't see Joyce, who apparently hadn't noticed her.

The platform is so full that no more people can fit on it without pushing someone onto the tracks. Renee is not a slim woman, and she feels the heat and crowding intensely. Next to her, a woman fans herself with a magazine.

"This is it," one woman announces to Renee. "I'm going up to take the express bus." With that, she climbs out of the station. Renee decides to give it a couple more minutes. When the train comes, she barely makes it inside. She didn't see any more of Joyce.

6:20 P.M., St. John's Hospital, Rockaway:
Kathy Quiles

At the hospital, Kathy Quiles goes into a visitor's lounge to watch the evening news, all of which carry accounts of the birth.

At that moment, in Bay Ridge, Joe Caracciolo waits for his girl-friend to come home. She walks in and asks him how his day was.

Before he can answer, she tells him about all the places she had been that day. He waits impatiently.

"I delivered a baby today," he says matter-of-factly, "then I went out to check on the manhole cover out at 90th Street in Rockaway."

Lorraine was about to say uh-huh. Then she pauses.

"You delivered what?"

"See, there was a manhole cover reported missing out on 90th Street on the Far Rockaway line, and things were a little slow, so I decided to go—"

"Did you say you delivered a *baby?*"

When the phone calls start coming from the press, Joe doesn't want to talk. So Lorraine does. When the reporters ask her how she is related to Joe, she's too embarrassed to say girlfriend. "Fiancée," she says. That was how Joe Caracciolo and Lorraine Tozzo got engaged.

6:25 P.M., Lower Manhattan: SONI and SLICK

A good long ride from Bushwick is The Door, way downtown on the cusp of SoHo and TriBeCa, two old industrial zones that recently went high chic. The L all the way to Eighth Avenue. Then an E train down to Spring Street, and a block south to Broome Street. There. The Door's banner hangs over the entrance, swaying lightly in the breeze. It took a solid forty-five minutes on the train, but AUDI and SLICK and SONI were members in good standing of The Door and made the trip three or four days a week.

Most youth centers are built on unkept promises. One night, a forgotten crisis commands the attention of the press and the politicians: a murderous rumble, say, or a wolf pack rampaging through a serene part of town. Let's get them something besides the street. Start some programs.

From these traumas is brewed a nostrum of jaded adults reading newspapers, a Ping-Pong table with chewed corners and a sagging net. Cast-off folding tables. A basketball court ruled by ten kids. Another handful who hang out near the Nok Hockey table. If a puck can be found. If the set still exists. Even with fists full of city dollars, most after-school programs are held in the same barren public buildings that, day behind day, exist only by the power of inert bureaucrats who fill out forms for books that never arrive, semester upon semester, in buildings that were new fifty years ago and haven't seen a roofer in twenty-five. Where teachers with a notion or two about how to engage kids are eaten alive. And where only those with enough political hooks can land a gig in the after-school youth program at $26 an hour, with little chance they will stir themselves or anyone else.

And here come the boys from Bushwick, killing an hour on the train to get to The Door.

At the very first, The Door surprises with the lavishness of its physical appointments. Why is so much money spent on these modular furnishings?—these corporate-style office pods where counseling is given, the oak banisters along the splashy mid-room stairways, the subtle but profuse lighting? This was the design vocabulary of a first-rate private school, the sort of place where you might find the children of the city's rich ghettos.

But just past the entrance, near the reception desk, a sign announces that this is not an exclusive holding pen for youngsters waiting to assume a position of comfort in life:

TRAIN PASS SCHEDULE:
7:15 P.M.
8:15 P.M.
9:00 P.M.
9:30 P.M. **Tues., Wed.**

See, the train passes provided by city schools are no good after 7 P.M. The city doesn't want kids riding the trains for free all night long. For The Door, the TA makes an exception, since its activities don't get rolling until two in the afternoon. Then, during the evening, an announcement is made for the Train Pass, an escorted walk to the subway, with a counselor who shows a clerk the proper papers for the students to pass through the gates.

Around the city, chartered buses shepherd privileged children to and from home, to avoid the dread subways. Not the kids at The Door.

At The Door, a kid can take a class in ceramics. Learn the double somersault. Act in a play. Meet a counselor about a bad situation. Find a job. Or, as Danny Gomez was doing, finish the courses for a graduate equivalency diploma, so he can become the first member of his family to apply for college. The Door, in short, is a department store for the emotional and social lives of New York teenagers. It has a nursery for teenage mothers, and a health clinic, complete with laboratory and pharmacy. Any teen needing a lawyer can find one here—and more to the point, a lawyer who would do more than try to beat a court case, would also help turn kids away from the uncaring arms of the law. The institution reports that six thousand kids a year visit, of their own free will, free of charge.

First stop for AUDI, SONI, and SLICK is the weight room downstairs. Sheets of paper lie along the walls for graffiti tags—authorized writing, with none of the hot outlaw flame of drawing on a train, but The Door is their place, and graffiti-free but for the assigned space in the weight room. "They want to be part of the system," said Elma Denim, The Door's associate director. "They're being held out of it. That's why there's all this rage. They're not breaking down the system."

SONI and SLICK have signed the paper on the wall. But they wanted more. They had to have more: SLICK has been humiliated.

"We could kick JA's ass if we ran into him," says SONI.

AUDI grunts and bench presses.

Fat chance. JA lived in an elegant apartment house in one of the finest neighborhoods in the city, the Upper West Side of Manhattan, and had gone to a high school where the tuition and fees were over $9,000 a year. That was just about a full year's pay in most Bushwick houses: the mean income there was $10,000, one-third that of the Upper West Side. A baby born in SONI's neighborhood had a 70 percent higher chance of dying before its first birthday than in JA's. A thousand buildings had been abandoned or torn down since 1970 in Bushwick. On the Upper West Side, condominiums had been pried into every square yard of space.

The murder rate for Bushwick was four times that of the Upper West Side, death by cirrhosis or chronic liver disease 70 percent higher.

In short, Bushwick had many of the earmarks of a third-world country. Once, it had been a great center for German immigration and for beer production, with fourteen breweries in an eleven-block area. It also boasted a dozen theaters, including the first in the United States to use electric lights. The Irish followed the Germans into the tenements, then the Russians and the Poles. After the Depression, the Italians arrived. In the 1950s, the area was cleared of middle-class whites in a spectacular housing scam: rampant blockbusting was accomplished by offering easy mortgage credit to scraping-by minorities at scandalously high rates. What banker could do this? None, without the help of Uncle Sam, which guaranteed the mortgages to people unable to carry them and thus oversaw the meltdown of the neighborhood.

Whites fled to the newly opened suburbs. Puerto Ricans, without jobs, without education, without English, settled the husk of Bushwick.

In this, Bushwick, like virtually all New York neighborhoods, is very much a historical shell through which great churnings of people pass: there are practically no old New York families, practically no New York neighborhoods where familial lines extend more than a single generation or two.

In the late 1970s, Bushwick changed again. Jose Gomez left the tiny village of Denares, near the city of San Francisco in the Dominican Republic, and found a home with other Dominicans among the cinders of Bushwick.

In time, the father sent for the rest of the family, his wife, the three boys and a girl, and scraped together the cash to open his own bodega in the East New York section of Brooklyn. (The supermarket, with sprawling aisles and acres of groceries, could not survive the New York real estate market, leaving thousands of tiny niches for all-purpose grocery stores, known in Hispanic neighborhoods as bodegas—crowded but complete Noah's arks of victuals.) Mr. Gomez spent nearly all his waking hours there, accompanied by his son, Ramon. But not Danny. He was SONI, he wanted more. He wanted to catch fame. He had gone part of the way through Bushwick High School, and along the way, made the friends who formed U5.

Maybe to the rest of the world, the graffiti scene was fading in the mid-1980s as SONI and SLICK and AUDI came of age. But U5, their crew, had a purpose. They were a loose grouping of teenagers going through high school in a decaying city, who could see ahead of them long hours in the bodegas with their parents, or car repair shops, or a job in one of the envelope factories still running in Brooklyn. In their generation were kids who could swing knives and bats and rampage through subway trains. Other kids could hang out on corners and wave 9-millimeter guns. The graffiti kids went to make their mark another way.

"There were a lot of crews here in Bushwick. I wanted a central crew, that would be known citywide, that would be powerful," said AUDI. "That's when I made up U5. Instead of two letters and three numbers, I decided to make a letter and a number. It was something new, that nobody ever had, a letter and a number. We caught fame. But we gained it, too."

They would meet on nights in the apartment of Jesus Torres, who could draw cartoonlike figures so well that he was commissioned to paint a line of sneakers for a company in Puerto Rico.

There, in Jesus's bedroom, they would plot their strategies. A subway map hung on the wall behind the door, so that routes could be studied. Soon, though, the map in Jesus's room started to look like the ones in the subway: so obliterated with tags that it was impossible to read.

"We used to go hit the trains every week," said AUDI. "We went on a frenzy. We used to go every week. Sometimes, even, like three times a week. We used to hit a lot. We wanted to give U5 a name. We wanted to catch fame among the young people, you know, the writers."

"In our school, there was at least fifteen people from U5—they was into graffiti," said Jesus Torres.

> Sometimes, there was problems with rival groups and things like that. But most of the people in U5, they're strictly into art. They're not into drugs. They're not into the streets. They don't be hanging out, or all that, none of that stuff. Most of them are well-spoken, they're intelligent people. They're striving for their goals. Most of them work, you know, and have decent jobs. I work as a cook. In the Empire State Building, Houlihan's. I cook shrimp— I'm in the mid-fry. Onion soup, clams, whatever.

SONI had his job at Pergament, a big home improvement and house-wares place. But after he started going to The Door, he wanted more. There, he was learning a few other ways of earning self-respect besides scrawling a name on a train. In a month or two, he'd be done with the courses, and could send in the application to Manhattan College. The graffiti scene was kind of dead.

But this stuff with JA. Man, he couldn't walk away from that.

They walked over to a pool on Carmine Street with one of the staff people from The Door. They'd take a swim and be about their business.

6:35 P.M., Lexington Avenue, Beneath Bloomingdale's: Joyce Bresa

At last Joyce Bresa has boarded a subway car. She would be home soon. She glances out the window at the first stop after her station. The crowd at Lexington Avenue is frightening. If I had been over here, just one stop away, I never would have fit onto the train, Joyce thinks. No train has come through the station in at least a half hour. This is a transfer point from the Lexington Avenue lines, and so in the meantime, hundreds of people have been funneling down the stairs from them—even though there is nowhere to put them.

The acceleration of any vehicle causes pressure on its occupants; subway riders are accustomed to being pulled back by their own inertia when a train leaves a station, or thrown slightly forward when their momentum continues to carry them ahead when the train is slowing down. This train is different. It bucks. It throws them back and forward, and makes horrible noises. No one likes the sound of it. Joyce closes her eyes and counts the minutes until she will be in Queens.

6:40 P.M., Upper West Side: JA

A surprising portion of the thirty thousand licensed liquor establishments in and around Manhattan have stayed afloat on the patronage of generation upon generation of affluent teenage prep school students. Rich kids have boozed away their parents' money in a succession of fashionable dives long before Holden Caulfield binged his way through midtown. Robert Chambers, the preppy murderer, spent the night of the killing in a bar crowded with underage drinkers like himself. Dorrian's Red Hand and the Wicked Wolf were at one time two of the Upper East Side perennials favored by kids from Dalton, Collegiate, Trinity, Horace Mann—the great names in New York high school education, at least among folks with nine or ten thousand dollars a year for tuition. They drank mixed concoctions like Singapore Slings and screwdrivers and Harvey Wallbangers and Kirs, or guzzled imported beers like Corona and Heineken.

Not JA. He curled his lips at the mention of the preppy bar scene. It was definitely out, especially after high school. He and his pals headed downtown, to the hot club—whichever one it was that season, for hot clubs had the half-lives of butane lighters.

A week ago, when it all came to a head between JA and the boys from U5, JA had spent a good part of the night at MK's—one of these firefly establishments. The $20 cover charge applied only to saps without a pass or a connection with the bouncer—a fee intended to keep out the "bridge and tunnel crowd," the people who had to come from somewhere else to the island of Manhattan, and who were congenitally unhip by club standards.

JA was drinking heavily. At the bar, he bumped into COCER, who ran around on the periphery of U5.

"You're JA?" said COCER. "Whoa, man. I know these dudes, SLICK and SONI. They been after your ass for the longest time. They say you been ducking them."

"Hey," said JA. "I'll take SONI on. Anytime."

"I don't know SONI so well," said COCER. "I hang with SLICK. He says you a pussy, a sucker."

"I'll fight either one of those guys—but where? I can't make them appear."

"SLICK says he's gonna fuck you up."

"Yo, let him name the time."

"Yo, let's go to his house, I'll show you where he lives."

Just before dawn, JA and COCER, along with REAS and VEN, two of JA's pals, drove through the dark streets of Bushwick. JA wondered about this move. But he didn't want COCER to think he was dodging a chance to go face to face with SLICK.

In the vestibule of the apartment building, COCER leaned into the buzzer for several minutes until a groggy voice answered.

"Yeah," said the voice.

JA pushed COCER aside and spoke into the mouthpiece.

"Yo, it's JA."

"Yeah."

"Come downstairs if you want to fight me."

"You got the wrong buzzer."

COCER shook his head.

"Yo, SLICK, come on down, man, and fight."

"You got the wrong place."

JA turned to COCER. "What's up with this kid?"

"It's the right buzzer—I been to his house before," said COCER.

JA buzzed again and spoke into the microphone.

"Yo, SLICK, you're fronting, talking all this jazz about how you gonna kick my ass and not backing it up. Well, come downstairs and back it up."

"Fuck that," said COCER. "Now he's going to call his boys."

In a bag, JA had a few spare cans of spray paint. He copped a few tags on the outside of the building. REAS and VEN watched. This was JA's beef, not theirs, and tagging someone's house was heavy. Very heavy.

Fuck SLICK, thought JA. Now it was brightening outside, and a man stuck his head out a third-floor window and hollered something at the kids in front of the building. They decided it was time to leave. Where am I, JA wondered. He looked at a street sign, and saw Empire Boulevard and Rogers Street. SMITH's name was Roger. The name stayed with him as he slumped into the seat and rode back to Manhattan. Otherwise, he had no idea where he was.

SLICK discovered the infamy scrawled on his house when he came downstairs that morning. Word moved quickly through Bushwick of JA's attack because COCER had seen the whole thing.

"Ten guys, they came in cars from Manhattan," SLICK explained to his friends.

6:42 P.M., Eleventh Street Cut, Queens: Joyce Bresa

To most subway riders, being in a tunnel 500 feet beneath the East River is roughly identical to being in a tunnel 20 feet below Broadway: you can't see anything outside, and you're not supposed to look at the people inside.

But to the practiced eye of a train operator, a dark subway tunnel is more than a closet of shadows. Niches are built into the walls where emergency exits can be found. The roadbed slants up and down, depending on the terrain. Tracks merge at switches. Certain signals, especially those at sharp curves or near a station, are set up on timers, so that a train moving too fast will be "tripped"— stopped automatically by a robot arm on the track that reaches under the track and pulls open a valve, releasing air from the brake lines.

For R trains coming out from under the East River, one landmark is the Eleventh Street Cut.

Ahead, motorman Mark Vales could see the cut, marked by a double signal and a wall of light as two tracks split. One broke from the tunnel and climbed to an el. The other continued underground into the busy Queens Plaza station. By then, he'd have the worst part of the trip over with.

Passing the Eleventh Street Cut, Mark Vales heard a loud bang from under the train. He released the dead man's handle and let the train coast for a minute. Then he pressed down, and felt the surge of power. Good. Now the train was climbing an incline, leading up from the deep river tube and toward the station. Home Signal GD139X42 was just ahead, with its top and bottom light both showing yellow. All signals control what's known as a block of track, and the light turns red if the block of track ahead of it is occupied. A home signal controls the track when two routes intersect.

The two yellows meant that the track was clear ahead, but proceed with caution to the next signal. Mark Vales could keep going.

But were they both yellow? You drive through the dark and you see all the lights, red and yellow and green, and the brain begins to tease itself. That one, was it yellow? Wasn't it red? What's that up ahead? Truck drivers call it white-line fever. Train operators call it tunnel vision. Now Vales was at an automatic signal, D21250, which was yellow—he could keep moving.

Instead, Vales stopped the train. He peered ahead, could just about make out the lights at Queens Plaza. There was no train ahead. He pushed down for power.

The train rolled back a few feet. Vales found circuit switches, reset them. Still no good. Again, the train rolled back. Then it did not budge.

Vales pushed the button on his microphone.

"Command, come into 6:05 R out of Canal."

There was no response.

"Command, come into the 6:05 R out of Canal."

The radio was dead. So was Joyce Bresa's train.

6:43 P.M., Eleventh Street Cut: Joyce Bresa

Joyce didn't bother looking out the window of the train. There was nothing to see. In her head, she had a clock that was pacing the trip, and she reckoned the train was not far from Queens Plaza when it stopped. No problem: so many lines meet at the station that it wasn't unusual to wait a minute or two just outside while earlier trains clear.

"Congestion ahead" is the usual announcement made by the conductors. It was a reason cited for every conceivable delay—to the disbelief of riders who, having spent twenty or twenty-five minutes waiting for a train, knew that there could be no traffic immediately before them. But it was the customary excuse made at a customary place, and even though the conductor didn't call it out on the P.A., Joyce assumed that was the problem. Annoying.

A man who worked for the post office was dressed in his letter carrier's outfit. When the train stopped, he looked down at the woman sitting in front of him.

"People should understand now why their mail is late," he said. She smiled.

"A hundred bottles of beer on the wall," someone sang out, "a hundred bottles of beer . . ."

"You take one down, you pass it around, ninety-nine bottles of beer on the wall," someone else answered.

They were interrupted by an announcement. This would be the "Congestion ahead" excuse.

"Your attention, ladies and gentlemen. Due to a signal against us, we are being held here temporarily.

"Ladies and gentlemen, we have everything under control."

Guffaws and general hilarity followed this. "Ninety-eight bottles of beer . . ."

Just then the train lurched, and Joyce felt a grinding under her feet. Then the train rolled back. She felt it push forward again and then roll back. The vibrations of the engine stopped. The train was silent. Then came a crackle over the P.A., and the conductor's voice:

"Motorman, where are you?"

A pause for an answer that did not come.

"Motorman? Are you there, motorman?"

There was a hush after this, but no one picked up the song about the bottles of beer on the wall. The fans stopped whirling. Then the lights flickered and died.

6:44 P.M., Flushing Avenue, Brooklyn: Scene from a Play

The Cast: Denia Brache, a tall woman with a waterfall of dark hair over her shoulders and down her back. Exquisitely fine features, highlighted with a few dabs of rouge and shadow. She carries a big leather pocketbook and a plastic bag. Also Assorted New Yorkers, including a teenage couple who appear to be in the usual state of adolescent heat, and a newspaper reporter in the usual state of rumpledness.

The Place: The elevated train platform at Flushing Avenue in Brooklyn.

The Time: A hot evening in spring 1989.

The Set: The audience is looking down at the elevated platform, so it can see the players, and beyond them, the cars threading around the girders of the Broadway el. The roof of a supermarket can also be seen, a long flat field of unbroken black tar, except where people on the el have thrown cans and bottles.

When the curtain rises, we see the young couple kissing passionately. The reporter is leaning over the platform rail, looking at the street. Denia Brache enters, right, from the staircase. She is frowning, and talking with great animation to no one in particular.

Denia: (*menacingly*) But don't you feel so safe.

Reporter: Huh?

Denia: I don't want to talk about this, because I am afraid of what you'll do.

The reporter retreats downstage, and positions himself on the other side of a big trash bin. From there, he eyes Denia, who continues to talk, at times, waving her index finger. The young couple, who have been in a clinch, come up for air. At once, they notice Denia.

Boy: Crazy bitch.

Girl: Who is she talking to?

Denia: (*oblivious*) Leave her alone.

They, too, retreat. Denia becomes increasingly agitated. She swings her hands, makes a fist, glares at the sky and continues to talk. Occasionally, the reporter can hear snatches of what she is saying. He wanders nearer to her.

Denia: Not in this house. Not while I am here.

Reporter: Are you feeling all right?

Denia: (*Her tone changes instantaneously.*) Just a minute. (*She returns to her agitated state.*) Not while I am here.

The reporter stares blankly.

Denia: I am doing La Poncia in *The House of Bernarda Alba* by García Lorca.

Reporter: Pardon?

Denia: I have an audition downtown in thirty minutes. La Poncia, she is the maid, the servant. It's a good part. She keeps all the secrets in the family, because she is very close to Bernarda—because, really, Bernarda knows her mother was a whore.

Reporter: Ah.

Boy: (*from the other side of the trash bin, referring to the reporter*) He's moving on her.

Girl: She's crazy.

Denia: I don't care. One time I was rehearsing the part of a lady who was completely nuts. You should have seen me then.

Boy: How about right now?

Denia: I don't feel any shame. If they want to laugh, let them have a good time. This is a very strong part, very dramatic. She hates Bernarda, but she is faithful to her. One day she is going to say whatever she has to say.

The J train pulls into the station. They all board. Denia sits down and takes off her shoes, which have low heels, and replaces them with flats. She finds a brush in her bag and vigorously strokes her hair, then ties it behind her. Apparently, it is an effort to age herself.

Denia: This is a character part of a sixty-five-year-old woman.

Reporter: How old are you?

Denia: We in the acting business never disclose our age; someone will say we're not right for a part even when we could do it. I'm in the range of twenty-five to thirty-five. I do voice-over work, some television shows and I have a part-time job, of course, for money. I rehearse wherever I am going, all the time when I am in the train. Now I am going to Fourteenth Street for this audition, for an out-of-town production in Minneapolis, Minnesota.

Girl: If she acts like that in public, in Minnesota they'll lock her up.

Denia: Some days I have to play very emotional parts, and I cry. People come over to me and ask, Is there anything I can do, lady? I say, What's the matter with you, you never saw someone talk to themselves? I'm just practicing.

Boy: She's rehearsing talking to herself.

Denia: (*in character, jabbing finger*) I said what I have to say. Wish me luck.

Exeunt, to the roar of the subway.

"Command Center," said the dispatcher on Jay Street.

"Queens Plaza dispatcher here, Command. South of Queens Plaza we have the 6:05 R out of Canal and it's not moving."

The stalled train was invisible to the people in the Command Center—just like most other trains, moving or stationary, that theoretically were under their control. They sat in front of a 70-foot board, the perfect scale model of every inch of the 731 miles of tracks in the city subway and elevated system. But no more than 50 track miles had been plugged into the circuits that would show trains passing: 93 percent of the system was invisible in the Command Center.

Still, to prevent a drastically bad night from getting worse, the Command staff needed information, fast.

Another train, a G coming from Brooklyn, was just one stop away and was ready to leave for Queens Plaza, where it would merge with the R. If the switch was blocked, the G would have to be held in the station. Otherwise, it would be stuck in the tunnel behind the stalled R train.

At Queens Plaza, a tower operator looked at his track board. Unlike the board in the Command Center at Jay Street, this one worked—though it showed only a few miles of track in either direction. Also on the display were the switches under his control. Four lines converged on Queens Plaza station, making it the busiest in the borough.

Of course, a train, by itself, can't turn left or right: it is steered by the switches. And the switches are run by the tower operator, who watches train movements on a miniature version of the model board at the Command Center.

A train on a switch blocks traffic on two tracks, because the signal system automatically prevents trains from converging on each other.

So it was critical for the Command Center to know if the R train was stuck on a switch.

At Queens Plaza, a tower operator—working a double shift—looked at his board. Somehow, he didn't notice that the R train was blocking the switch.

"It's clear of the switches," said the tower operator.

The G train from Brooklyn was sent on toward Queens Plaza.

6:46 P.M., Eleventh Street Cut, Queens: Joyce Bresa

"How long do you think we'll be here?" Joyce asks.

He's a middle-aged, working-class African-American, stuck in the same place on the train with her, and he doesn't have the first idea about what is wrong. But he sees the beads of perspiration on her face and panic beneath the thin ice of her eyes.

"This? Oh, this should be about forty-five minutes," says the man, improvising. "But it probably wouldn't take that long." He looks her over, and begins to worry. "So you don't take this kind of thing really well, eh?"

"No."

"So, what do I do—how can I help you?"

"Well, talking to me would help a lot," says Joyce.

"You know, I been riding the trains a long time," the man begins. "Fifty years. All my life. I remember when the train used to be a nickel and service used to be better. We used to take the subways everywhere then, any time, day or night. You could go to see a show, come home by yourself after midnight. Even the ladies would do that. Not a worry in the world."

He pauses a minute. Joyce is staring, trying to focus on his words about bygone days.

"We used to have Miss Subways back then."

"Oh, really?" said Joyce.

"You're probably too young to realize it."

"I'm not too young to realize it, I'm too young to remember it."

"You could have been Miss Subways. You never know. Anyone could have been a Miss Subways. They just took a nice face off the train and made you Miss Subways."

That was sort of how it worked. In 1941, the city had just taken over the operation of all the formerly private subway lines, and revenue was desperately needed. To promote advertising space on the trains, the Miss Subways contest was invented, with posters made of young working women, detailing their aspirations, their backgrounds, their availability. (One was fired when it was discovered she was actually a Mrs. Subway.)

"A little girl with big ambitions!" read one ad. "Thank County Mayo for this Washington Heights beauty" said another. One contestant took to the stage of the Apollo Theater in Harlem, where she urged the audience to send postcards supporting her candidacy. In the musical *On The Town,* a beauty contest winner is dubbed Miss Turnstiles, and she is pursued by a lovelorn sailor who sees her in a station, then spends the rest of his shore leave trying to find her. The contest ended in 1976, after the faces of two hundred women had rolled across the decades.

All before Joyce's time in New York.

"You didn't have to do anything nice to win?" she asks.

"You didn't have to do a damn thing. You only had to live in a borough."

"I would have missed that because I grew up upstate," she explains to the stranger on the train.

It was far away, on an afternoon long ago when Joyce was five. She and her sister were playing in the family's little Cape Cod house in Hopewell Junction, and at the top of the stairs was a bay window with a small cabinet underneath. Wouldn't it be fun, said her sister, to crawl into it? Joyce thought so. She wedged herself into the cabinet. Her sister closed the doors and giggled. Then she locked the latch, ran off and was distracted. Two hours later, her frantic mother opened the cabinet. Joyce was curled up in a ball. Awake.

As an adult, she squirmed off crowded elevators. She wouldn't go into submarine rides at amusement parks. She let overcrowded trains pass by. Usually.

"YO, move the Fuckin' TRAIN!" holler the boys. They're coming home from a softball game. They have their bats and are banging them on the floor of the car.

"Listen, fellows, we have to wait here, it's not going to help any by your screaming," Renee Guttierez admonishes.

6:48 P.M., Eleventh Street Cut: Joyce Bresa

As soon as they spotted the R train stuck in the tunnel near Queens Plaza, Veamon Sanders and Reginald Edmondson, a pair of roving troubleshooters, headed along the catwalk to see if they could get it moving.

"What's the matter?" asked Edmondson.

"She won't take power," said Vales.

Edmondson tried for himself but could not raise the dead train. A typical on-the-spot subway train repair involves resetting circuit breakers, much like those in a home. That didn't work. Then he walked toward the rear to try starting the train from the fifth car.

There were serious problems with this train, and in a dark, hot tunnel, it was next to impossible to discover them, much less repair them. Edmondson was hoping to get the power in the rear five cars on the chance that they could push the train as far as the station. But the fifth car was as dead as the first.

He climbed back onto the catwalk. That was when he saw the passenger, walking along as if he owned the place.

"Hey, man," said Edmondson. "Get back in the car."

"Later for that," said the man, who kept walking.

"It's not safe out here."

The man ignored him. A moment later, he passed the conductor, Edgardo Febles.

"Come on back in here," said Febles. The man stumbled in the dark, but did not fall. Febles had been a conductor for two weeks. In conductor school, they'd taught him that a train should not move with a passenger on the roadbed. The public address system was dead, which meant Febles couldn't contact motorman Vales in the first car. He could barely move inside his own car, much less walk through five more to the front. So he pulled the emergency brake cord.

He needn't have bothered. That train wasn't going anywhere.

Just a week ago, the lead car, No. 3734, had been checked out in the Jamaica yard by Inspection Team 14. There were breaks and cracks in the trolley lead—a condition that could mortally wound the car and the train connected to it. New York subway cars take their power from a third rail that carries between 600 and 750 volts of power. Two "shoes" on each side of the car grip the third rail, and the trolley line carries the electricity from the shoes to the motors.

A cracked trolley line is approximately the same as a tourniquet on a limb: it blocks the flow of vital juices.

But this car had traveled 1,166,332 miles in its twenty-five years of service. It was long past due for a major overhaul, and was scheduled to receive one in a couple of months. Meanwhile, it was in such bad shape that for the regular inspection team to do a fair repair job, the car would have to be lifted with a crane and its undersides removed. Fat chance.

Instead of going to all that bother, someone found a roll of electrical tape and wrapped it around the cracked trolley line. It was a patchwork job. But, hey, the car was going out for overhaul soon. And there was a lot of pressure to provide cars to make service. Making the score, it was called in the barns: supplying all the cars necessary to make the schedule.

So no one on Team 14, none of the managers who had been installed at great expense by David Gunn, troubled about water in the batteries, either. Half of the shoes were misaligned. Insulation on the electrical portion of the third car was frayed.

By the time the train got to the Eleventh Street Cut, seven of the ten cars had dead motors, thanks to low water in the batteries. That meant the first car was pulling most of the train by itself. And when it rolled across the switch, the first car no longer was attached to live power—because of its gaping trolley line.

Normally, the rear cars could supply adequate juice—but their motors had expired.

The bottom line was that the train should not have been put into service. But on a hot evening in 1989, with a billion dollars worth of new and overhauled cars not available because they were in for repairs, something had to be put out on the road. The TA had to make the score.

Cracked cables, dead motors, a useless radio, average mileage on the ten cars of 1,181,514, and it was going on the road to take working people home from the steamy night. Only one thing could have kept this train out of service: a teenager with a can of spray paint. The dispatcher who put a graffiti-ed train into service could look forward to a few days in the street. Without pay.

6:56 P.M., Command Center: Scene

"Command Center, come in to the 6:22 G."
   "Command."
   "South of Queens Plaza, we have a signal D2-1248 red against us. It appears that there is an R train over the switch."
   "Stand by. Queens Plaza tower, come in to Command."
   "Queens Plaza."
   "Is that 6:05 R over any switches?"
   "Affirmative. The 6:05 is over switch 33."
   "Thank you."

7:05 P.M., Eleventh Street Cut: Joyce Bresa

"Police, Blakely on the B2 at 05."
   "Police."
   "We need police help at Queens Plaza right away. We got passengers leaving a stalled train south of the plaza."
   "Police."
   "B2, come back for police."
   "Blakely on the B2, police."
   "At Queens Plaza, what is the interval on that train?"
   "I don't know. It's a northbound R train south of the Plaza."
   "People are detraining onto the roadbed?"
   "Yes."

People may be evacuating from the front cars, but in the dark of Joyce's car at the rear, no one is moving. Who can see?

A couple of people flick butane lighters.

"Put it out—hey—put it out," says an authoritative voice.

"We don't know what kind of gases are down here," says another.

The lights disappear. But the mood in the car turns sour. The man who had comforted Joyce with tales of Miss Subways is getting dry in the throat. Not from talking, either. He's getting worried.

"Miss?" A young black man in a suit, who had been chatting with an older man, places his arm on her elbow, gently, to get her attention. "Are you feeling all right?"

"I wish I had a Life Saver," says Joyce.

"Would a Life Saver help?"

"You wouldn't believe it, but I would have something to concentrate on doing. Anything. To concentrate my mind on anything."

"Why don't you have a seat here on my briefcase a little while," says the man. "Take the load off your feet."

Joyce is grateful. The train has died on a curve, with the tracks banked to one side. People have to lean against the tilt. All day on her feet and now she's standing on a hill in hell.

Even before he offered his briefcase as a seat, Joyce had been trying to figure out the relationship between the younger man and the older. Lawyers, she thought. The older one is definitely a professor, and the other, a former student. They met each other in this boiling dungeon. They said something about Fordham. She tried to keep her thoughts on the two men, but panic began to climb along her back. She was sweating heavily.

The advertising posters, on the walls where Miss Subway once reigned, were being torn off the walls and used as makeshift fans. Now the older man was fanning her.

It was not long before everyone in her car had heard Renee Guttierez talk about the problems with the trains, things that ought to be done, and how it was best to REMAIN CALM. Finally one man spoke back to her.

"Lady, that voice, if I were married to you . . ." and people around him giggled. Renee did, too, even though it wasn't really a funny joke, in her opinion.

7:11 P.M., Police Radio Room, Jay Street, Brooklyn: Scene

"Okay, that was the original 6:05 Extra out of Court. That train did recharge, they found a pulled cord and then they tried to move and lost power."

"At this time, he still is not moving, correct?"

"Oh definitely. As a matter of fact, I am letting everybody know as of 1909 we have power off on the Dog-2 track from Eleventh Street to Holt at 1911. We have power off on the GD2 track from Eleventh Street to Austin, that's due to passengers going onto the roadbed and the catwalk."

"All right, in English, that's the northbound local and express?"

"No, that's northbound local. Both tracks. The express is still alive, the reason for that is we have trains coming in from crosstown line and the Broadway subway. Okay, listen, I got three officers standing on the platform. I want these officers to stop these passengers from getting off the train if we can."

"Okay. Any part of that train in the station at all?"

"No, that's why we are evacuating it."

"You are evacuating it or just people trying to jump to the tracks?"

"The passengers have taken it upon themselves to leave the train. They are jumping between the cars. They have broken out windows. They are generally leaving of their own accord. We have not officially told them to get off the train."

7:15 P.M., Eleventh Street Cut: Joyce Bresa

The temperature in the cars is approaching 115 degrees. The fans are not moving, and the windows are open only the slightest crack, if at all. The voices rise in anger.

"Shut up."

"Get away from me, you're too close to me."

"You don't know what you're talking about."

"Let's not fight, we're in a bad situation, we're all in this together."

The voices, soothing and angry, drizzle down the car.

Then someone mutters it. Just a few words. The name of a movie that every subway rider has seen.

"It's like *The Taking of Pelham One Two Three*."

Hardly anyone laughs. Something has happened on the street, Joyce decides. She glances at the man who had tried to soothe her with the tale of Miss Subways. He is rocking against the door, back and forth. Why can't people come from the station to help us? she thinks. Someone has taken over the station. With guns. No one can get by the guns to help the people in the tunnel.

Something terrible.

Renee Guttierez gazes at the steamed-up windows on the train. That woman who didn't get on the train back at the station under the Plaza. The one who gave up waiting, and went to get the express bus.

It wasn't her time to go, Renee Guttierez thinks. But it's my time. I never even thought to tell anyone goodbye. Hail Mary, full of grace, the Lord is with thee. Blessed art thou among women, and blessed is the fruit of thy womb, Jesus.

Holy Mary, Mother of God, pray for us sinners now, and at the hour of our death.

Amen.

"Police."

"I understand from my motor instructor on the scene that your officers are helping the passengers off the train and onto the platform. That's not what we are requesting. We are requesting that they stop the passengers from getting off the train."

"All right, I'll let them know."

"Police Stack on the IND."

"Police."

"All right police, the motor instructor on the scene south of the plaza is reporting we need medical assistance there. We have a passenger who fell and we have some people that are overcome by the heat."

"Okay, thank you."

"Police, come into Darby on the IND."

"Police."

"Police be advised that in regard to that 6:05 R that lost power with the passengers on the roadbed, we have the 6:22 G out of Fourth Avenue stuck behind him with power off. Also, passengers are misbehaving on the 6:22 G."

"I'll make a note of it. Thank you."

"All concerned come into Stack on the IND at 1928. We got a report that people are roaming all over the tracks south of Queens Plaza, we are going to have to remove the power on the northbound express track. We will have no E or F service in or out of Queens Plaza. We need a lot of assistance over there. We just can't stop the people getting off the train. Nobody's there allowing them to get off. We want to stop them."

"Police. We got everybody available in the area responding. We don't have a whole lot of people out there."

7:35 p.m., Eleventh Street Cut: Joyce Bresa

Joyce is wobbling a bit when she hears the shatter of glass, somewhere in the distance. Then another window, closer. She snaps straight up. What now? My God, has someone flipped out?

"The kids are out there," someone reports. "They have a bat. They're breaking the windows."

"See if they'll come here and do it."

The boys arrive with bats on shoulders.

"Stand back, folks, we don't want no one getting hurt," says a big kid of about fifteen. "Getcha little bit more air in here."

With a mighty swing, he knocks out a window. A draft of the rank tunnel breath comes in, and everyone breathes deeply, then lets out big sighs. They feel a little better. It's still pitch black.

Out there, in the dark, is the G train, blocked by their own R train. An F train, a big hulking shadow, is stranded by the power removed from the tracks because of the people wandering on the roadbed.

Joyce can't see out to the other trains, to the several thousand people also stuck in the dark. Abandoned. There is a good possibility that she will not get out alive. A woman sitting on the bench catches her eye for a long minute, then asks, "Do you think we are going to die here?"

Joyce can't bring herself to lie. She says nothing.

7:37 p.m., East Harlem, Manhattan: Scene

Three kids barrel down the stairs at 96th Street and Lexington, flashing subway passes at the token clerk.

"Hey, guys," says a transit cop, pointedly looking at his wristwatch. "What's the problem? It's after seven o'clock, your passes expired. Why are you so late?"

"Officer, we were at play rehearsal," says Gardell Betancourt, fourteen.

"Okay," says the cop. "What's the name of the play?"

"Joseph and the Amazing Technicolor Dreamcoat," says Ray Santa, thirteen.

"Never heard of it," says the policeman. "What part do you play?"

"I'm Levi, one of the brothers," says Gardell.

"I'm Jacob's nephew, and one of the guards," says Ray.

"Stage manager," says the third member of the trio, Eson Chan, twelve.

"Let's have some proof," the cop asks. "What are your lines?"

"It's a musical, all songs, there hardly are any lines," says Ray.

"How about you?" the cop asks Eson.

"He's the stage manager," says Ray. "He doesn't speak onstage."

"You better manage something," says the cop. "Let's hear one of the songs."

The three boys huddle on the station mezzanine. As students at De La Salle Academy, a private junior high school for kids rich in spirit and brains but poor in the pocket, they travel the city to a splendid education. There's very little that a subway ride can throw at them that they can't handle—even when their embarrassment glands suddenly are pumping lethal doses of mortification through their adolescent veins.

"Are we really going to do this?" whispers Eson.

"Yes," says Ray. "What're we going to sing?"

"Let's do 'One More Angel,' " suggests Gardell, who has a starring role in the production and knows the song well. Ray and Eson agree.

"Hey, guys," the cop hollers around the station. "These kids are going to sing for us."

Another cop saunters over. An elderly couple heading for the No. 6 train pause. The token clerk sticks his head out the door of the booth.

"Okay," says Ray, snapping his fingers, bending at the knee, bouncing a foot until he finds the beat. Gardell opens:

"Father, we have something to tell you . . ."

There are a number of silly little gestures that must be done in the performance of this song—palms out, waving back and forth, pointing to the sky, heads rocking in unison. All this the boys do as they sing, with Gardell leading:

"Of manhood in its prime . . ."

Their audience claps, hoots and wishes them well as the boys head for the train, three kids who sang for their subway.

7:44–7:51 P.M., Police Radio Desk, Jay Street: Scene

"Hello, police, Blakely on the B2."

"Police."

"Be advised that we are now requesting medical assistance over there at the plaza. I got a report from the motor instructor passengers are feeling faint."

"Okay, I got multiple medical buses en route."

"Okay, by the way, I lost contact with my train operator. I don't know what's going on now."

"I'll see if I can get an update."

"All departments, Blakely on the B2."

"Track and Structures."

"Stations."

"Electric."

"Okay, we are setting up a command post at the south end of the northbound platform. Train dispatcher Flores, RTO [Rapid Transit Operations] will be the man on the command post."

7:58 P.M., Police Radio Desk, Jay Street: Scene

"Police, Blakely on the B2."

"Okay, Mr. Blakely, go ahead."

"Okay, listen, we have a report now on the 6:22, which your personnel are walking to, my motor instructor has not seen them yet. But on that train there is a female passenger who is pregnant and getting nauseous."

"Okay, I'll let them know in the tunnel. Our radios don't work too well, but I'll try."

"I understand."

8 P.M.
MAY 12

A MAP
THAT TELLS
A STORY

Token clerks will hand out more than 8,000 free subway maps today and every day, some 3 million a year when business is booming. The current edition is a sterling piece of design that, in 1979, replaced something that belonged in a gallery at the Museum of Modern Art, not on a subway wall. It wrestles the geography of the city and the spaghetti of the subway into a single, nearly sensible package. When you crack the code, it unlocks the city like nothing else.

The careful map reader will find an entry for a Brooklyn stop called Empire Boulevard. Until 1918, it was known as Malbone Street. The events of November 1, 1918, would drill the name Malbone Street into the consciousness of New Yorkers. That morning, motormen with the Brooklyn Rapid Transit stopped work because the company was firing people who joined the Brotherhood of Locomotive Engineers.

To keep service going, the BRT sent an overtired and untrained dispatcher to drive a train from Manhattan to Brighton Beach. In his fourteenth hour of duty, he took a curve at Malbone Street too fast and derailed. The worst acci-

dent in the history of the subways killed 102. Dozens who survived the collision were electrocuted because dispatchers thought the power had been shut off by strikers as a prank. They restored it as the dazed riders staggered in the dark. The crash forced the transit company into bankruptcy, and made Malbone Street a synonym for horror. A few years later, the city changed the name of the stop to Empire Boulevard.

8:15 P.M., Eleventh Street Cut: Joyce Bresa

"They would have a much calmer person on their hands if they would just tell me why I was sitting here," says Joyce.

"It could be anything, but I'm sure it's nothing," says the young man, his tie loosened.

"You told me that an hour ago. I don't think I believe you anymore."

"I probably don't blame you."

"I've been riding the train since the day they opened," says the professor, "and I've never been stuck on a train this long."

"Oh really?" says Joyce. This is not a young man. He might have told me, Oh yeah, two years ago, I was on the train for three hours. No cheap little comforting remarks.

8:25 P.M., Under Herald Square, Manhattan: Scene

At last, a phone that works. Richard McDonough has to make a call back home, to Phoenix, and the first three pay telephones he's tried in this subway station gave no dial tone. At the fourth one, McDonough punches the number for Phoenix to give a fast report on his trip to New York.

"Really," he says into the phone. "People have been quite nice. Not what we've been told at all."

Over his shoulder, McDonough can see another man trying the pay phones, each one in turn, just as he had. Then the man reaches over to a metal conduit that fed the entire bank of telephones. He lifts a section of it away. A rope of wires dangled inside. Maybe he will fix the dead phones, McDonough thinks. No, he doesn't seem to be doing that at all. Watching the man from the corner of his eye, McDonough is having a hard time concentrating on the conversation.

"If I sound real strange for a moment, it's because there's a guy next to me chewing on the phone wires," McDonough explains into the phone.

There may be madness on the streets of New York, but in the subways it usually comes complete with an instruction manual on method: as McDonough watches the man gnaw through the telephone wires, he hears silver cascading into the coin returns of three nearby phones. The man scoops the change out of the phones and heads into the night.

"It was like a slot machine paying off," McDonough explains into his phone, which, thanks to precision wire chewing, was unmolested. "He knew exactly what he was doing."

The lines for most of the 2,500 pay phones in the naked subway system are available to the cunning of the New York hustlers, a breed that has been finding ways to jimmy and rig them over four decades. Unlike their cousins upstairs, the subway phone wires often hang in exposed places, while lines for street phones run underground to the booths.

Because the wires leading up to the subway phones are accessible, the crooks are able to tamper with them. One way is to chew the wire insulation.

"They are fooling with the wiring—either in the handset or in the wiring leading up to the phone booth," explains Richard Edney of the New York Telephone Company. "They are shorting out the telephone. This knocks out the telephone's ability to return money because an electric impulse triggers the coin return."

Now the phone won't return coins and won't make phone calls. The wire chewer waits nearby for people to fill it with change.

"Then the thief 'unshorts' the telephone line," says Edney, "and the machine tells itself to give back the dough. And the money drops out."

Some $15 million drops out—over the course of a year, and a dozen other scams, run by a hundred other scam artists.

While the phone company offers a $2,000 reward for tips on phone bandits, McDonough is not tempted, as he explains after his call out west.

"I considered saying something to the guy—but I figured, well, if he chewed on wires, he might start on me next," says McDonough.

8:30 P.M., Eleventh Street Cut: Joyce Bresa

A man with a flashlight appears at one of the broken windows.

"We'll be going out through the door in a couple of minutes," he says.

What door, Joyce wonders. God. She was so glad to see him.

"Someone's having a heart attack," a voice says.

The stretcher comes through. Fifteen minutes later, they lead people from Joyce's car to the catwalk, but the riders swoon and collapse. Joyce slips and bangs her knee.

She hardly feels it, but she decides to step back on the train and walk through the cars to the front, 600 feet. Along the way, she sees men and women sprawled on the floors. One man is clutching his fractured knee. A few people stay with a woman who has two children, to help them out. A short man, who can't weigh more than 130 pounds, puts his determined shoulder under a woman 60 pounds his better and half drags her to the front. Casualties.

8:56 P.M., Command Center: Scene

"Police, come in for Blakely."

"Police."

"Okay, police, do we have request to restore power on the local track two, south of Queens Plaza. We are looking for a reason to do that. I understand everybody is off the R line at D2 track."

"Okay, stand by."

(A pause in the transcript record, which resumes at 9 P.M.)

"B2, come in for police. B2, come in for police."

"Police, go ahead for B2."

"Okay, B2, be advised I am being advised by my supervisor Geere, supervision in the field, they do not, I will repeat, do not want power restored at this time. Any questions, please contact my supervisor 3860."

"All right, police. This is Goldberg at 2101 hours."

(A pause in the transcript record, which resumes at 9:12 P.M.)

"Police, come in for B2."

"I need you, police, also. I have a confirmation from Captain O'Hare on the scene at Queens Plaza to restore power to all tracks at that location."

"Okay, all departments, Blakely on B2, restoring power all over Queens Plaza area. I will give you details later."

"Track and Structures."

"Shops."

"Station."

"Electric."

It was over.

9 P.M.
MAY 12

THEY
MOVE
IT

The IRT for many years was known as the Irish Rapid Transit. When the first successful transit union was forming in the 1930s, the driving forces were members of Clan na Gael, a secretive Irish brotherhood that had started in America in 1867 to back Irish independence from Britain. In the 1930s, after revolution and civil war in Ireland, many members of the Irish Republican Army had moved to America and joined the Clan. They were key players in the founding of the Transport Workers Union. It was not until 1985 that Local 100 of the Transport Workers Union would have its first president born outside Ireland. Probably more than half of the city's transit workers through the 1940s were Irish, with most of them coming from Galway, Kerry, and Cork, the poor western and southern counties of Ireland. Most of the Irish had not seen a telephone before coming to the United States and had little formal education. The entry-level positions in transit provided a quick path into the lower ranks of the middle class.

Today the ascension of a black middle class can be gauged by watching the faces in the token booths, the conductors' cabs, or behind the wind-shield of the train operators' cars.

David Wilson, the son of a slave, finished eighth grade in Baysville, South Carolina, and was one of a family of fifteen that came north in the early 1930s to New York. Wilson was part of a great historical tide: machines had ended cotton pick-ing as a way of life in the South. He went to work in 1946 for the city's Board of Transportation and stayed three decades. He married Dovetta, who finished fifth grade in Alabama and worked in New York as a cafeteria aide, and they lived in a place called the Lincoln houses in Harlem, a public housing project filled with sure-footed climbers. The Wilsons raised nine kids. They ate dinner together every night at 6 P.M. Chores on Saturday, church on Sunday, homework from the public schools every night. One hour of television a day for the kids—provided there was no fighting. The nine kids grew to be nine professional adults, living across the United States.

"He was a track man the whole time he was there," said Timothy Wilson, the fourth of the clan and a city accountant. "The subway, that was his thing; he was always on those trains. He was proud of it. He'd have to be on his deathbed before he'd take a day off."

David Wilson retired in 1976 after thirty years with transit. By May 12, 1989, he has been dead four years. But one of his dying complaints rings in the ears of his children—those best able to give something back to Harlem had moved on. "He named off certain families that had left, including us," recalled Carolyn C. Blair, twenty-eight, the youngest Wilson who is now an actress and singer. "He said, 'Don't be like that. This is where you grew up, got your roots, your training. Give some-thing back.'" And so they decided to pool their funds and create a family scholarship fund, named for David and Dovetta, that would help another generation of youngsters make it into college.

An arc of American history, running from starving Irish immigrants to the children of black slaves, curves up when it reaches the subway.

Today, there may be a sprinkling of Irish-born subway work-

ers, but by far the largest group are American-born blacks. Since the migration north in the 1940s, blacks have grown from about 10 percent to 42 percent of the 51,000 transit workers. Hispanics are now about 10 percent, and Asians, 4 percent. They have health insurance and sick leave, paid vacations and good pensions. Their base wages range from $19,000 to $35,000 a year.

They have their chance at an American dream because they went down to climb up.

9:20 P.M., Queens Plaza:
Joyce Bresa

This really is the worst thing that has ever happened to me, Renee Guttierez decided when she got to the top of the stairs. People in uniforms were running around. Not a cab or bus anywhere. She'd walk. The air would be good.

They didn't even have a person there to say sorry.

Ten minutes later, Joyce staggered up to the street. It seemed there were fifty rescue vehicles on the street, the ambulances, the fire trucks, police emergency trucks. Mayor Koch was out for a drive, heard the news on the radio, and went to the scene. He was leaning over one of the people on a stretcher, and speaking into a cellular phone. Television cameras filmed the mayor in action. How wonderful, Joyce thought.

Lines of people waited at the pay phones near the station. She crossed Northern Boulevard and found a phone. No dial tone, and then she noticed a metal hood across the coin slot. She hung up. She would never get home. A car rolled past, and from the corner of her hungry eye, she saw it. Reno. She ran half a block, futilely, waving, trying to yell. Maybe it wasn't him. She found herself in front of a bank with a phone. Reno answered the first ring.

"Hi, it's me."

"Are you all right?"

"I'm at this bank on Northern Boulevard. Near the Queens Plaza station. Come get me."

A young girl wandered down the street. Mascara streaked her face. No one was wearing dark glasses now: the hour of avoiding eye contact had long passed.

"Where are you going?" asked Joyce.

"I've got an aunt here in Astoria. I'm going to go there, to her house, and get a ride home. Or something. I don't know. I can't think."

"My husband will take you there."

"You're sure he doesn't mind?" A pure New Yorker.

"No."

The car pulled up in five minutes. Joyce opened the door.

"Reno, I have this girl here, who needs a ride."

"Oh, of course, I'll take you where you want to go."

Joyce sat numbly in the front seat. Reno's eyes shifted from the road to her knees, where blood had soaked through the stocking from her slip on the catwalk. He looked at her face.

The girl got out of the car with effusive thanks. As Reno pulled away from the curb, Joyce dissolved in tears.

"How is your mother?" she sobbed.

"You know, Joyce, it's amazing, she was a real trooper. I don't know if it was because I was just a mess."

They reached the door of the house. Her mother-in-law walked to the door and fell to her knees, wailing and weeping between bursts of Italian.

"I thought I was never going to see you again, I sat out on the porch looking at Daddy, saying, Reno doesn't know but she's never coming home."

"Yeah, well, I'm fine."

Joyce went upstairs. The refrigerator door was covered with phone numbers of police precincts, hospital, the Transit Authority. Reno fixed her a bourbon and soda. She downed it. Then he made another and told her about a phone call he'd gotten earlier in the evening.

"Your sister called. They thought they'd come into the city for the weekend. I told them you hadn't come home yet, I didn't know where you were. But I said her clothes are still here, so I know she hasn't left me. I know Joyce. She'd *never* go anywhere without her clothes."

10 P.M.
MAY 12

PARKING THE SUBWAY

Only in New York would subway trains have a hard time finding a parking spot. At ten o'clock, a Brooklyn IRT train shoves off for the Bronx, not because the schedule really demands another train to move north now, but because there's nowhere to put it tonight—or any other night. The Livonia yard in Brooklyn, which houses parts of the IRT fleet, is full up. Every night, seventy cars have to go to the Bronx just because there's no room in Brooklyn. Of course, they pick up passengers along the way, but over the course of a year, the trains log 1.5 million miles of service that's really not necessary.

10:19 P.M., Canal Street, Manhattan: SONI and SLICK

They pay your way home from The Door at night after the train pass is no good. They have to. You run a school that doesn't open until two in the afternoon, nobody goes home until eight or nine o'clock, the subway pass has been dead for two hours already.

A man from The Door had escorted them to the subway station. He handed them tokens and watched them pass through the turn-stiles.

"JA's got this tunnel on the Number One line between Columbus Circle and 66th Street," says SLICK. "He hangs out there. We go fuck him up."

"How we gonna know if he's even there?" asks SONI.

"He's got a whole wall of tags there in the tunnel," says SLICK. "The whole thing, man, every piece of it is his. We could buff him good."

"Yo, we don't know that area too good," says AUDI. "I'm not down for that."

"Nah, man," says SLICK. "We got to."

"Yo, he tagged up SLICK's house, we gotta come back at him," says SONI, who, though dubious, is sensitive to his friend's slight. After all, SLICK has gotten into this thing because of SONI. This has been SONI's beef with JA, and SLICK sort of got dragged into it. Now he has been dissed, seriously. That's the lowest thing you can do to another writer, paint on his house.

AUDI should know this, man. SONI couldn't say it in front of SLICK. It's bad enough for SLICK.

"See? All right, man, be that way," says SLICK.

"Yo, man, I gotta go," says AUDI.

He leaves them as they wait for a train uptown, to JA's turf.

"Later," says SONI.

"Later," says SLICK. "Let's find JA."

10:30 P.M., Upper West Side, Manhattan: JA

A retarded move, JA tells himself. At least from what he had been told. Personally, he doesn't remember anything before he woke up on the road, cars screeching to a stop near his head. But SMITH had been there, watched the whole thing. And SMITH said when he saw JA take the leap, he thought about having to call JA's mother and tell her that he had died.

Ridiculous fucking thing to have done.

JA had been drunk. Spifflicated drunk. All he knows is that he had been with SMITH, on the ramps approaching the Lincoln Tunnel, scoping out places to tag. There was a very sweet-looking highway sign, directly above the six lanes of traffic leading to the tunnel. To get there, he'd had to jump about four or five feet from a street that overlooked it, then land on the frame of the sign.

"You almost made it," SMITH had said.

The moment he hit the pavement 15 feet below, trucks careening and cars screeching, marked the end of a forty-eight-hour frenzy of graffiti tagging all over the city. It had started on that predawn morning he'd tagged SLICK's house. "When you get the momentum going, it's like a fuel—you go on like a crack binge—with graffiti, not crack," JA later explained.

That was six days ago. So tonight, he is staying home in the splendid apartment on 86th Street, where a decorator's hand shows in every room. Except his lair. He keeps the mattress on the floor. In his oak rolltop desk are spray cans of paint. The oak cabinets built into the wall hold giant cans of spray paint, collector's quality: very hard to purchase, heavy-duty industrial-size cans that you could never find in the store. JA is king.

With a flick of the remote, MTV barrels into the room, through the stereo speakers of the television. He turns the page on a magazine, and wriggles his toes. They're sticking out of the plaster cast they'd put on to keep his knee in one place. Pain in the ass.

11:35
P.M.
MAY 12

BOOKING
THE
GAME

At the end of every work day, each transit department produces a report on its activities for the day.

These tend to run along dreary lines: the station department, for instance, lists the number of fires in trash cans and how many turnstiles have gone out of order.

But just about the last item in its eleven-page report on May 12, 1989, is entitled "Ball Game Summary." Shea Stadium had been built near the site of the 1963–1964 Worlds Fair, in Flushing, Queens—naturally, and necessarily, near a stop on a train line. When the Mets won the pennant in 1986, the fans celebrated by moving a good part of the outfield into the No. 7 train. The next morning, Vilma Newton, who supervised the cleaning on the line, got up early to make a huge tray of fried chicken. Then she called in crews to shovel out the turf and infield dirt, offering her own down-home reward for their efforts.

Today, there is little risk of over-exuberant fans: it's too early in the season. And as the stations department report shows, the Mets didn't bring any joy to Mudville—or the subways—on this night.

Time	*7:35-11:35 p.m.*
Attendance	*33,325*
Passengers exiting	*5,748*
Passengers entering	*4,377*
Bags Deposited	*3*
Amount	*$3,514*

Mets 3   Padres 4

Everything but the box scores.

11:45 P.M., Broadway, Manhattan: SONI and SLICK

The musicians from Lincoln Center are saying good night. Tonight, the opera was *Don Giovanni*. At the Vivian Beaumont, *Anything Goes* was selling out at $50 a ticket. The Mostly Mozart series had begun. Even with all this, it was a quiet time of year for the high-culture scene, in a way, since the ballet company was closed. Once, the choreographer Twyla Tharp put on a ballet with graffiti writers, on-stage, painting the set, while the dancers went through their steps. It was a smashing success nearly twenty years ago, with Manhattan people paying good money to watch these ghetto kids from the Bronx and Harlem.

The centerpiece fountain had been turned back on only a week or so earlier; the city had ordered all ornamental water displays shut off because of a drought scare. Even though its water was recycled, the dry fountain was a powerful symbol. A burbling fountain would be a soothing presence in the wicked heat of the city.

The pit musicians, the orchestra players, were walking into the warm night, the men in black tie and jacket, the women in long dresses. Even without the instruments, you could tell they were working people, despite the formal gear, because they walked across the plaza of the arts center and down to the Broadway subway station.

There, you could stare into the tunnel and see all the way to the lights of the station at Columbus Circle, 59th Street. When a train approaches, its headlights come together like a rising line drive off the bat of a mighty hitter.

It is just seven blocks from the Lincoln Center stop to Columbus Circle, a distance that two quick, strong young men can cover in a few minutes. The way the light falls, the boys in the tunnel are swallowed in shadows. And they have business to do. There are probably fifteen tags on the tunnel wall between the two stations. It is hard to see them all, but they get most of them. Buff them. Stomp on his shit. That was one wall. Three spray cans of gray paint already are beat. Only one left. Now they have to do the other side. Have to.

The musicians peer into the darkness. Ah, there's the No. 1. Good ol' No. 1. They're lucky to get out of work before midnight. The trains start slowing down after 12:00. This one, the 11:59 out of South Ferry, was going up to the Bronx and into the 240th Street yard. Yardmaster Darrell Williams is waiting there to get it to the car wash. Now, from the 66th Street platform, the musicians see the train leave the Columbus Circle station, starting up the rise to Lincoln Center.

Later, when he was able to talk about it without weeping, the motorman would say that before the train brakes went into emergency mode, he thought he saw a bundle of clothes on the roadbed. That wouldn't be enough to trigger the automatic brake under the car. Needed something more solid. He climbed down on the roadbed and started looking. He had to go back eight cars before he found the . . . obstructions.

At Lincoln Center, the waiting riders stare out into the darkness and see the headlights have stopped their approach; they wonder why the train isn't moving.

The police told the newspapers that the writing on the walls was just scribble, that there was nothing to it at all. When JA was off the crutches, he went and saw with a glance. Those tags. SONI and SLICK. Their last ones.

Midnight, New York City

Now the day makes its closest approach to peace in New York. A pump in Brooklyn draws 1,000 gallons of water a minute away from the subway. The tunnel won't collapse today. In St. John's Hospital in Rockaway, Joseph Ramiro Casiano, a half day old, has long since been changed from Muria Acevedo's new white pants into a receiving blanket and lies in a tiny plastic crib. His mother, Kathy Quiles, is stretched between crisp hospital sheets in a room with just one other person, for a change. They are sleeping.

In separate holding pens at the Manhattan Criminal Court building, Anna Lans and Darrell Hawkes are awaiting their arraignment on charges of grand larceny. Having escaped her prison, having had a good long shower, Joyce Bresa has decided that being alive is a pretty good thing, all in all. At 520 First Avenue, they are sending the mortuary wagon out to pick up two from a subway tunnel. Tom Thomasevich is singing to himself, softly, so as not to wake anyone:

> *Who knows where or when*
> *We'll meet again*
> *This way?*

Along Post Avenue, a window is open on the seventh floor of number 130. The night is fresh and as the city breathes its evening airs, Rene Ruiz, the perpetual innocent who made his first solo subway flight today, lies in bed and can hear the clatter of the el a block away. It is carrying the No. 1 down to the tunnels that irrigate the skyscrapers and skyline of a city owned by the world. Deep in the half-dark sky of a city night rides the thunder of his train.

Some Days Later

Anna Lans and Darrell Hawkes were charged with grand larceny and eventually pleaded guilty in State Supreme Court. She was sentenced to five years probation and fired from the Transit Authority. Hawkes was sentenced to six months in jail.

Kathy Quiles and Ramiro Casiano moved out of the welfare hotel room and into a five-bedroom house in Far Rockaway, renovated by the city, which is paying their $800 rent. Baby Joseph was burned and scarred when he was placed under an incubator at the municipal hospital. Kathy was a guest on the "Joan Rivers" show and was given a baby bottle with 150 tokens inside. Ramiro occasionally handles odd jobs. **Joseph Caracciolo** continued to work at the Transit Authority, although after his numerous television appearances discussing the birth, he was encouraged to take up a career in modeling. His fellow transit workers call him Baby Doc.

Joyce Bresa became an assistant buyer at Bendel's after serving her time on the sales floor. The Transit Authority announced that the R train was stopped in the tunnel by a malicious prankster who had pulled the emergency brake. In the face of reports to the contrary, the TA recanted, admitted the train failed because of poor maintenance, and said it had botched the evacuation. But responding to a class action suit filed on behalf of riders, the Authority said there was "an assumption of risk" in boarding a subway train, and that the passengers knew "the hazard and dangers thereof and that they assumed all the risks necessarily incidental to such an undertaking."

Tom Thomasevich was trailed by internal transit investigators, who cited his singing as "bad conduct." He was ordered to platform duty. When he returned, the investigators continued to follow him and accused him of several minor infractions. On one occasion, Thomasevich walked off the train in frustration, for which he received a fifty-day suspension. He no longer sings in the train. After several more encounters with transit supervisors, he was brought before an arbitration panel and fired on February 6, 1990.

David Gunn resigned as president of the Transit Authority in February 1990 and said he was moving to a family farm in Nova Scotia to chop wood for a while. In 1991, he became the chief operating officer of the Washington Metro.

Robert Kiley resigned as the MTA chairman in January 1991 and became the chief executive officer of Fischbach Corporation, an engineering and construction concern that was digging itself out of financial trouble.

Daniel Gomez, SONI, was waked in an open coffin, wearing a Panama hat and dark glasses to cover the trauma of his death. His father closed the bodega to take the body to Santo Domingo for burial. The remains of **Rubin Fernandez,** SLICK, also were returned to the Dominican Republic. **John Avildsen,** JA, sporadically wrote graffiti in the subway until he returned to Los Angeles to resume his film career. U5, the Bushwick graffiti crew, no longer is active.

The chicken that escaped ritual slaughter on the D line was spotted, pecking along the trackbed, several days later by Alan Carey of Albany, New York, while he, Carey, was waiting for a train at the Prospect Park station. The hen's destination and whereabouts are unknown.

As of this writing the subway remains graffiti free. During the time you took to read this epilogue, 10,276 people paid their way onto the system. Another 456 jumped the turnstile.

Notes

11   **Rule 117 (I), which says except in an emergency:** Official
      Rules of the New York City Transit Authority.

15   **subway toilet facilities were closed:** Oliver Leeds of Brooklyn
      brought suit in Federal District Court in 1987, demanding that the
      Transit Authority reopen at least some of the bathrooms. The TA
      responded by saying it had no duty to provide such facilities, citing as
      its legal authority a previous court case over the conditions in the
      cages at the Central Park Zoo in which a judge had held the munic-
      ipality free of any particular standards of care for orangutans and
      walruses. A winning argument. The TA then sought to recover legal
      fees against Mr. Leeds, calling him a "self-styled crusader" of "ma-
      licious" intent. Leeds, a man genuinely devoted to the life of the city,
      had brought the suit because as he was getting older and his health
      was failing, he found it hard to complete a trip without access to a
      toilet—and also because he thought the city was surrendering to
      barbarians by letting vandals decide policy. Leeds once had been
      threatened with arrest when he led a group into the subway station
      near his home and they started scrubbing grime. The judge said he
      did not have to pay the TA's legal fees. Leeds died in 1989.

16–17 **"It apparently has not occurred to the CIA":** "Observer,"
      September 23, 1975. Ellis Henican researched and recreated the
      CIA testing story in his column in *New York Newsday,* January 22,
      1991.

18   **In a single decade, the black-car business:** The estimate of
      6,000 vehicles is contained in "The Private Sector in Public Trans-
      portation in New York City," January 1990, an interim report pre-
      pared for the U.S. Department of Transportation, Urban Mass
      Transportation Administration by E. S. Savas and others.

26   **The young men pleaded guilty:** William Prout and Peter Grassia pleaded guilty to second-degree murder in December 1979. They interrupted their trial to plead guilty because Linda Krauss suddenly entered a plea of guilty to attempted manslaughter, and was due to testify against them. They were sentenced in State Supreme Court in January 1980 to fifteen years to life.

28   **The halon didn't come on:** A memorandum, dated April 13, 1988, from Albert Dzingelis, the assistant vice president for system safety, was sent to Carol Meltzer, the chief stations officer, warning of the unreliability of the fire extinguisher. The message was not passed to the clerks until after Mona Pierre died on June 4, 1988. Then the Authority began to improve the fire extinguishers.

29   **"The only parts":** Quoted by Don Terry in the *New York Times*, June 3, 1988.

29   **Noting that the booth was not destroyed:** "It works. Clearly, it works, because the booth is still here," said David Gunn, president of the Transit Authority, on June 4, 1988, during press interviews. What appears to be a callous remark is actually a product of Gunn's reflexive defensiveness whenever any part of the system was questioned. Gunn had spent the night of the attack in the hospital with the dying clerk.

29   **the system discharged more than nine hundred times:** Cited by Charles Seaton, *New York Daily News*, June 19, 1989.

29   **By 1989, token booth clerks were being robbed:** In 1989, 102 clerks were robbed while inside the booth; 204 were robbed when they went outside.

32   **Someone did a study:** The study is not available; Daniel T. Scannell, the chief operating officer of the subway system during the 1960s, recalls it.

32   **the radiance of the cargo:** The standard values for release of heat by a standing person, not active, is 400 to 425 British thermal units per hour; seated, a person will release approximately 350 BTUs per hour, according to the American Society of Heating, Refrigeration and Air Conditioning. On average, then, 400 BTUs are generated per person per hour. During the morning rush hour, 559 trains are operated. Each carries, on average, 2,000 passengers. Ten hours of that works out to 4,472,000,000 BTUs generated by the New York riding public on its way to work. This calculation assumes very little stress, which would increase the BTU output.

33   **the crime reports generated:** Source: Annual Reports, Board of Transportation, New York City Transit Authority, New York City Transit Police. The categories for robbery don't include purse snatches, wallet grabs, and other forms of what most people think of as robbery; these are classified as larcenies. In 1989, there were 4,493 larcenies; in 1946, there were 167.

33   **But a postmidnight rider:** Memo from city council president Carol Bellamy, June 11, 1981, to members of the New York City Board of Estimate.

41   **reduced-fare groups alone could:** APTA 1989 Annual Report on Fares, nationwide. The fare increased to $1.15 on January 1, 1990.

41   **At 181st Street in upper Manhattan:** New York City Transit Authority, Revenue Department, Total Registration by Booth for May 12, 1989.

44   **no transit planner dared:** Interview with Howard Benn, assistant vice president for planning and operations, February 6, 1990.

56   **a city commission confidently:** Norval White and Elliot Willensky, *AIA Guide to New York*, third edition, 1989. Harcourt, Brace, Jovanovich, p. 458.

57   **Manhattan's population in 1850:** Donald A. Mackay, *The Building of Manhattan*, pp. 38–40.

57   **On its streets:** Peter Derrick, "Catalyst for Development: Rapid Transit in New York," *New York Affairs*, vol. 9, no. 4, Fall 1986.

58   **While the route of the subway:** Clifton Hood, "The Impact of the IRT on New York City," *Historical American Engineering Record*, 1979, p. 185.

62   **In the first five decades:** City Planning Commission.

62   **"All of the net population":** Peter Derrick, "Catalyst for Development."

62   **Between 1913 and 1927:** Clifton Hood, *Underground Politics: A History of Mass Transit in New York City Since 1904*, Doctoral Dissertation, Columbia University, 1986, p. 218.

63   **This was a poison pill:** Peter Derrick, "The NYC Mess: Legacy of the 5 Cent Fare," *Mass Transit*, July 1981.

64–65 **"The IRT rapid transit system always":** Joshua B. Freeman, *In Transit: The Transport Workers Union in New York* (Oxford University Press, 1989), p. 5.

65   The outcry against the original transit: Clifton Hood, *Underground Politics*.

66   On December 23, 1946: New York City Transit Authority, *Facts and Figures*, 1987.

66–67 At the same time, a movement: Robert Caro, *The Power Broker*, Vintage Books, 1974, p. 757.

67   "The subways were built under pressure": Clifton Hood, *Underground Politics*, p. 388.

67   "The whole program is clear:" Cited in Hood, p. 389.

69   a decade-long frenzy: "The Corcoran Report 1989 Year-End Study: An In-Depth Semiannual Survey and Analysis of Conditions and Trends in the New York City Luxury Co-Op/Condominium Marketplace," published by the Corcoran Group, New York, New York.

70   Loudly opposed to the taxes: Press release, July 9, 1981, issued by the New York City Partnership, David Rockefeller, chairman.

70   Koch hosted a breakfast: *New York Daily News,* July 8, 1981.

70   the mayor hailed the act's passage: *New York Daily News*, July 9, 1981.

71   "SAVE A BUNDLE": *New York Times*, September 6, 1981.

72–73 A sampling of the contributions: Campaign contributions compiled by Michael Weber, now a reporter for *New York Newsday*, while he was a special assistant to state senator Franz Leichter.

73   the value of its real estate increase: Department of Finance, City of New York.

73   The price of a room: The Corcoran Report 1989 Year-End Study.

73   Some 45 million square feet: Jim Sleeper, "Book and Bust with Ed Koch," in *In Search of New York*, Jim Sleeper, ed. (Transaction Publishers, 1989). Originally a special issue of *Dissent* magazine, Fall 1987.

75   "Level F allows two square feet": From the Draft Rapid Transit Service Guidelines, August 29, 1987, prepared by Michael Grovak, Department of Operations Planning, New York City Transit Authority. Actual observed capacity of 60-foot B-division car: 230 people. Of these 44 were sitting, leaving 186 standees. Total standing room in car: 305.3 square feet. Actual standing room per person: 1.641 square feet.

75 **Stockpens must "have sufficient space":** Title Nine of the code of federal regulations, 91.1 (B), cited by Michael Gerrard in the *New York Times* on May 9, 1979, "It Means B(ruise) M(aul) T(ransit)."

76 **Nelson Rockefeller . . . had declared:** *New York Times*, October 22, 1981. The article cites Rockefeller making the statement in Rochester, New York, while campaigning for bond issue.

77 **by 1940, the New York City subway system:** The city did acquire existing rail lines—a section of the Long Island Rail Road, out to the Rockaways, that was connected with the Independent system, and a stretch of track in the Bronx. The city also built, among others, a small but vital connection, near Chrystie Street in the late 1960s. Essentially, though, the subway system was finished before World War II.

79 **engineering to figure the true costs:** "New Routes Capital Construction Program, New York City Transit Authority," Audit Report NY-AUTH-30-79, Office of the State Comptroller, filed February 7, 1980, p. 17.

82 **He immediately placed a call:** Steve Isenberg, Lindsay's chief of staff, recounted the story to the author in 1990. The Whitneys have never had much luck with the subway; an ancestor apparently was jobbed out of the construction contract for the IRT, the city's first subway, by the financier August Belmont, who could play machine politics better than anyone in his era. (See HAER for full particulars.)

85 **spiraling inflation radically unlike:** Audit Report NY-AUTH-30-79, op cit, note on p. 16.

86 **delivery receipts to show 44,000 cubic yards:** Testimony of Joseph Welsch, Inspector General, U.S. Department of Transportation, Field Hearing before U.S. Senate Subcommittee of the Committee on Appropriations, November 2, 1985.

88 **world's only city with a shrinking rapid transit:** *A Framework for Transit Planning in the New York Region*, by the Regional Plan Association, April 1986. Prepared under contract to the Metropolitan Transportation Authority.

88 **"two tunnels under Roosevelt Island":** Editorial, "The Tunnel Fiasco: Graft or Just Stupidity?" *New York Daily News*, June 30, 1985.

88   **protests over the construction work:** Office of the Inspector
       General, Metropolitan Transportation Authority, MTA/IG 87-7,
       "Review of the 63rd Street Tunnel Project," pp. 9, 10.

89   **seventeen levels of government:** "The Capital Project Pipeline:
       An Analysis of Spending for New York City Public Transportation
       Improvements" A Report by City Council President Carol Bellamy,
       December 1978.

89   **the subway fare was abruptly raised:** See Jack Newfield and
       Paul DuBrul, *The Abuse of Power: The Permanent Government and
       the Fall of New York*, pp. 188–90. The authors cite minutes of the
       Municipal Assistance Corporation meetings which indicate that the
       move to raise the fares had more to do with reassuring the invest-
       ment community of the city's fiscal "discipline" than any analysis of
       the transportation budget.

90   **The Beame shuffle meant no federal funds:** "New Routes Cap-
       ital Construction Program, New York City Transit Authority," Audit
       Report NY-AUTH-30-79, Office of the State Comptroller, filed Feb-
       ruary 7, 1980, p. 24.

90   **carried as an ongoing project:** Testimony of Joseph Welsch,
       November 2, 1985.

93   **The sum was astonishing:** The Wales Hotel, on 93rd Street and
       Madison Avenue, a small European-style hotel, was charging just
       over $2,400 a month in the spring of 1990, which is high season in
       the Manhattan hotel business. Payments on a 30-year, $262,000
       mortgage at 10.5 percent are $2,396 a month. And despite New
       York's reputation for hyperbolic housing prices, the top rental mar-
       ket in most middle-class family neighborhoods hovered no higher
       than $1,500 a month, much less 60 percent higher.

94   **$300-a-month apartments were vanishing:** In 1984, the city
       had 681,206 apartments that rented for $300 or less. At the begin-
       ning of 1987, it had 409,459, a decline of 39 percent, or 271,747 in
       two calendar years, according to the New York City Housing and
       Vacancy Report for 1987, cited by Robert Friedman in *New York
       Newsday*, January 22, 1989.

95   **funds for new housing declined:** Robert Friedman, *New York
       Newsday*, January 22, 1989.

102   **"Between 40th and 60th Streets":** Regional Plan News, No.
       71–72, December 1963.

104   **102 years to finish:** Molly Gordy, "TA Abandons Rebuilding Plans; Subways to Get Paint Job," *New York Newsday*, August 25, 1987. Instead of major renovations, painting, better lights, and, yes, new tiles were planned. And in some places, they actually were installed.

105   **chewing gum motif:** Meltzer cited by Molly Gordy, "Though TA Fights Hard, Gum Still Holds the Floor," *New York Newsday*, January 16, 1989.

Another problem: the floors were laid with quarry tiles, which require grouting and masonry at joinings. Gum that attached to the grout was even harder to remove. Terrazzo tiles, which are more expensive, have smaller joinings, less of a target area for the gum. And in the stations where they have been installed, they haven't popped up.

111   **Total Summonses:** Source: Annual Reports, Board of Transportation, New York City Transit Authority, New York City Transit Police. Between 80 and 90 percent of summonses issued in the last two decades have been ignored. The transience of the population makes them difficult to enforce. However, their utility as a budget-balancing gimmick was seized on in the cash-starved 1970s and clung to until late in the 1980s, when the dismal annual return rate was widely known.

115   **"Do you know how black people":** Tony Jones, quoted by Caryn Eve Wiener in *New York Newsday*, June 29, 1989.

115   **perhaps ten thousand vans:** This includes estimate of commuter vans, jitneys, and feeder vans in "The Private Sector in Public Transportation in New York City," January 1990, an interim report prepared for the U.S. Department of Transportation, Urban Mass Transportation Administration, by E. S. Savas and others.

123   **A fifteen-minute train ride:** The distance from 46th Street in Astoria to Fifth Avenue in Manhattan is 3.97 miles of railroad track, and the running time is listed as 13 minutes at midnight, 16.5 minutes during morning rush hour, and 15 minutes during the evening, according to "Distance and Maximum Running Time Between Stations," published by the TA Operations and Planning Department, January 22, 1989. That works out to a speed of 15.88 miles per hour in the evening, and 14.43 miles per hour in the morning—when the schedule is met. It's about three times faster than surface traffic, such as buses and automobiles—when it's working.

131   **"a cool little vaulted city":** Cited in Benson Bobrick, *Labyrinths of Iron* (William Morrow, 1986), p. 262.

131 **"sealed like King Tut's tomb":** Norval White and Elliot Willensky, *AIA Guide*, p. 62.

132 **design should incorporate "beauty":** "Ceramic Ornament in the New York Subway System," by Susan Tunick, a pamphlet published by Assopiastrelle, the Italian Tile Center, New York.

132– **The Mineola emerged:** E. J. Quinby, "Minnie Was a Lady," *Rail-*
133 *road*, February 1956.

138 **taxi service in New York:** The relationship between the taxi industry and the government is useful to both. The chief regulator for the taxi industry, appointed by Mayor Koch, had obtained free cab service for Koch voters during the 1985 Democratic primary. The services, valued at $45,000, were not disclosed on campaign finance reports. The mayor acknowledged the helpfulness of his regulator, Jay Turoff, who was later indicted and convicted of tax fraud in other shenanigans.

140 **To save labor costs, Belmont installed:** Clifton Hood, *Underground Politics*.

141 **Joseph Spencer had had a brainstorm:** What was Spencer's reward for saving the TA over $4.5 million a year in slugs? He had formally submitted the idea in spring 1983 to an employee suggestion program, gotten a receipt, and developed and monitored a prototype bull's-eye until November of that year, when he retired after 34 years of service. About three years later, he saw his idea put to excellent use. When he requested a cash award from the employee suggestion program, he was turned down. He went to court, seeking $10,000 for his multimillion-dollar invention, and after a nonjury trial, lost. Civil Court judge George Wade in Brooklyn found that Spencer did come up with the bull's-eye idea, but he had so many duties that he was "holding a managerial position and thus was ineligible to receive an award." The thanks you get.

142 **One clerk filled the slots:** Dennis Duggan, *New York Newsday*, January 6, 1986.

143 **manufacturing jobs in New York:** Data supplied in an interview with Samuel Ehrenhalt, regional director of the U.S. Bureau of Labor Statistics.

143– **"Once, the garment industry, teeming":** Saul Friedman, "The
144 City Swings to Service," *New York Newsday*, June 29, 1986. A major discussion of the conversion of New York's economy from manufacturing and industry to services.

144   **about 44 percent of the population:** "The New Century—Forecasts for the Tri-State Region," April 1989, published by the Regional Plan Association.

144   **"It's hard to build an economy":** Saul Friedman, *New York Newsday*, June 29, 1986, quoting Glenn Yago, director of the Economic Research Bureau at the State University of New York at Stony Brook.

144   **cost to business of delayed riders:** "The Economic Costs of Subway Deterioration," Federal Reserve Bank of New York Quarterly Review, Spring 1981.

147–   **"Beach was a nineteenth-century":** Robert Daley, in "Alfred
148   Ely Beach and His Wonderful Pneumatic Railroad," *American Heritage*, December 1961, gives a colorful account of the Beach episode.

161   **The TA was taking twice the time:** Speech by Robert R. Kiley, at a meeting of the Association for a Better New York, February 14, 1984.

162   **Kiley had publicly—and mistakenly:** "The New York Underground," an address by Robert R. Kiley at the New York Public Library, February 9, 1988.

164   **"like buying automobiles":** The Council of the City of New York, First Interim Report, Special Committee on Public Transportation, September 1970.

164   **longer trains would slow down:** "Notes from Underground," June 1971. Published by the Committee for Better Transit.

166   **the R-44s were virtually dead:** "New Technology Test Train," a paper presented by Charles Monheim, chief mechanical officer of the Transit Authority, to the American Public Transit Association Conference, June 5, 1989.

186   **"only the Smiths went and did it":** In March 1990, Roger Smith became the first writer to be indicted for felonious graffiti writing. He was accused of causing property damage in excess of $500. The dollar amount was not uncommon; the attention, by press and prosecutors, was.

193   **ten thousand signs:** Studies by the Permanent Citizens Advisory Committee to the MTA in 1989 found that in nearly every station, some sort of officially wrong instruction was given to the passengers, whether it was a light globe outside the station signaling red—no access—when it should have been amber—some access—or signs pointing the way to train lines that had been closed for half a century.

198– **these factors affecting ridership:** "Transit on Track, Paper No.
199 1: MTA Transit Ridership: Trends and Prospects," a joint project of
the Regional Plan Association and New York Citizens for Balanced
Transportation, March 1985.

199 **The fare has increased seven times:** Subway fares: October 27,
1904 to June 30, 1948: 5 cents. July 1, 1948 to July 24, 1953: 10
cents. July 25, 1953 to July 4, 1966: 15 cents. July 5, 1966 to January
3, 1970: 20 cents. January 4, 1970 to January 4, 1971: 30 cents.
January 5, 1972 to August 31, 1975: 35 cents. September 1, 1975 to
June 27, 1980: 50 cents. June 28, 1980 to July 2, 1981: 60 cents. July
3, 1981 to January 1, 1984: 75 cents. January 2, 1984 to December
31, 1985: 90 cents. January 1, 1986 to December 31, 1989: $1.
January 1, 1990: $1.15.

202 **hair they have braided:** Joanna Molloy, "Notes from the Underground," *New York* magazine, February 27, 1989.

202 **E. B. White wrote:** E. B. White, "Here Is New York." The Curtis
Publishing Co., 1949.

203– **a third of the population of the city:** Frank Vardy, a demogra-
204 pher for the City Planning Commission, says foreign-born people
were projected to take 30 percent of the city's population in 1990.

212 **"who have no conception of":** Carol Polsky, "Red Light, Green
Light," *New York Newsday,* March 20, 1989.

214 **All those rush-hour car czars:** Howard Benn, the TA's vice
president for operations planning, said that about 3,000 people per
hour use the FDR Drive in rush hour—mostly single-occupancy
vehicles. The capacity of an IRT Lexington Avenue train, the near-
est subway line to the FDR, is 2,000 people, so just 1.5 additional
trains would be needed. However, the Lexington Avenue line operates during rush hour close to capacity—30 trains an hour, one every
two minutes, which is the minimum headway. Unless the Second
Avenue subway is built, there's not much space to put those people
from the FDR Drive.

214 **reduce noxious emissions:** Testimony of Mortimer Downey before the U.S. House Ways and Means Committee, March 14, 1990.

214 **the mass transit network saves:** *Power for the MTA,* Regional
Plan Association, June 1977, p. 4.

214 **over 2 billion gallons of gasoline:** Conversion factors from the
Transportation Energy Data Book: Edition 10, by Stacy C. Davis and
others, Oak Ridge National Laboratory, September 1989.

214 **Manhattan's ozone pollution is second:** Richard Levine, "Region's Boom Brings More Road-Choking Traffic," *New York Times,* April 10, 1990. Levine reports an additional 2.5 million car registrations during the 1980s.

214 **National subsidies for automobiles:** Speech by Robert R. Kiley at the annual meeting of the American Public Transit Association in Atlanta, Georgia, September 25, 1989.

214 **trains have become less efficient:** The *Transportation Energy Data Book: Edition 10,* by Stacy C. Davis and others, paints a stark picture. In 1970, cars used 5,471 BTUs per passenger mile; by 1987, that had declined to 3,481. Rail transit had gone in the opposite direction: in 1970, BTU consumption was 2,453 per passenger mile; in 1987, 3,534.

215 **they chose thirty-year-old models:** In 1981, the MTA rejected suggestions by Jerrold Nadler, an assemblyman from Manhattan, that it consider the subway car being bought by the Chicago Transit Authority, which was 44 percent lighter than those now in use in New York, and took that much less energy to move. And before making the largest purchase of new rapid transit car equipment in the nation's history, it didn't investigate regenerative braking, a technology then being used in Europe to capture with a flywheel some of the friction forces in stopping the car. People at the TA had been scarred by the 1970s adventure of its parent, the MTA, in purchasing new technology and were reverting to the tried and more or less true.

219 **the MTA was a creature of the governor:** There are seventeen people on the MTA board, but only fourteen votes. Four of them are appointed by the county executives of the northern suburbs of Rockland, Orange, Putnam, and Dutchess; each, however, has only a quarter vote, which is not counted unless the vote is unanimous. These four are known as the quarter-pounders. Three others, with full votes, are appointed on the recommendations of the county executives of Westchester, Nassau, and Suffolk. The mayor of New York City, the largest mass transit city in the world, with a bus and subway system ten times the size of all the rest of the MTA together, is allowed to appoint four members of the seventeen. The governor controls by appointing six, including the chairman. All are subject to confirmation by the state senate, which frequently holds up the process by tying it to such matters as legislation aiding cheese factories near the Canadian border.

220   **the Central Intelligence Agency had launched:** From documents submitted at a Joint Hearing of the Select Committee on Intelligence, the Subcommittee on Health and Scientific Research, 95th Congress, First Session, August 3, 1977.

224   **the cost overruns had been:** Katherine Foran, "Subway Car Fix Late, Over Budget," *New York Newsday*, August 13, 1989.

227–
228   **Bishop DeVernon LeGrand had:** Joyce Young of the *New York Daily News* wrote about the LeGrand operations in an article published April 3, 1988.

232   **known evermore as** TAKI **183:** Today, he runs a repair shop for foreign cars in Yonkers. In May 1989, he told Joel Siegel of the *New York Daily News* that he was amazed by what he had started.

238   **wasn't just a group of transit managers:** Minutes of the Car Appearance Security Task Force, August 16, 1985, p. 2.

241–
242   **overtime worked by employees in "safety sensitive" positions:** Most of the information about the increased hours worked by employees in safety-sensitive positions comes from a series by the author published in *New York Newsday* on March 5, 6 and 7, 1989. Mark Vales's time cards for the period covering June 18 through July 7 were obtained from the Transit Authority under the New York State Freedom of Information Act. By the way, on the night of the incident involving Joyce Bresa, the Transit Authority kept Vales for an investigation until nearly 6 A.M., fourteen grueling hours. He was back at work before 5:00 the next evening—his sixteenth consecutive day of work. The report by MTA inspector general John S. Pritchard III is entitled "The Impact of Long Work Hours on the Safety of the NYCTA Bus and Subway Service," February 15, 1990.

243   **Granville T. Woods devised:** "Black Inventors," *Amsterdam News*, February 9, 1991. Woods's Electrical Railway System premiered at Coney Island in 1892.

248   **Bushwick and West Side statistics:** Michael A. Stegman, Housing and Vacancy Report, New York City, 1987, and Summary of Vital Statistics, Department of Health, City of New York.

248–
249   **a great center for German immigration:** *The Brooklyn Neighborhood Book*, 1985, published by the Brooklyn Borough President's Office.

272   **Until 1918, it was known:** Brian J. Cudahy, *Under the Sidewalks of New York* (The Stephen Greene Press, 1988), pp. 71–80.

278   **first president born outside Ireland:** Sonny Hall, a German-American, became president May 20, 1985.

278   **more than half of the city's transit workers:** Joshua B. Freeman, *In Transit*. This book is the definitive work on the role of ethnicity in the subway labor movement.

292   **During the time you took to read:** At 3.7 million riders per day, 2,569 riders per minute pay their way into the system. At the 1991 estimate of 60 million fare beaters a year (164,383 a day), 114 jump the turnstile per minute. The epilogue is 518 words long, which takes about four minutes to read.

Index

tunnels, 23, 174–175, 254
  depth of, 56, 170
  first, 63, 147–148
  63rd Street, 79, 80, 82–83, 86–88, 90, 91
tunnel vision, 255
turnstiles, 46, 113, 139, 141, 287
  first, 140
Tweed, William Marcy, 57, 146–148

U5, 12, 188–190, 239, 250, 252, 292
Urban Mass Transit Administration
  (UMTA), 162

Vales, Mark, 240–241, 242, 254–255
Vanderbilt, Cornelius, 58
vans, 115
Velez, Marisol, 152, 158, 178, 182, 191
VEN (tag name), 252, 253
voodoo, 2

Wagner, Robert, 140

Walton, Exree, 107
Washington Heights, see stations, 181st
  Street and St. Nicholas Avenue
water main breaks, 4, 24, 151
"wheel," 46
wheels, 126, 128, 160
White, E. B., 202
White, Norval, 56
Whitney, John Hay, 81–82
Willensky, Elliot, 56
Williams, Darrell, 38–39, 289
Wilson, David, 279
Wilson, Dovetta, 279
Wilson, Timothy, 279
windows, 129
Windels, Paul, 66
Woods, Granville T., 243

Yankee Stadium, 65, 93

Ziegler, George, 76